I dedicate this book, in blessed memory, to my mother, Genia Gross, for her ever-enduring love, her strong work ethic, her love for her family, and her undying faith in God—even after experiencing the atrocities of Nazi Germany as she barely survived Auschwitz.

Contents

Acknowledgments

This book is an effort of many months, and there are some special people who deserve special thanks for helping me bring it to fruition. Many thanks go to my mom and dad who taught me to take responsibility for myself at a very early age. This early independence allowed me the freedom to grow, gain knowledge, and garner insight. My editor at Sourcebooks, Peter Lynch, who believed in me and this book, encouraged me to make the book a reality, and would always amaze me with his prompt response to my questions. To Michelle Schoob, who helped make my words clearer. Thanks to Duane Newcomb, who always made time to talk to me about my progress and made me feel as though I knew what I was doing. I also want to thank my administrative assistant and right-arm, Melodee Hunt, for her professionalism, support, organization and love; Lee Ann Martin, Cheryl Lopez, Miranda Collard, David Hille, and Ben Mahill at the Country Rose Tea Room for their coffee fill-ups and encouragement; Carolyn Temple, a dear friend who provided me with insightful feedback; Dan McNeill, whose support, promptness, and incredible knowledge helped make my words dance; Teresa Jelletich, my fitness trainer, who was there to offer great insights and allow me to pitch ideas and brainstorm with her during workouts; Teresa Mawson and Jill Thayer, two dear friends whose support and love were always present; Yossie Ziff who was my champion and cheering squad; Bob & Elaine Steinberg for nurturing me and my "newest baby" along the way with their unconditional love, encouraging words, and friendship; to my beautiful Judy Fairchild, who regularly checked in on me to make sure my spirit was joyful and my emotions were unblocked so that I could be a better person and live a more authentic life during all of this; Alan Klein for his enduring support and genuine love; to my gorgeous nieces, Shelly and Sarah Gross, whose genuine concern for how their "Aunty's" writing was coming along always put a smile on my face; and a very special thank you to my three wonderful children who help nourish my soul, strengthen my patience, and inspire me—my daughter Naomi, whose love and confidence helped keep my spirits high and whose spunk kept me smiling; to David, whose thirst for knowledge and experiences lovingly reminded me that each day is a new day and should be taken as it comes; and to my youngest son, Daniel, who is a daily reminder of sensitivity and sensibility and whose work ethic is an inspiration.

In addition, a big thank you to all the women, the everyday heroes whom I admire and who have shared a bit of their lives with me through interviews, seminars, consulting, coaching, and friendship.

I am greatly indebted to all of you.

Introduction

Because I grew up with two parents who worked full-time, I learned to become self-sufficient and independent when quite young. My parents are immigrants, having come to America after World War II. They were not familiar with American culture, values, time-pressures, and, most importantly at the time, games and toys. If my brother and I wanted to play games, we had to develop them ourselves. Since my brother had nice printing, he was in charge of constructing board games. I was in charge of the creative games, like Restaurant, Hollywood, and others I'm sure you haven't heard of.

As I grew older, finished school, and got married, I found myself, like most women, taking care of the house, grocery shopping, cooking, raising a family, and working. I became what *Redbook* magazine calls a juggler. I juggled my business, children, home, husband, and all my other activities in a limited time frame.

I found myself uptight and extremely stressed. If I had kept juggling, I probably would have had some sort of breakdown. Instead, I realized that much of my problem stemmed from not properly organizing my time. But when I started looking for help, I found that though much had been written about time management, almost no authority had addressed the special problems facing working women.

For instance, men rarely have to figure out how to do the wash, keep the house clean, and still work late at the office. The book *The Second Shift* states that the changes in women and the absence of change in men creates a situation where men simply aren't really helping.[1] These time-management problems are as real today as they were when the book first came out and need to be seriously addressed. Time issues not only affect our daily twenty-four hours but also the quality of our work, our lives at home, and our overall health.

This started me on a search to discover how to use my time more effectively, cut down on the stress and guilt that comes from having to neglect something or someone, and still accomplish what I needed to accomplish—every day, week, and year.

To do this, I read everything I could find on time management, observed my own life, and interviewed numerous working women. What I discovered was that the issue of time tends to be a common denominator in the lives of all working women. It is also the one thing that keeps most working women from leading stress-free and guilt-free lives.

I find that women view time far differently from men. Women often perceive time as an enemy that prevents them from getting it all done, all the time. For some reason society has decided that even when a woman works she is still responsible for making sure that everything gets done at home—and to this end she never has enough time. It's true that men also want to accomplish more in less time, but that nearly always means accomplishing tasks at work, with their hobbies, or with outside interests at home. Men's concerns rarely include the day-to-day tasks of running the house and the family. I have found that

---

1. Hochschild, Arlie, and Anne Machung. *The Second Shift: Inside the Two-Job Marriage.* New York: Viking, 1989

this concern that women have for home tasks, family, and work are at the root of much of their concern about time.

These special time-pressures cause many working women to feel overwhelmed, guilty, and stressed. Because they don't have the time to get everything done, they tend to put off those things that are really important to them. The focus is to "embrace" rather than "tackle" this time challenge. Working women usually give top priority to the family or others.

I find that the underlying passion that fuels me to write this updated book is to share how each one of us makes a difference. However, the challenge is to make a positive difference in our lives, our children, significant others, colleagues, friends, and the community at large. This book is designed to help you balance priorities and live a spirited, joyful, and quality life. In it, I will ask you to decide what you want to accomplish in your life. Then I will offer a number of suggestions to help you manage your time as a working woman (inside or outside the home) so that you can live your life productively and happily twenty-four hours a day.

One of the problems I found when doing the surveys for this book was that not every working woman had the same objectives. Some wanted to put their entire time emphasis on taking care of the home and children, yet work everything else in. Others weren't quite sure what they wanted, and some wanted to put all their time into their careers.

The study "The New Diversity: A *Self* Magazine Report on American Women" helped me greatly as I grappled with the matter of women's differing objectives.[2] The study defined several types of women who shared the same priorities in regard to how they wanted

2. This study was analyzed in "Transition," *Marketing Insights Magazine*, Fall 1989, p. 27.

to use their time for work, home, and personal activities. This study supported my own view that time management must be powered by personal values—that no one system would be right for every woman. In my work, I simplified the typology presented in the *Self* study. I offer three categories—the Traditional Homemaker, the Transitional Woman, and the Achieving Woman—as categories for discussing distinct attitudes and paths to happiness. I have also added different generations of women; from Seniors to the quarter-life crisis Twenty-Somethings, including three stages of Baby Boomers in the mix.

As you read *Time Management Secrets for Working Women* you will be able to see which category you fit into and determine if you are using your time in a way that matches your values and makes you happy. You may be surprised at what you find. For instance, the Traditional Homemaker is happiest when she spends about 20 percent of her time on professional tasks, 50 percent on home-related tasks, and 30 percent on personal activities. If you are a Traditional Homemaker and find yourself spending 50 percent of your time on professional activities, 20 percent at home, and 30 percent on personal activities, you may well be chronically unhappy and frustrated. Similarly, an Achieving Woman will find nothing but frustration if she tries to spend 50 percent of her time on home activities. You will also find a pattern to each generation.

The first step in achieving what you want to achieve with your time is to discover what category you fall into and what you want to accomplish. This means developing goals, since goals are the blueprint for change.

In approaching *Time Management Secrets for Working Women,* I want you to keep a positive attitude toward change. What does not seem possible to change at first glance may well be just what you need to change. For instance, I remember speaking to a working mom who was picking up her daughter from a birthday party. She mentioned how tired she was and how she didn't have the energy to go home and clean the house but that it "had to be done."

Upon direct questioning she told me that her husband doesn't help around the house because he keeps their two cars clean. I pointed out to her that cleaning cars is a weekly job but housework is a daily one. She also realized, however, that she wasn't going to get extra help from him, so she would have to deal with the problem herself.

I suggested that she consider having a cleaning service come in once a week. She protested: not only could they not afford a cleaning service, but her husband would consider it out of the question. In cases like this I feel it is important to keep a positive attitude toward change. I realize that a lot of women wouldn't consider a cleaning service, but what about a house helper? Perhaps she could trade off for help with a neighbor or friend or maybe she could hire a teenager a few hours a week. Either one of these alternatives would solve a lot of problems.

I want you to stay flexible and open to new ideas as you read *Time Management Secrets for Working Women.* Flexibility means maintaining an internal feeling that everything will work and using whatever method you find necessary to make it work. You may think you can't change something as basic as the time you spend taking care of the children or cleaning the house. But consider what you and your friends have already done. Remember back a few years, when eating "healthy" wasn't even thought of. Many women have made basic changes, and today they are eating more fruit and vegetables, serving balanced meals, and eating a low-fat cholesterol-free diet. If you and others can make basic changes like these, you can also make the changes that will free you from anxiety and guilt and give you a chance to spend your time in those activities that mean the most to you.

I also want you to keep the Integrate or Suffocate idea in mind. Forget about multi-tasking as it only leaves you with less energy, not attentive to what you're doing, and disorganized with what comes next. But rather, focus on the concept of combining your values, passions, and the people in your life with innovative ways to answer the question: "How can I make this work?"

The last section sets up a six-week Balanced and Joyful Life Program with skills that lay the groundwork for living a more balanced, calm, joyful, and productive life. I use this program with my coaching clients, whether they contact me for life balance, executive coaching, or marketing strategies implementation. It identifies your values, emotional patterns, time skills, attitude awareness, health and fitness, and financial health.

A mathematical equation may equal eight. But there are several ways to reach that number: four plus four, five plus three, two plus six, eight plus zero, and seven plus one. They are all correct; it is the choice of which to use that is different. Throughout *Time Management Secrets for Working Women* I will offer you a number of choices to solve individual time problems. To get the most out of the book, you must stay flexible. Don't reject any solution out of hand; consider all of them and pick those you think might work.

Finally, *Time Management Secrets for Working* Women will not do you a bit of good if you read it and then put it back on the shelf. This is an *action* book. Its purpose is to change your life. Nothing, however, will happen unless you take action. Just as a composer may have but one melody in mind, as he or she begins to write, one idea seems to inspire another and an entire symphony comes to life. Mark some of the suggestions you want to try as you go through the book. When finished, go back and actually try them. In addition, I suggest you consider this a reference book that you refer to over and over.

This book encourages you to open your mind to new ideas and tactics. Feel free to think about them and to modify them. But, whatever you do, pinpoint which group of women you fall into, then decide on the changes you want to make, then *make them*. Remember, without action, nothing at all can happen.

Few women would say that they have achieved time equality at work, at home, or in their personal activities. *Time Management Secrets for Working Women* gives examples of how to balance your time. I believe it can help you create a future filled with a new perception of time, a positive attitude toward defining priorities and living your values, and a more flexible schedule filled with fresh possibilities. Try to stay open to some of these ideas—and make an internal and soulful pledge with yourself to make a difference and embrace a new mindset that allows for integration fueled by positive energy and quality choices. Enjoy!

Chapter One

How to Make Time for the Time of Your Life

Y ou've seen her in magazines: Superwoman. She's wearing beautiful, expensive clothes and not one hair is out of place. She's smiling as she holds a briefcase in one hand and her three-year-old daughter in the other. You've seen her on television, where you could swear that her clothes had just arrived straight from the cleaners after being worn by a top-notch, well-endowed model. She walks into a clean, two-story, organized home where the children are happy to see Mom and dinner will be prepared within minutes.

A more realistic scenario: Diane Keaton's face fills the screen and we see a woman touched by anguish. Her sensitive features contort with pain, causing a shudder of compassion to ripple through the audience. Is this woman facing political ruin or untimely death? Hardly. In this poignant scene from *Baby Boom,* Keaton must make the wrenching choice between meeting with her star client or babysitting a newborn. As a seasoned executive but inexperienced full-time mom, her dilemma is excruciating.

For most working mothers, Keaton's situation is business as usual. Like Keaton's character, they are fighting a losing battle to juggle the one thousand and one tasks demanded by job, home, children, husband, friends, and family.

A woman who signed her name "Tired in Texas" summarized the problem in a letter to Ann Landers:

> I put in forty hours a week downtown and just as many at home…My job as a supervisor is stressful. The demands on me are awesome. Everyone wants something. When I come home, I must prepare supper, clean the house, wash clothes, pick up the kids from their daily activities, help with homework, and see that they are bathed and put to bed. By then I'm dead tired. And each day is busier than the day before. I'm totally shot and feel as if I'm sinking into quicksand. My body says *rest,* but my mind says *get ready for tomorrow.* And the real problem is that there isn't enough time to do it all.

This story is typical of working women all across the globe. Most women work out of necessity. Some work so that the family can enjoy niceties such as a bigger home or an extended family vacation. The problem for most, however, is that the time crunch is killing women physically and emotionally.

What these women want most is the time to handle, without always rushing, all the tasks they deem necessary. The need for time management comes as no surprise to women, who have traditionally been the ones altering their schedules to accommodate daily activities, errands, and special projects. Men, traditionally, have not had this burden. As Gloria Steinem said several years ago in an interview, "I have yet to hear a man ask for advice on how to combine the time for marriage and a career." And yet people who teach time management expect working women to allocate their time in the same way a working man does. Stated simply, it doesn't work that way.

Women, at all ages, enter or leave the job market; change careers; have children; marry or remarry; start, complete, or add to their educations; run their own businesses; and more. Many of these varied roles are simultaneous, and the result is a *severe time crunch*.

Establishing Your Own Personal Motivational Lifestyle

As a working woman, you have surely felt the crunch: meeting the needs of your job and your family threatens to take all your time; with no time for yourself, you may feel as if you are about to disappear altogether. How can you resolve conflicting demands and maintain some sense of personal peace? The first step is to define how you want to allot your energy. Let your own values determine how you balance work, family, and personal time and then develop a lifestyle that reflects your priorities. Only by incorporating your own values can you maintain a lifestyle that will seem fulfilling to you and motivate you to grow as an individual.

A study published in *Self* magazine defined seven such lifestyles, which the study called Personal Motivational Lifestyles. Each one reflects the values of a certain type of woman. My own experience in working with women's time-management issues led me to simplify the *Self* model by distinguishing three categories. By choosing the category that best reflects your values and then restructuring your schedule according to the time-allotment percentages that accompany each category, I feel confident that you can improve the quality of your life.

The three categories of women are the Traditional Homemaker, the Transitional Woman, and the Achieving woman. See which one best reflects your views and values. In addition, each of the generations offer their own twist to the general lifestyle.

The Traditional Homemaker: "I Do Have a Career!"

Most Traditional Homemakers plan their lives around marriage and family, and they always wanted to be mothers. For these women, caring for home and family takes priority. Today, when most families need two paychecks to survive, 65 percent of Traditional Homemakers are employed, 35 percent of them full-time. Two-thirds of the women working full-time would rather stay at home. However, most do not see themselves as full-time homemakers for the rest of their lives. Three-fifths of the Traditional Homemakers who are not working currently plan to return to work when their children start school.

For Traditional Homemakers, work outside the home is a nine-to-five job, not a career. Many of these women feel that the desire to have it all is unrealistic. They believe a woman can't be her best as both a mother and a career woman. Their sense of accomplishment comes from taking care of their home and raising a family. Their traditional values and attitudes lead them to believe that the husband's job is more important than the wife's. Because of the consistency between their attitudes and lifestyle, these women seem to be happy. Their good feelings come from knowing that they won't always be at home. Many feel that a new life will begin for them in later years. They feel they have control over their lives, health, and well-being. All, however, believe they need extra time to do everything they want to do, both inside and outside the home.

Many of the women who stay home or work part-time feel that society as a whole does not take them seriously or see them as being as competent as career women. This is especially true for traditional women who worked—who were career women, in fact—but then opted to stay at home to raise their families. They do not want to be looked down on because they are "only housewives." Traditional Homemakers, in their view, do a very worthwhile job by taking care of home and family. They view the transitions from work force to home to work force as career changes.

The Transitional Woman: "I Feel Trapped."

These women have their hearts in neither their work nor their homes. Most Transitional Women are married and many work outside the home. Only 28 percent stay at home full-time. A large percentage are forced to work because of economic pressures. Many are employed in jobs they don't particularly like. This in itself creates a strain, and the strain is intensified by the pressure of having to cope with home and work and the guilt of having to neglect the family.

Women in this group lack a feeling of control. They are traditional in their values and attitudes, but they feel forced into working. As temporary escapes, they tend to be impulsive spenders, watch a lot of television, read magazines for guidance, and change hair and makeup regularly. These stress reducers, when used in excess, only cause more stress in their lives. Over 50 percent of Transitional Women live from paycheck to paycheck.

Because they perceive that they lack control, women in this group tend to lack confidence in their own ability to find solutions to their conflict. Transitional Women need consistent doses of support and information to help them make life choices. These women haven't decided whether to focus on homemaking or their career. They feel extremely ambivalent.

The Achieving Woman: "Of Course I Can."

Those who are Achieving Women are career-centered. They put their hearts and souls into their work. If asked to chair an event, be on a committee, or accept a new assignment or client, these are the women who say, "Of course I can." These women find themselves overcommitted, overwhelmed, and overworked. Their greatest fear is loss of control—professionally, personally, and at home. They feel that, if their juggling act misses a beat, then everything will come crashing down.

Yet 85 percent feel that their lives work well. Both the Achieving Women and the Traditional Homemakers find consistency between their values, attitudes, and lifestyles. Of all the groups, the Achieving Woman rate themselves the highest on self-confidence. However, the serious time pressures they face cause them frustration, anxiety, and conflict.

Achieving Women do not believe, as the Traditional Homemakers do, that the home is the center of life. Rather, they view their homes as an expression of who they are and as a refuge from their busy schedules.

Over 64 percent of Achieving Women feel they could live comfortably on their own salary. They tend to be extremely self-reliant and independent in a relationship. Because they are fiercely independent and financially secure, they tend to leave a bad marriage sooner than women in the other groups. In spite of the high percentage of failed marriages among Achievers, family is important to them. But their strongest sense of competence and accomplishment comes from their careers.

More than any other group, the Achieving Women would like to start their own businesses, if they had the money.

Looking at the Generations…from Seniors to Twenty-Somethings

Besides these similarities, each generation of traditionalists has their own interpretation.

Seniors (1922–1943)

This more mature woman (sixty-two to eighty-three) has respect for authority, has worked hard, is dedicated, and retains traditional views. Their numbers are expected to double from nineteen million in 2000 to about thirty-seven million in 2030.

These women have expendable income and they are most likely to upgrade their homes, much of their income going into appliances and electronics.

Ken Dyshtwald, president of Age Wave, a marketing consulting firm in Emeryville, California, calls this senior group the nineteen trillion dollar consumer because it represents 70 percent of the total net worth of U.S. households. Senior women are used to getting their information from newspapers, television, and radio. Therefore, those are the sources to which they respond. The sixty-five plusers, however, want to keep the technology simple, although many now have mastered the Internet and save time as a result.

"Many of these senior women are grandparents and the role of the grandparent is changing," says Rebeca Chekmuras, vice president of research for Age Wave. "Grandparents as a whole may be becoming secondary providers. They may be caring for the child while Mom is at work, and they may be the financial safety net of the child."

The largest majority of senior women are Traditional. An estimated 2.3 million American children under age fifteen were cared for by traditional grandmothers in 1993. Grandmothers today tend to be deeply involved in their grandkids' lives. According to a recent AARP national survey of 823 grandparents over the age of sixty, 78 percent have seen a grandchild in the past month or talked with them over the phone—and 65 percent say they speak at least once a week.

My research and case studies have shown that most Senior women are either Traditional Homemakers or Achieving Women. The Achieving Women are still working and enjoy their time at work. Many Senior women are in their own businesses or have developed their hobbies such as painting or knitting into a business while continuing to be a Traditional Homemaker.

Baby Boomer Women (1945–1958)

Baby Boomer values are health, youth, personal gratification, and material wealth. According to SRI consulting, Menlo Park, California, the "traditionalist boomer woman tends to be cautious, moralistic and patriotic. This group acted like the nine hundred-pound gorilla through most of the 70s, 80s, and 90s. The number of fifty-five to sixty-four-year-olds will grow to thirty-eight million during the next decade. Older boomers will work longer…some long after retirement age. Many of the traditional are now becoming grandparents, but they are a new generation of grandmothers. Today's traditional grandmothers are vibrant and alive, do yoga, and are proactive in wanting to be part of their grandchildren's lives.

There are three groups of baby boomer women: Empty Nesters, Still Have Kids at Home, and Women in Midlife Crisis.

The Empty-Nester baby boomers have time and financial freedom for the first time in many years. The transition from being an active mom to having an open void as the children leave the nest is especially heartfelt for the Traditional and Transitional Women. The Achieving Women feel the absence of children and "loss" of not having them at home, but feel a certain amount of freedom to pursue their careers and hobbies. All three groups of women feel much freer to pursue their hobbies and activities they have "put off until the children are out of the house."

The second group of Baby Boomers, the Still Have Kids at Home, are looking forward to their children leaving the nest so that they can also enjoy the time and financial freedom of their counterparts. The Traditional, Transitional, and Achieving Women in this group of Baby Boomers still feel the necessity of putting children's needs before their own.

The third group are Women in Midlife Crisis. In past decades women have dreaded going through the late forties and fifties. But today Baby Boomer women are turning this period in their lives into a golden opportunity. According to a recent *Time* magazine cover story, there are roughly forty-three million American Women ages forty to sixty. Instead of stagnating when they hit the midlife hurdles—divorce, disease, an empty nest, or the loss of a parent, many now have a tremendous urge to help others and surprisingly, at the same time help themselves. As *Time* reports, a hospice nurse is now running a consulting firm to help women handle their aging parents; a doctor is building a second career selling clothing for upscale middle aged women like herself; and a pharmaceutical company representative has turned a long-held idea into Abby's Idea Factory to help inventors turn their ideas into products. As *Time* says, women from coast to coast, of all backgrounds, are essentially opening up the Great Midlife Lemonade Stand and this applies to all three groups, Traditional, Transitional, and Achieving Women.

Generation Xers (The pragmatic generation, 1960–1977)

Gen Xers believe in diversity, are motivated by money, are self-reliant, and value free time. This generation, however, believes they are entitled to a job that is fun.

Many Xer women are married and living with their spouses; 55 percent have at least one child. Their experience in growing up in boomer families—divorce, day care, and latchkey kids—has made them more independent and self-reliant.

Generation Ys (also referred to as Millennials, Generation Next, 1977–1994):

This generation was caught in the dot-com demise. This group is self-reliant, family oriented, brand conscious, consumerist oriented, mobile, and connected to others.

They want to keep a kid-like view of the world and have the freedom to follow their dreams. Casual is in. Most Gen Ys prefer a relaxed, dressed-down look. Both men and women are likely to wear a piercing—not only in each ear, but in other parts of the body.

Twenty-Something Quarter-Life Crisis

Most Twenty-Something women are going through a quarter-life crisis, as referred by the authors Abby Wilner and Alexandra Robbins.

This crisis is centered around taking longer to grow up and become independent, whereas this twenty-something age group in my generation (Boomer) was somewhat clearer. Many of us knew that we wanted to become mothers, work at careers, and get jobs at this age. It was a little easier because it was expected of us by society.

However, the Twenty-Somethings are taking longer to make up their minds as to what they want to do. This gap between adolescence and adulthood is a worldwide shift, not only found in the United States.

Frank Furstenberg Jr., a University of Pennsylvania sociologist who headed a research team says, "It isn't just an aberration. It's become normal behavior." In addition, these Twenty-Somethings are sometimes referred to as the "boomerang kids" because they return home after college. According to Twentysomething Inc., a market researcher that tracks youth trends, 65 percent of this year's grads expect to live with their parents after earning degrees.

It seems that when my generation started out we knew we had to start at the bottom and work up. I have worked with many Twenty-Somethings that have an entitlement view and expectation when first starting out; buy a nicer home even though it may be their first, spending money daily on the "latte factor," as coined by David Bach, *The Automatic Millionaire*, expect and start anywhere but the bottom of a new career or job.

Returned Decade

In addition to the generational values and perceptions of the four demographic groups, there is an additional culture change emerging that transcends all of these generations and that is what I refer to as the "returned decade," whereby there is about a ten-year span where each generation acts, behaves, thinks, and looks a decade younger. Twenty-Somethings act, behave, think, and look like teens; a Thirty-Something as a Twenty-Something; a Forty-Something as someone in their thirties; a Fifty-Something as someone in their forties; a Sixty-Something as someone in their fifties; and a Seventy-plus-Something as someone ten years younger.

Why these emerging trends now?

There are several reasons for these new trends and new culture for women. First and foremost is the technology boom which allows women to gather more information from a larger source than ever before. There is also an increase in healthy lifestyles, an increase in medical breakthroughs, an understanding and appreciation to live a purpose-driven life, and the realization that life on this earth is shorter than we thought and no one has guaranteed us any extra time.

Give Yourself Permission to Live the Life You Want

When children are young, we teach them to ask permission to do things and go places. Many women have internalized the childhood requirement for asking permission. They think they must ask before they get a job, change careers, go on an out-of-town business trip, leave for a vacation with a boyfriend, husband, or girlfriend, or take time for themselves.

To make lifestyle changes, women must learn to give permission to themselves and then turn "permission to…" statements into formal action. Setting goals is one of the best ways to give yourself permission, lay the groundwork for your ideas, and turn a desire for change into action.

Set Goals

Achieving goals takes thought and effort. The *American Heritage Dictionary* says that a goal is (1) a desired result or purpose, an objective; (2) the finish line of a race; (3) in certain sports, a structure or area into which players must propel the ball or puck in order to score.

Webster's New World Thesaurus offers other words to replace goal: *object, aim,* and *intent.* Goals offer us a way to aim toward our desires and give us a way to grant ourselves permission to do what we need to do. It's referred to as *intention.*

Intent or intention goes beyond our concept of goals. Your subconscious mind believes whatever you think to be true. So, if you believe that you can't do something or perhaps you have placed limits on what you feel you can do, then your subconscious mind believes you. For example, Emily, a Fifty-Something Achieving Woman, owns a small business. She says, "I can't believe how limiting my ideas and vision for the business were—I would immediately think 'can't do that' and then there was no chance of me thinking beyond that." Emily stood in her own way in reaching her goals. Therefore it becomes important for us to think of our goals and what we want to bring into our lives in a positive, no boundaries way. Imagine it already accomplished.

Intention can also be thought of as energy. Quantum physics has shown us that everything is energy. For example, if we were in a very large auditorium and we both had tuning forks calibrated to middle C and I tapped mine on a table, your tuning fork, provided it was calibrated to middle C as well, would vibrate. However, if your tuning fork was calibrated to middle E, it would not vibrate. This is why positive energy attracts positive energy and negative energy attracts more negative energy. Have you ever wondered why when something you perceive as negative happens to you there are usually another one or two negative things that happen as well?

How can we break out of this negative energy system that attracts negative people, feelings, activities, etc. and change them to attract positive energy?

First, get connected with your genuine inner self. We attach judgments of "bad," "awful," and "stupid," to behavior, thoughts, and feelings for ourselves as well as others. Instead, you may want to say to yourself, "It is what it is." It makes such a difference in the way you see and feel about things with that simple statement. It neutralizes a potentially damaging view.

When we're young we may look to the outside world to find out how we need to feel by how others act or react. My oldest son, David, was about twenty months old when he was sitting at the edge of the pool with his dad and accidentally fell into the pool. As his dad quickly pulled him out of the pool, he looked a bit dazed and didn't know what to think of what just happened. We had smiles on our faces, even though I was frightened out of my mind. It didn't take long before David began to smile and all was well in his little world.

For over fifteen years my goal was to live in another city two hours away, overlooking the ocean, with much higher housing costs. I always knew that I would live there but I never knew how that would happen, quite honestly. However, I knew the power and strength of intention and also knew that the details would take care of themselves as long as my intention was focused. So, setting goals and writing them down is important. I sit here now writing this overlooking the ocean, living in the city I dreamt of.

Once you have written down general goals which also, by the way, serve as permission for you to do what you want, write down your motivations for these goals. Note specifically how you are going to reach them and then write out the intention statement. These statements are written as though they have already come true. Remember that the subconscious mind doesn't know what is "real" or "non real." The subconscious will act as though what you say and think to yourself is true and will help you materialize your wishes, goals, and desires.

Here's how Jenny wrote down her goals and her intention statements.

 **GOAL SHEET**

GOALS	INTENTION STATEMENTS
Make More Money	"I have an abundance of money flowing in."
Take Vacations	"I enjoy three vacations a year."
Lose Weight	"I love my beautiful slim body."
Stay Healthy	"I am healthy in body, mind and spirit."
Find My Soulmate	"I am in a loving and passionate relationship."

Goals are a way to turn your desires and intent into meaningful results and define your purpose. To set a goal, you must determine what you really want out of your twenty-four hours—what you want for you and your family, at work, and in your romantic relationships. Most women spend more time thinking about the weekly grocery and errand list than thinking about what really counts in life.

To set your goals, follow these steps:

1. Start a goal sheet with four headings: "General Goals (Permission to…)," "Intention," "Motivations," and "Specifics."
2. List five general goals—five things you want out of life.
3. Under Intention write your goals as though they are already true.
4. Write down your motivations; ask yourself *why* you want each goal. A good way to do this is to talk into a tape recorder about your goals and why you think you want them. When you play the tape back and listen, the motivations behind your choices may become clear.

5. Under the heading Specifics, list *how* you can reach your goals.
   Be creative; brainstorm.
6. Start now!

Most women have no trouble stating general goals, such as saving more money, having nicer or cleaner homes, taking more vacations, or getting a good job. Writing down general goals such as these is the first step in the right direction. Writing down your goals increases your likelihood of achieving them. Seeing your goals in print helps you organize your priorities and reinforces your commitment. In addition, it activates your subconscious in regard to finding ways to reach your goals.

Once you have written down general goals (which also serve as permission to do what you want), write down your motivations for these goals, and then note specifically how you are going to reach them. Jenny, a pharmacist, listed her five major goals: to make more money, take vacations, lose weight, stay healthy, and find a lover. After discussing these general goals, she discovered that she wanted and needed to give herself permission to make more money so that she could have a weekly housekeeper and buy more clothes. She discovered that she needed to give herself permission to go on vacations so that she could get away from the stress at her job, give herself permission to lose weight so she could feel better about her body and feel more sexually comfortable with men, give herself permission to stay healthy in order to keep up her busy schedule, and give herself permission to find a lover to share and discuss her thoughts and fears.

Jenny now had general goals ("permission to..." statements) and the motivations behind them. At this point she needed to fill in how she would achieve her goals.

Jenny's goal sheet looked like this:

GOAL SHEET

General Goals (Permission to…)	Motivations	Specifics
Make more money	Cleaner house Expensive-looking clothes	Save $50 out of each paycheck Hire a housekeeper Shop sales at quality clothing stores
Take vacations	Relief of work-related stress	Go to bed early on Friday nights; Enjoy Saturday breakfasts alone
Lose weight	Feel better about my body	Start a diet; Lose 17 pounds Walk 3 times a week (25 minutes before work)
Stay healthy	Ability to accomplish all the activities on my busy schedule	Walk at lunch Bring sack lunch from home
Find my soulmate	A man to share my life	Feel good about myself sexually; Indulge in new, sexy undergarments; Join a singles group

You can also put your goals on tape as already accomplished projects. Since the subconscious does not know what is real and what isn't, it is a very effective tool to reaching your goals. A business woman, for instance, may want to see herself as well-liked, be thought of as a leader in her field, get along better with her husband and children, franchise her business, and become an in-demand speaker. Yes she can put these on paper, but it is much more effective when you put these goals on tape in your own words and play them back as you walk, garden, or drive to work each day. After awhile, your words on tape become you.

Set Aside One Hour a Day

Just as physical exercise is important for keeping physically fit, mental exercise is important for keeping mentally fit. We all know that everyone has twenty-four hours in a day, but the way we *use* and *perceive* our twenty-four hours either stresses us out or rejuvenates us.

Most women have heard the saying "An apple a day keeps the doctor away." The updated version for working women is "One hour of personal time a day keeps the time crunch away." We have approximately six thousand waking hours in a year. About two thousand are used on working eight-hour days. That leaves four thousand discretionary hours left (including sleep time).

Certainly you can find seven hours a week to sit quietly and think. Set aside one hour a day—preferably the same time each day, to establish habit—and *just think*. Think of ten ways to improve an activity, a relationship, a belief system, or anything else you find yourself worrying about. Write your ideas down on a legal pad. You do not have to resolve the situation at that moment. Just think and organize your thoughts. You may want to walk and exercise while you're thinking.

You will find that each idea triggers a new idea. This is what happens if you feel comfortable and not pressed for time—your mind wanders. You will find yourself thinking creatively. Most women do not take the time to think creatively about a situation or activity; they are pushed, by others or themselves, into making a decision or solving a problem immediately.

Everything you need to make a decision, change a belief system, or improve a relationship is within your grasp if only you think constructively about it. Something that you can do while you're taking time to think is to visualize the outcome you want in each situation and of reaching your goals. So, for Jenny, she would visualize the following:

Visualize more money: She would "see" herself receiving larger monetary checks, going to the bank and depositing large sums of money, "see" a checkbook with large sums of money in the register, and "see" her paying the housekeeper without any monetary worries.

Visualize taking vacations: Jenny would "see" herself on the beach relaxing in a swimsuit with the sun warming her body and giving her a golden tan.

Visualize losing weight: She would "see" herself wearing fitted skirts and tops, going to the gym wearing slimming fitness clothes, going out wearing a sexy dress, and anything else she would like to do with a slimmer body.

Visualize staying healthy: Jenny "sees" herself eating healthy meals and has the energy that good health brings.

Visualize finding a soulmate: She "sees" herself interacting with her lover, even though she may not know exactly what he looks like—feeling warmth and love between the two of them, doing fun activities together, and other ideas of what a loving relationship would look like to her.

Think, Don't Worry

Most women tend to worry, rather than think, about situations. A lot of this worrying comes from the feeling that women need to make the "right" or "perfect" choice. Remember, however, perfection is not real.

Trying to achieve it will stall your creative process. Avoid trying to achieve perfection; just think clearly. If you think chaos, you get chaos. If you think of staying calm and making the best decision at the time, you will stay calm and chances are good that you will make a wise decision. *You are what you think!*

Our thoughts are very powerful. In fact, what we think affects our body, our spirit, and our environment. Someone said that 50 percent of the time we worry about things that never happen, 30 percent of the time we worry about things that have passed, 12 percent of the time about health issues, and only 8 percent of the time about real problems. Of the real problems, half of them we can solve and the other half, we can't. This means we spend 96 percent of our time on unnecessary worry.

The comic strip *Cathy* said it best:

Oh, Irving…I'm sorry! I've been worrying about myself and ignoring you!

Oh, Charlene…I'm sorry! I've been worrying about Irving and ignoring you!

Oh, Electra…I'm sorry! I've been worrying about Charlene and ignoring you!

Oh, Mom…I'm sorry! I've been worrying about Electra and ignoring you!

Oh, Dad…I'm sorry! I've been worrying about Mom and ignoring you!

(Pant, Pant, Pant, Pant)

Oh, Self…I'm sorry! I've been worrying about everyone else and ignoring you!

HERE WE GO AGAIN…

Two Great Expressions to Keep Perspective

Both of my parents are Holocaust survivors and have seen a lot of misery, pain, and atrocious behavior. Growing up as a child, I often heard my parents use a Yiddish expression when things did not go as planned or there was a minor accident (this minor accident once included a totaled car, but my daughter was okay). The expression, roughly translated in English says, "This break over another one." In other words, if something needs to happen, let it be this rather than something worse.

The other Yiddish expression I heard a few years ago and I think of it often and helps me keep things in perspective and my thoughts calm during a problem or small accident (as in my extremely strained ankle last year), is "Gam zu la tov," which roughly translated means, "This too is for the best." For some reason these two expressions help me put problems into perspective. Find one or two expressions that resonate with you and use them when you feel stress and need to calm down. There's a reason they resonate and help you calm down and think more clearly. I believe it's because they touch on a real truth for you. I also believe this is why we get "tingles" when someone says something— what they are saying signals the truth for us.

Visualization Exercises

I believe the mind is the best computer available to date. Just as your computer is not judgmental, nor is your mind. This is a wonderful gift that our minds give us. We, by our thoughts and emotions, place a judgment on an action, comment, or thought. As a result, without giving judgment to things, our mind picks up what we are truly thinking. It is imperative that we guard our thoughts so that they are not filled with judgment, such as "awful," "anxious," "bad," "ugly," etc., but rather turn these thoughts into loving, kind, compassionate, calm, harmonizing thoughts.

Our mind interprets our thoughts and our spirit brings our intentions into being. The subconscious mind takes the things we say to ourselves as well as others literally, just as a younger child might do. I remember when my daughter was about three years old and she spilled grape juice on the floor. I said angrily, "Look at what you've done," and she lowered her head to stare at the mess on the floor. She took what I said literally. Some women I work with feel that the men in their lives take their comments literally as well and this causes all kinds of problems, because we know that what we say sometimes comes from raw emotions and we don't think about what we are truly saying or how we are saying it—we are just emoting. This is particularly true when we're pressed for time and feeling overwhelmed.

Meditation

A perfect time to meditate is after you have looked at your goal sheet daily. Your meditation may take the form of reading inspirational quotes or passages of books that uplift your spirit and attitude. You may also want to include a phrase or mantra that you say everyday at the beginning or during or at the end of the day that may quiet your mind or alleviate the anxiety you feel. The mantra I use most mornings is, "I have enough time to do what needs to be done." This phrase helps me to calm down and focus on my day. It helps put me and my time in perspective. I know from previous times that I will get done what needs to be done—not everything that I want to do, but certainly the things that need to get done today. So much of our time stress is activated just by the thought that we have so much to do and not enough time to do it.

In effect, our self-talk sets us up to feel anxious. It is this internal dialogue that places added pressure on the day and on our perform-ance. I have another mantra that I repeat when I feel overwhelmed working on a project and that is, "I can if I think I can." I love the book by Dr. Norman Vincent Peale, *You Can If You Think You Can*. The words of wisdom are just as applicable today as they were when Dr. Peale wrote them in the fifties.

Important Points to Remember

It is important to establish your own Personal Motivational Lifestyle. The lifestyle models this book presents are the Traditional Homemaker, who is family-centered; the Transitional Woman, who may not be fulfilled by her job and feels guilty about the time it takes from her family; and the Achieving Woman, who is career-centered.

To know what you want in life, you must develop goals. In addition, you need to give yourself permission to reach these goals. When developing your goals, remember to be specific. The more specific you are, the easier it will be to achieve what you want in your life.

Chapter Two

Where to Put
Your Time Emphasis

A working woman's time is divided into professional, personal, and home time. However, *how* a woman divides her time should depend primarily on what motivates her. Once the working woman identifies her Personal Motivational Lifestyle, she then needs to take stock of how much time she allots to each of these areas and compare her tally to what her motivational lifestyle dictates. If an Achieving Woman puts the major emphasis on the home while her real interest and motivation is work, then the result is stress and unhappiness.

Distinguishing Professional, Home, and Personal Time

This section will elaborate on the motivational lifestyles described in chapter 1, so you can see the time allotments that each type of woman tends to feel satisfied with.

The Traditional Homemaker's primary time emphasis is in the home. Traditional Homemakers see themselves as managers of the home and want to be valued for this. They derive self-confidence from their role as home manager, but they are dependent on positive reinforcement from family and friends. Traditional Homemakers feel that taking time out for themselves is selfish, that they must keep busy with the cleaning, wash, or children to make everything work in time.

A statement from Nancy, a homemaker and substitute teacher, typifies the homemaker's view: "I'm happiest when I'm home playing with my kids. I like substitute teaching because it leaves me time to spend with my children. I'd hate to leave the kids every day—they need me at home."

According to informal surveys conducted by the Marketing Time Source of Santa Monica, California, most Traditional Homemakers would like to spend 50 percent of their time at home, taking care of the house or children; 30 percent on personal activities, such as shopping, hobbies, or lunch with friends; and 20 percent on professional activities, such as working part-time at an office to supplement family income.

A strong work-at-home cottage industry is springing up among the Traditional Homemaker group. These cottage industries revolve around the family and home, from sewing personalized T-shirts for cheerleaders, knitting scarves, jewelry making, interior design, to eBay retailing.

The Internet has opened huge possibilities for women who prefer to stay home with their children and share their "domestic" talents with others, earning extra cash on the side.

Entrepreneur.com (www.entrepreneur.com) offers twenty-five part-time businesses that traditional women can start today and promote over the Internet. This includes computer tutoring, medical transcription, records searching, and many more.

The Transitional Woman's time is split between her professional and home lives. She is torn: her value system says that women need to take care of the home first and then work if necessary. The Transitional Woman's inability to fulfill the traditional female role makes her dependent on others for satisfaction and happiness. In addition, compared to Traditional Homemakers and Achieving Women, Transitional Women are usually less satisfied with their relationships. This group needs to know that positive changes are possible and that they deserve the good things in life. They need to learn that they have choices.

Elaine, an executive secretary who is a Transitional Woman, feels hurried all the time. "I enjoy the people I work with, clothes hunting, and getting my very own paycheck…but some days I hate to leave my little baby and a messy house."

The Internet and home business, however, can be a safety valve for Transitional Women just as it is for Traditional ones. Judy, for instance, works as a medical transcriber from her home office, transcribing patient medical records for hospitals, doctors, dentists, chiropractors, and veterinarians who need outside help transcribing patient medical records. Before launching her home business, she took several classes in medical terminology from a local college.

Most Transitional Women like to spend 35 percent of their time at home, 35 percent of their time working, and 30 percent of their time on personal activities.

The Achieving Woman's primary time emphasis is in her professional life. She derives self-confidence and a feeling of control from her career. Without a career, most of these women (all generations) feel they have no purpose, even though they may have a family. Her strongest needs are the need to succeed and the need for independence. She is constantly on the go, always trying to make situations better and events bigger. She wants to know how and where to go to get something done.

Janet, an accountant, loves her career. "I look forward to going to the office. In fact, sometimes I feel a little guilty that I enjoy my career so much. Some Saturdays I prefer to work at the office instead of staying home."

Trish, a Thirty-Something attorney, found that working outside the home full-time was just too much for her three children, husband, and herself. She and her husband decided she would work part-time from home. Trish is an Achieving Woman and found that her work at home was closer to full-time even though she was doing most of the work in her home office. Trish found that her computer gave her as much access to office resources as working at the office did. As a result she spends only a couple of hours there a week to catch up, and the rest of the time she works out of her home office which has been completely remodeled to meet her needs. Many builders today, especially those designing smart homes, specialize in building home offices with their homes and provided specialized wiring for computer needs. This is especially true for Generation Xers and Achieving Baby Boomers.

A typical Achieving Woman wants to spend 50 percent of her time engaged in professional activity. She would like to spend 25 percent of her time on personal activities and 25 percent of her time or less at home. She tries to cut her home chores by assigning some tasks to other family members, leaning heavily on convenience or prepared foods, or by hiring part-time help. They are also the impetus behind the "smart appliances" being developed by Whirlpool and others so that a working woman can program her refrigerator and oven over the Internet from the office and have dinner ready by the time she comes home.

Determining How to Divide Your Time

In this section, you will identify what you're doing for a two-week period and with those results, determine your present time emphasis by listing the time spent on all activities, totaling the time spent by category, and then entering the totals in the chart on pages 27–28.

Begin by writing down what you're doing during the day in thirty-minute intervals, starting with the time you wake up and tracking until you go to bed. This is your Daily Time Sheet and it looks like this:

5:00 a.m.—wake up

5:30 a.m.—shower and listen to the news

6:00 a.m.—grabbed an apple for breakfast and left for work

6:30 a.m.—dropped off kids at school and commute to work

7:00 a.m.—commute still in progress

7:30 a.m.—arrive at work

Continue at 30-minute intervals until bedtime

Once you have your daily time sheets filled out for an entire two weeks, including weekends, then it's time to total the time in your Activity Time Sheet. I know it can be a bother to do, but the information that you discover doing this is worth the time and effort.

Activity Time Sheet

Begin by adding all the activities you performed that day that would go under the headings of Home, Personal, or Work. Round off your time to the nearest hour—the total for each day will not add up to exactly twenty-four hours. Circle all work times in yellow, home times in green, and personal times in red from your Daily Time Sheet. Add all the times circled in the same color, and write each total in the appropriate column of the chart. Determine your total time by category for each day for two weeks. You can do this on your computer as well.

ACTIVITY TIME SHEET

Professional Time	Home Time	Personal Time
Monday		
Tuesday		
Wednesday		
Thursday		

⏰ ACTIVITY TIME SHEET continued

Professional Time	Home Time	Personal Time
Friday		
Saturday		
Sunday		
Monday		
Tuesday		
Wednesday		
Thursday		
Friday		
Saturday		
Sunday		
Totals		

For example, Sheila works from 8:00 a.m. to 5:00 p.m. every day, with one hour for lunch. She draws a yellow circle around the amount of time she spent at work. If she runs errands at lunch, that hour is considered home time. She circles the "home" total in green. If she takes her lunch hour with a friend, has her hair trimmed, or shops for clothes, the time is personal time; she circles the "personal" total in red.

Preparing dinner, washing dishes, or putting the children to bed is home time. Reading, watching television, or going to the movies is personal time. If, however, she goes to the movies just for the children, then the activity is considered home time.

You will not only see where you are spending your time, but more important, you will be able to decide if your time emphasis is in balance with your motivational lifestyle. You will know you are balanced when you feel peace within, rather than constant turmoil.

When finished, decide what percentage of time you have invested in professional, home, and personal time. Then compare your time with the averages for each type of woman. For instance, suppose you're a Transitional Woman who spends 60 percent of her time at work, 20 percent at home, and 20 percent in personal activities. Compared to the typical allotments for a Transitional Woman—35 percent professional, 35 percent home, and 30 percent personal—your schedule is out of balance. You probably feel the strain it is imposing on you.

You are "wasting time" if your time emphasis is not consistent with your motivational lifestyle. This inconsistency brings general anxiety, fatigue, and time tension, which is an intrusive concern about having the time to get things done.

The standard of 30 percent personal time may seem overindulgent, selfish, or not possible. Look at the reality, however: after you subtract seven hours from twenty-four for sleeping and twelve hours for professional and home activities, you have approximately five hours left daily for personal activities. In the remainder of this book, you will learn how to capture these hours.

How to Achieve the Balance

You have just learned where the different types of women usually feel comfortable putting their time emphasis. Now you'll look at a few examples to see how time use and lifestyle can be mismatched.

The Traditional Homemaker

Situation Sylvia, a Forty-Something Traditional Homemaker, volunteered over twenty hours a week outside her home. "I stay at home and volunteer at my daughter's school, in organizations, and do the books for our family business. The more I do, the more I'm 'volunteered' to do. I'm away from the family on the average of two nights a week and most mornings. I constantly try to find time to do the things I need and want to do—gardening, making crafts, and taking care of the family. I feel like I'm ready to snap."

Time Mismatch Sylvia is a Traditional Homemaker, but she spends 50 percent of her time outside the home, volunteering. According to her Personal Motivational Lifestyle, she needs to spend 50 percent at home, 30 percent on personal activities, and 20 percent on outside work.

Time Balance Sylvia needs to say no and reprogram her schedule.

Time Interpretation Here is what she had to say after she made the necessary changes: "I chose the one organization I enjoyed most and only volunteer five hours a week, during the day. I started a small vegetable garden with zucchini, tomatoes, and peppers. I still don't have all the time I need to do what I want, but I don't feel like I'm ready to snap, either."

Sylvia changed her time emphasis to reflect her motivational lifestyle, Traditional Homemaker. By combining her personal interest in gardening with her home interest in cooking, she balanced home and personal time. By choosing only one volunteer organization, she was able to spend her work time in a way she thought important, freeing her to do other activities consistent with her lifestyle.

Situation Liz, a Thirty-Something Traditional Homemaker, works twenty-four hours outside her home each week. "I work part-time so that our family can have a few extras…summer camp for the girls, and nice clothing for the children. By the time I come home and do every-thing that's needed, I feel anxious and crabby."

Time Mismatch Liz is a Traditional Homemaker, but she spends over 50 percent of her time outside her home and less than 20 percent in her home. She needs to reverse these two time allotments.

Time Balance Liz needs to work fewer hours in her present job or find a position that will allow her to work part-time at home. Many jobs fit nicely into this pattern—typing, bookkeeping, proofreading, and design work.

Here is Liz's explanation of the changes she eventually made: "I asked my boss to let me do some bookkeeping at home. We worked out a plan so that I can do this one day a week. I'm able to take on book-keeping for two new clients now, since I don't waste my time getting prepared in the morning, taking a thirty-minute lunch break, or driving to and from work. I keep the same child-care schedule, but get a lot more done."

Time Interpretation Liz changed her time emphasis to reflect her motivational lifestyle, Traditional Homemaker. By combining her part-time job with slightly more responsibility and staying home one day a week to work, she increased her time emphasis in the home while actually increasing what she accomplished for her employer.

Situation Allison, a Thirty-Something Traditional Homemaker with two children who was a teacher before her children came along, started an online children's store selling baby bibs and accessories that she and her partner make at home. "I'm thrilled to stay home with the children, but I really need to spend a little more time with the business if I'm going to make any money at it. I don't need to make a lot of money, but at least help my husband out with some of the bills. I feel torn working the business when the kids are awake and need me."

Time Mismatch Allison spends her time at home, but spends only 15 percent of her time at home working her online business, 20 percent on personal activities, and a whopping 65 percent focused with her children. Since her generation feels adamant about spending quality time with their children, she is torn and feels guilty with this time mismatch.

Time Balance She needs to plan her week with specific times set for her online business. She can plan to work while her young children are napping, or plan to work her business in the evenings when her husband comes home, or work at certain times during the weekend. She can also work more in the business when her youngest child is in preschool and get a babysitter "playmate" to play with her youngest child two or three mornings a week.

Time Interpretation Allison chose to work specific times on the weekends and find a partner to help her out during the week. She found a "grandmother" figure to babysit and play with her youngest child three mornings a week. Since the babysitter comes to Allison's home, she feels as though her son now has another person who loves and adores him and not really an outside babysitter. Since Allison is a Gen Xer, she feels more responsible for bringing in money than her younger sister, who would prefer to spend any extra time with her friends and all the children.

The Transitional Woman

Situation Lillian, a Transitional Woman (a thirty-five-year old Gen Xer), works constantly and relies on babysitters to watch the children. "I am spending money for someone else to get to know my children while I work. When I have any time at home, I'm too busy washing and cleaning to share any good family time. I'm always rushing and fitting in errands."

Time Mismatch After charting Lillian's schedule, she found that she was spending 45 percent of her time at work and with work-related activities, 35 percent of her time at home, and 20 percent of her time on personal activities.

Time Balance Lillian must find a way to spend less time on the job and more time with her family.

Time Interpretation Lillian's boss would not accept flextime. So she changed to a job that allowed her to keep a flexible schedule, even though the new job paid less. "I couldn't keep up the pace. Even though I make less money, I don't need to use the sitter as much. I've worked a deal out with my neighbor—I take care of her little boy Saturday mornings, and she watches my daughter Wednesday evenings, when my husband and I go to a movie. I pay a neighborhood teen to iron twice a week. During 'iron' time, the family sits at the kitchen table talking, with the television off and the answering machine on. So far, it works out well."

Situation Karen, a Transitional Woman, works all day long. She picks up items around the house in the morning as time allows, works at her full-time job, and comes home, prepares dinner, and continues to straighten the house. "I feel like I'm a walking and talking cleaner-upper. I'm always picking up toys, wrappers, lint, shoes, and other stuff. I need *help* in the house."

Time Mismatch Through charting her time, Karen found that she was spending 50 percent of her time at work and 50 percent of her time at home cleaning up. She had no time for personal activities.

Time Balance Karen must decrease the time she spends on housework by hiring help, asking her family for help, or changing her standards.

Time Interpretation Karen delegated some household responsibilities to other family members. She could not afford outside cleaning help, so she turned for help within the household. "I am responsible for the kitchen and the bathroom, my ten-year-old takes the family room, and my boyfriend takes our bedroom. I tell them how much it helps and how I have more time for them. I didn't know if it was going to work at first, but the more time I spent with them, the more they made the effort."

Situation Millie, a Fifty-Something Transitional Woman, works as a sales representative for a department store and takes care of her ailing mother. "It's been very difficult working full-time and taking care of my mom. I visit her every evening when I get off work and stay with her for a few hours. My husband is very understanding but it's taking its toll on me and our relationship. If I miss a night my mom complains and I wonder if she is okay."

Time Mismatch Through charting her time, Millie found that she was spending 90 percent of her time outside the home between work and visiting her mom.

Time Balance Millie has dabbled on eBay and really enjoyed the experience. Millie may want to explore the possibility of working on "eBay" activities so that she has a good income and the flexibility of checking in with her mother earlier in the day.

Time Interpretation After several months of finding more ways to make money on eBay, Millie now makes two-thirds of her past salary. "At this rate I'll be able to make financial ends meet 'almost,' and visit my mom. I'm finding I have a lot more energy for my relationship with my husband. I feel like I have a life again," says Millie.

The Achieving Woman

Situation Janie, an Achieving Woman, does not spend what she thinks is enough time at work; this causes her stress. "My mother needs more health care since my dad passed away. I take her to most of her doctor appointments, testing, and such. I have a demanding work schedule that I can't keep up with. I have to come up with something, but don't want to give up my job or sacrifice my mom's health."

Time Mismatch Janie spends 40 percent of her time at work, 45 percent of her time at home and with her mom, and 15 percent of her time on personal activities.

Time Balance Janie must find a way to delegate her mother's care, work more efficiently, or do both.

Time Interpretation "I asked my boss of eight years if I could work at home one day a week. She was not in favor of the idea at first. I explained to her that I would not need to take as much sick leave with this new schedule. We tried it, and it worked. I spend five hours on

Wednesdays with Mom. It gives me two days, Monday and Tuesday, to get involved in work and two days, Thursday and Friday, to complete what I've started. I check up on Mom during lunch or after work on the other days. I have a college student come in the afternoons to provide companionship for her."

By negotiating a flexible work schedule with her boss to suit work and her mom, Janie feels that she has more control over work and her mother's care. She takes less sick leave and is able to concentrate more fully on work when she is there.

Situation Louise, an Achieving Woman, is spending most of her waking hours with work-related activities. "I started waking up at 5:00 a.m., going for a walk (on the days I thought I could spare thirty minutes), scheduling business breakfasts at 7:00 or 7:30, and then getting to the office by 8:30. I would come home around 6:30 and plop down. I forced myself to stay up until 11:30 so that I could spend time talking to my husband, who was watching the news on TV. I probably would have kept this up, but I came down with an inner-ear infection. This caused me to lose my equilibrium and *forced* me to take it easy."

Time Mismatch Louise found that she was spending 65 percent of her time at work or work-related activities, 20 percent at home, and 15 percent in personal areas.

Time Balance To decrease the number of hours she spends on her career and to preserve her health, Louise must find a way to work more efficiently or take on fewer projects.

Time Interpretation "I realized that my work was getting done but that I wasn't creating new projects as rapidly. I started focusing on one project at a time, rather than several at once, putting all my effort into one area. My husband and I set up time to talk before the news. I went to bed earlier, slept in later, and made only one early-morning business breakfast a week. It has been almost seven months since I last lost my equilibrium, and I hope to keep it that way. I now feel more in control of my life at work and at home. The doctor wants me to spend more time on myself relaxing…That's my next project."

Situation Janet, a Twenty-Something divorced mother of an infant son, decided to stay home after working in the pharmaceutical industry for seven years. "I find I am spending so much of my waking time with my online business. It is doing so much better than I thought it would and I need to spend time on it. I feel guilty that I'm not spending enough time with my son. It seems that my weekly housekeeper and babysitter are raising him."

Time Mismatch Janet is spending over 65 percent of her time on her online business, 10 percent on personal activities, and only about 25 percent on her child and home activities.

Time Balance Janet needs to scale back on her work and increase the time she spends with her son. Having spent so much of her time working outside in the field, Janet was able to have a flexible schedule, work long hours, and still have enough time to have a life. Now, she needs to become familiar with a schedule that allows her to work full-time from home, placing time boundaries on her work time so that she is home focused on her baby more often during the day.

Time Interpretation "Now that I keep specific 'office hours' and turn off the computer every day at 3 p.m. to enter the 'home zone,' I feel much more balanced and not as guilty. I go back to work three evenings during the week and find time to have friends over for dinner for 'my' time a couple times a week."

As you review your own time allotment, remember: Everything you need to make a decision, change a belief system, improve a relationship, or redivide time is within your grasp *if only you take the time to think constructively about it.*

Finding Your Peak Time

Imagine that each daily square on the calendar is divided into four parts: morning, afternoon, late afternoon, and evening. Until you train your mind's eye to automatically separate the day into four parts, manually draw in dotted lines to differentiate the sections. With your PDA or hand-held computer, visualize these four imaginary sections.

Dividing your day into fourths is also helpful when we identify our energy levels. What part of the day do you find your energy the highest? To identify our energy levels and embrace the results helps us to accomplish our everyday tasks with less stress. For example, much of our energy depends on our circadian rhythms.

Circadian is Latin for "around the day." These rhythms change depending on what the three basic cycles are doing; physical, emotional, and intellectual. Our physical cycle takes twenty-three days to complete. It controls our energy, coordination, resistance to change, and other physical points. This is why we may need more sleep depending on where our physical cycle lies. It's important that you honor your body if it is telling you it needs more time to rest. Many of us think that we shouldn't be tired, we had enough sleep…but the body doesn't work that way. Our bodies do tell us when they're tired, sleep deprived, hungry, etc. When we don't listen to these incredible and sensitive "computers," they cause problems and break down. This breakdown comes over a period of time if we have not been listening to our bodies; as a result we get sick, exhausted, become emotionally and physically burnt-out, and experience other present day maladies, such as autoimmune diseases.

The emotional cycle is twenty-eight days and is tied to creativity, mental health, and our temperament, and the intellectual cycle takes thirty-three days to complete. Our intellectual cycle regulates memory, alertness, and other intellectual pursuits. When our intellectual cycle is high we are more likely to remember things better and do well on tests.

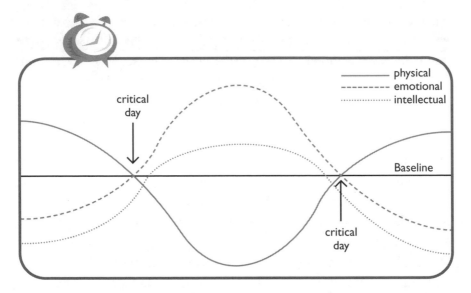

critical day

physical
emotional
intellectual

Baseline

critical day

Positive is anything above the baseline and negative is anything below the baseline. However, the critical days, when we feel more "out of whack," are those when any cycle crosses the baseline, switching from positive to negative, or negative to positive. On critical days there is a greater chance that things will go wrong and we are more likely to have an accident. Pilots in Europe have their biorhythms checked and if there are two or more lines in the critical zone they are not scheduled to fly the plane.

The number and severity of workplace accidents also tend to increase during the night shift. Major industrial accidents attributed partly to errors made by fatigued night-shift workers include the Exxon Valdez oil spill and the Three Mile Island and Chernobyl nuclear power plant accidents. One study also found that medical interns working on the night shift are twice as likely as others to misinterpret hospital test records, which could harm their patients. It may be possible to reduce shift-related fatigue by using bright lights in the workplace, minimizing shift changes, and taking scheduled naps.

Many women who travel from coast to coast, with the three-hour time changes, experience disrupted circadian rhythms, which causes the feeling of jet lag. This feeling of jet lag is even greater going from California to Italy, for example. Your physical, emotional, and intellectual cycles are out of sync with the new time schedule. It is important that you prepare in advance of your long-distance trip. There are things you can do to make the time lag less dramatic. You may want to go to bed thirty minutes earlier every other night until your time schedule is closer to that of your destination. This is a benefit of using a month-at-a-glance calendar so you can see when you're traveling next and make the changes at bedtime. If that proves to be too difficult, there is another solution to reduce the effects of jetlag with light therapy. This therapy exposes people to special lights, many times brighter than ordinary household light, for several hours near the time the person wants to wake up. This helps them reset their biological clocks and adjust to a new time zone. This is especially beneficial if you travel very long distances. Some people take melatonin, but there are no studies of its long-term effects.

But what about children who routinely stay up late at night, starting at a young age? Our biorhythms are responsible for these night owls as well. My daughter, Naomi, loved staying up late as early as I can remember. I thought she didn't want to go to sleep because she didn't want to miss anything that was going on around her. No matter how I scolded or told her to go to bed, she would be awake past 11 p.m., while she was in grammar school and beyond that to high school. Now, as a young adult, she frequently stays up until 1 or 2 a.m. Thank goodness she found a career that allows her to sleep in.

The bottom line: Be kind to yourself and your body. Listen to what it needs, i.e., more sleep, relaxation, healthy foods, water, "zone out" time. The more we learn to embrace our biological rhythms the more they will work with us rather than against us. If you are a night owl, you may want to consider finding a job or career that embraces these hours. Otherwise, you will be walking, talking, and working on automatic pilot during the mornings.

Night Owl Careers

Since it is difficult at times to live and work in an eight to five business world, what jobs or careers are available to night owls so that they can live a quality life without living on autopilot during the weekdays?

Here are a few great careers for night owls:

- Outside sales
- Real estate
- Accountants
- Most online businesses
- Afternoon and evening shift workers, nurses
- Artists, writers

In addition, many businesses such as banks, insurance companies, software companies, and others that stress twenty-four-hour service hire many people for night shifts.

Using Your Energy to Your Advantage

If you have high energy during the morning, plan to do your "brain work" during this time. For you and most women, mornings are the worst time to have meetings; instead, schedule concentration activities during morning hours. Place or return phone calls around 11:30 a.m.

During the lunch hour, give yourself permission to hit a few balls against a wall (playing tennis well is not necessary), take an aerobics class, window-shop, or read for pleasure at a park or cafe. Plan Fridays as business-lunch days. Remember to be flexible. For example, you do not need to stay the entire hour of aerobics. Health experts agree that twenty minutes of aerobic activity is productive (and much better than nothing).

You may want to exercise during the lunch hour two or three times a week. During the other lunch hours, you may want to do errands, attend a club meeting, or schedule a business lunch. Remember, be flexible!

If your high-energy time is in the afternoon, this is a good time to start major projects. Do not, however, start a major project and think it will be finished by the end of the day. To do so would be setting yourself up to feel overwhelmed. Plan for in-office time the morning after you start a new project.

Late afternoon is ideal for starting a new project, if late afternoon is your high-energy time. If not, it is an excellent time for placing or returning calls. Late afternoon is also a good time for morning people to follow up, read, analyze computer printouts, or write correspondence.

During the evening you might plan to attend a class once or twice a week, do errands one evening a week, have a personal-needs night, stay late at the office, or enjoy a weekly family night, depending on your professional, home, or personal requirements. Remember to be flexible.

Dividing the day not only allows you to see how and where you are spending your time, it helps you to get going when you're at peak energy. You can see if you're spending your high-energy times in long, drawn-out meetings, in running errands, in accomplishing trivial things, or in putting out fires.

Matching Needs and Motivational Lifestyles: Time Tips

The need to expand time in a particular segment of your life may be chronic or it may arise in special situations only. Whatever the case, the tips that follow can be useful for all types of women.

Tips for Expanding Professional Time

The two tips of expanding professional time include a way to share burdens and a way to use time more effectively by organizing it better.

The SWAT Team

The SWAT team is a tool for managing both work time and home time, and it is uniquely adapted to the working woman. (Chapter 4, "The Big Glitch," talks about how to develop a SWAT team.) In effect, it helps a working mother be in two places at once by recruiting a group of other women who will fill in for her in many ways. A SWAT team can take the children to the dentist while the working woman performs an essential work task or, conversely, fill in at work while the working mom takes care of a sick child or herself.

With the baby boomers increasingly taking care of their parents, there needs to be another type of SWAT team available for this sandwich generation. This SWAT team may be made up of other men and women who have elderly parents they take care of and you can have an exchange going on during an emergency. There are also agencies available to help out during an emergency, although many of them do charge top dollar.

The Traditional Homemaker needs to use this tactic if there is an emergency or some kind of deadline approaching. This is also helpful if Mom wants to spend some special time with a newborn or other children individually. Because Traditional Homemakers spend most of their time around home and family activities, they feel they "should" be able to do it all, all of the time. Sometimes it takes others to show the Traditional Homemaker that burning the candle at both ends takes its emotional and physical toll on the family and herself.

The Transitional Woman may think a SWAT team is a good idea, but she may doubt she will find women who will participate. She barely has the time to think about it, let alone plan and make the calls necessary to get one in place. If she looks hard enough, however, a SWAT team emerges.

The Achieving Woman invented this concept. Achieving Women would not be able to enjoy their careers as much if various child-care and elder care options were not available. They are always interested in new SWAT team ideas.

The Month-at-a-Glance Calendar

A month-at-a-glance calendar is a must. It displays project due dates and reminders about letters to write, appointments to keep, and home and personal commitments that may cut into work time. This smoothes out the week and month, and prevents overcommitment during heavily scheduled weeks. Chapter 7, "Taking Control of Your Schedule," details the use of the month-at-a-glance calendar.

The Traditional Homemaker finds the month-at-a-glance calendar helpful in all areas of her life. The Transitional Woman finds the calendar helpful once she decides to purchase it. It helps her visualize her cluttered schedule. The Achieving Woman finds she can't live without a month-at-a-glance calendar once she has started using it.

PDA'S and Hand-Held Computers

Chapter 7 will go into detail as to best use your PDA and hand-held calendars. Whether you use a paper calendar or an electronic one, it is vital to be able to see the whole month at a glance.

Tips for Expanding Home Time

Management of home time constitutes a serious problem. Yet, with a little ingenuity and a few tips, working women can learn to handle most home chores in much less time.

The Mini-Office-Kitchen

Women, unlike men, spend hours in the car taking and picking up and running other home-related errands. One time-saver that works especially well is the mini-office-kitchen car trunk, which is an office- and home-supply store on wheels. As chapter 16 will discuss, if you have supplies with you, you can work anywhere and save many trips to your home, the office, or the store. You can use the trunk of your car to store paper clips, stapler, folders, scratch paper, newsletters, and other items you need repeatedly. Whether or not you have children, having healthful snacks and drinks in the trunk can be a time-saver in the face of a road delay. Keeping nylons, a mirror, and tennis shoes in the car can enhance your image, increase your flexibility, and improve your efficiency. The Traditional Homemaker originated this idea. In most cases, she needs to expand her supplies.

The Transitional Woman thinks it's a good idea, but she has doubts. She thinks the lip balm will spoil in the car, or the baby's toys will get dirty in the trunk, or the color of the wrapping paper will be wrong. The Achieving Woman needs to expand her mini-office-kitchen and remember to use it.

Bedtime Show-and-Tell

Let the children know that your late night at the office or the time you spend with a friend is the same night as bedtime show-and-tell. That is, after you get home, you spend a little extra time with each child at bedtime. You read a story, let the child read to you, or simply talk about the day's events. The catch is that the children must be washed up, in their pajamas, and in their rooms by the time you come home. It is a pleasure coming home to children who are all ready for bed when you are late and tired. To allow the children time for bedtime preparations, you may have to plan a simple dinner for them. A breakfast dinner—that is, a dinner that consists of typical breakfast fare, such as scrambled eggs with spinach—is quick, nutritious, and can be made by a husband or children. Or make easy sandwiches on show-and-tell night, or make arrangements with a babysitter to come every Tuesday night. Another option is to ask a neighbor or a SWAT team member to have your children over for dinner one night a week. You can spend that time with your sweetheart!

The Traditional Homemaker sometimes finds that declaring a bed-time show-and-tell night is the only way she can get her few hours a week of personal time.

The Transitional Woman thinks bedtime show-and-tell is a good idea, but she hates to impose on the neighbors or she feels that her children are burnt out on babysitters.

The Achieving Woman feels this tip offers a great way to enjoy both her professional life and her family life.

Dinner Time to Connect and Reconnect

One enriching way to expand home time is to place having everyone at the dinner table as a high family priority. I know it's difficult with everyone's schedule, but except on occasion, dinnertime is for everyone to be home. You may have to work with schedules on certain days of the week, but it's worth the energy and effort to do so. Sandra, a Forty-Something fitness trainer with three active children in sports says, "Most nights we sit down for dinner at 6:45 p.m., but on two nights a week, because of my son and daughter's soccer practice, we sit down at 7:30 p.m. I usually make lighter meals on those days. This is about the only time we're all together as a family and I love it."

Integrate or Suffocate™

There just isn't enough time to do everything we want to do, plus help our families, and the list goes on. If we try to do everything we will feel as though we are suffocating from more things to do. That is why I suggest to my clients the "Integrate or Suffocate" approach. This approach helps women meet their goals while living their values. It is not trying to do a number of different tasks at the same time while not being present or doing any of the tasks well. You know you're multitasking and not integrating when you feel anxious and pressed for time while you're doing the tasks. The difference with Integrate or

Suffocate is that you may be doing a few things at once but you are present and thoroughly enjoying each task. For example, Shelley, one of my clients, is a Thirty-Something Traditional Homemaker, did all her own housecleaning, wash, and ironing. She just couldn't find the time to iron. So, now she combines her ironing with testing her children for school tests and discusses their day. "I actually look forward to ironing now because it is our family time together," says Shelly.

Let me give you a perfect example of how you can use the Integrate or Suffocate approach in your life. In fact, this event is when I coined the term "Integrate of Suffocate." Many years ago, when my children were small, I tried not to make evening meetings. However, there was a dinner meeting two hours away that I really wanted to attend because of the wonderful speakers. I commonly ask myself, "How can I make this work?" After a few days I figured it out. My husband and I and the kids drove down to the meeting. The family dropped me off while they had soul food and went miniature golfing. When they picked me up at 10 p.m. they were already in their nighties. We were so excited to share our evening with each other. At first, all three children were telling me about the evening, and then one dozed off and then the second and then the third child was asleep. At that time my husband and I were able to connect. I knew I had made a good decision to take the family along when my children asked when I was going to the next meeting. This is a perfect example of Integrate or Suffocate. If we don't integrate what we really want to do in our lives we end up feeling frustrated or resentful, two very damaging emotions.

Other ways you can "Integrate or Suffocate"

- Exercise while watching a morning news show or any television show. You can do stretches, tummy crunches, use a torso machine, or a stationary bicycle.

- Do kegel exercises, squats, and lunges while talking on the phone.
- Exercise is part of your work day. Think of exercise as your creative buddy. It will help you de-stress, and think of creative ways to handle situations or complex events. It takes you away from the situation for a short while and allows your subconscious to work things out for you.
- Meditation is part of your work day. It is similar to making a thirty- or forty-five-minute meeting with a coworker or client. The meditation time will allow you to gain new insights and also help you de-stress which allows your body and mind an opportunity to work things out.
- Reading the *Wall Street Journal* if you're in business or the *New York Times* or a fashion magazine if you're in that field is part of your work day. Looking through a magazine or reading a newspaper is the same, if not better, than listening to a one-hour speech or seminar. It allows your mind to learn information and also stimulates your creative juices. Why reinvent the wheel when there are so many places that the wheel resides?
- Use TiVo for shows you want to watch later while you exercise and save time watching commercials.
- As you're waiting in line, do kegel exercises, take deep breaths, and think positive thoughts.
- As you're making breakfast for the children in the morning, make their lunches and yours as well.
- Bring your children along as you do errands and make the time pleasant and positive. Listen more than you speak. Encourage your children to talk—it's amazing what you'll find out about their day, attitude, and friends.
- Look at your birthday and anniversary list and buy cards at the beginning of the month for the entire month of activities, including a sympathy and congratulatory card as well.

Tips for Expanding Personal Time

Working women often overcommit to work and home activities and neglect personal time. Psychologists tell us that to stay mentally healthy and happy, everyone needs personal time—time for themselves.

The "Mom Is Off-Duty" Solution

The working mom or woman simply lets the kids, herself, and her husband know that the time for "Mom, I need…"; "Janet, you must…"; and "Honey, where is…" is over. Mom is going off-duty to read or do anything else she wants. Some women just disappear into a den or bedroom—children and husbands enter at their own risk.

The Traditional Homemaker welcomes this off-duty period, since she recognizes that she is on call most of the time.

The Transitional Woman would like to use this tip, but she feels guilty that someone will really need to say something to her and she won't be "there" for them since she is out of the house working during the week.

The Achieving Woman often uses this off-duty approach with her children, but she forgets how useful it is to have time away from other adults.

The "Erase the Chalkboard" Approach

Take one day a month to regroup, take a look at priorities, or do nothing but things you enjoy. Look at this day as "preventive sick leave." You will benefit because you are erasing nonessentials from your mental chalkboard and making room for essential mental notes. Your boss will benefit, because you come to work refreshed rather than working on overload, which is counterproductive. Your family will benefit because of your positive attitude.

The Traditional Homemaker has a hard time justifying this time away. Once she tries it, however, the benefits overshadow any negatives.

The Transitional Woman has a difficult time justifying sick leave if she is not ill and especially if she is not paid for this time off.

The Achieving Woman likes the idea but keeps putting it off. She is constantly on "fast forward."

Ten Minute Meditative Time Out

Taking "timeout" is crucial for your mind, body, and spirit. I know that the days I dash out of the house without my meditative time are those days that I feel a bit out of kilter. Meditative time allows me to sit quietly, clear my mind, and allow my creativity to "think." This time allows me to get grounded and I set the mood and energy for the day. Often I want to stay in this frame of mind longer because for me, it is a good, peaceful, calm, and safe place to be. I try to take ten minutes of meditative time out in the afternoon as well—it helps me get grounded and focused for the rest of the day. Often I ask myself one question: "How could I have made today better?"

The Traditional Homemaker may think she has all day to do this, but because it hasn't been scheduled in during the mornings, it may not happen. In addition, she may forget because she is busy placing the family's requests first.

The Transitional Woman welcomes this time but needs to make sure she takes the time first thing in the morning for herself. Once she recognizes how calming this is for her, she will find the time to take these special ten minutes.

The Achieving Woman welcomes this meditative time out but is frantic in getting her work day started. Once she commits to doing it and guards her time accordingly, she'll find that this precious time helps focus her day.

Get in Touch with a Youth Activity

Would you like to bring some good feelings into your personal time?

Give your spirit a chance to soar for one hour or so each week? Then I would suggest that you get in touch with an activity you loved or enjoyed in your youth. It could be writing, dancing, tennis, riding, running, playing with Play-Doh, sculpting, playing an instrument, skating, painting, or anything else.

Start a group, take a community class, or do it privately. The activity you choose connects to something deep within you that provides a safe, fun, protective, and happy place for you. If you can't think of anything, then try something that you have always wanted to do—but start it NOW!

It will brighten your days and week and you will find that you look forward to it. It also serves as an excellent role model for your children—to keep active and involved in something that you enjoy. The time is now—it is not about "someday, I will,"… "when the children are grown," or "when I remarry," or "when I make more money." We never know what lies before us tomorrow and that is why we need to make today a present and give ourselves the gift of personal time.

When considering your time and tips for improving your use of it, focus on your lifestyle motivation and be careful to match your needs with your interests. It does work—give it a try!

When classifying yourself or using these tips, remember your generational differences. Seniors need to allow more time to carry out tasks, Baby Boomers are more competitive and want to be the best at what they do. Generation Xers are more focused on getting ahead and Gen Ys need lots of personal communication with others.

Important Points to Remember

Where you put your time emphasis is of great importance. A working woman's time is divided into professional, personal, and home time. How a woman divides her time needs to depend primarily on what motivates her—her Personal Motivational Lifestyle. Most Traditional Homemakers would prefer to spend 50 percent of their time at home, taking care of the house or children, 30 percent on personal activities, and 20 percent on professional activities. The Transitional Women prefer to spend 35 percent of their time at home, 30 percent of their time on personal activities, and 35 percent of their time working. The Achieving Woman's primary time emphasis is on her professional life. She is most happy when she spends 50 percent of her time engaged in professional activities, 25 percent on personal activities, and 25 percent of her time at home.

It is best to determine how you are spending your time by writing it down in thirty minute intervals—what you're doing from the moment you wake up to the moment you go to bed. Do this for two weeks and you will see where you are presently spending your time and can then make changes in your time emphasis if it is not consistent with your motivations.

Become conscious of your peak times during the day and understand that we are affected by our circadian rhythms: physical, emotional, and intellectual. Be kind to yourself by understanding these energy levels.

You can help expand your time by:

• Creating your own SWAT team
• Using a Month-at-a-Glance calendar
• Using a PDA
• Organizing a mini-office-kitchen in your car
• Having Bedtime Show-and-Tell with your children
• Using dinner time to connect and reconnect with loved ones
• Integrate or Suffocate

Chapter Three

Avoiding the Guilt Trap: Self-Indulgence Is a Necessity

odern women find themselves trying to play demanding multiple roles. One woman may find herself meeting the responsibilities of a wife, mother, lover, and career woman—not to mention those of a friend, daughter, hostess, child schlepper, housekeeper, recreational director, nurse, cook, and amateur shrink. Having to divide her attention between so many roles makes her feel guilty, so she redoubles her efforts by trying to excel in every one. No one can live happily or healthily under such stress, which can only lead to exhaustion. To break the cycle of guilt, stress, and exhaustion, self-indulgent activities are essential. They help the working woman balance all her roles.

Balancing Time Rather than Juggling It

Most working women try to juggle their time between work, home, and personal activities. Just as in a juggling act, if one item is off balance, then the entire group is in danger. It is one thing to plan your time, but another thing to juggle it. Working women need to learn how to balance time, not juggle it. Juggling requires perfect timing but not flexibility. Balancing requires timing and a great deal of flexibility.

Sally, an attorney who is married and has two small children, shares how she turns time juggling into time balancing. First, she refuses to work on weekends and does little travel, unless it's a must. "I hire a babysitter to come along on my out-of-town cases, which I keep to a very few. My children have a good understanding of what I do and how important my work is to me. They also know that my love for them is even more important. My favorite holiday is Valentine's…I have this 'thing' for Valentine's. I wonder how many male attorneys go home at the end of working an eight-to ten-hour day and bake Valentine cookies?" Sally keeps her plans flexible on her out-of-town trips. She knows flexibility is a must as a working mom.

Tammy and her husband have four children and own their own business. Every school day, from 9:00 to 10:30 a.m., Tammy spends about twenty minutes in each of four classrooms helping out with her children. Tammy is there to make sure they obtain a good education. "All they want is attention—they don't want a tutor or a private school. They want a mommy and daddy involved. I am not only tutoring, but giving love."

Including the time she spends traveling to and from the school, Tammy spends almost eight hours a week in her active involvement with her children's education. Most working parents can't take the time off their jobs to be with their children during the day. "When I leave the office," says Tammy, "half the work force is gone." Asked how she is able to accomplish this task, she says, "I made it an obligation, like work. Their grades have gone up and up, and it's changed their attitudes."

How can working women define their priorities and act in accord with them even though major obstacles exist? To help women do this, I have used five major reference points as tools.

Define Your Priorities

In my life-management workshops, I ask women to use their imaginations to determine:

- Charactcristics thcy would likc to dcvclop
- How they really want to spend their time and with whom—not the way they would spend it to avoid guilt
- What they would do if money were not an issue
- How they would like to be remembered
- What they would do if they had three extra hours a week.

The information gained from each of these determinations provides an important reference point in the landscape of time management. With reference points to outline priorities, time-management decisions become less difficult.

This section will present the questions used to determine each reference point. Use your imagination to answer each one, and see what priorities take shape.

Reference Point 1: Who or What Would You Be?

If you could be anyone or anything in the world, who or what would that be? Once you have decided, write down as many phrases as you can that describe your choice. By studying your descriptions, you will probably get an idea of why your choice appeals to you. A good friend of mine, a Forty-Something Achiever, would like to be a computer.

Who/What Would You Be? An IBM Computer
Describe:
- A Baby Boomer Achieving Woman
- It's small, streamlined, and fits comfortably on my desk or anywhere
- It's fast, powerful, and full of information
- It's not sensitive to others' emotions, only statements and directions

Another friend of mine, a masseuse, would love to be Elizabeth Taylor.

Who/What Would You Be? Elizabeth Taylor
Describe:
- A Mature Baby Boomer
- Transitional Woman
- She has seen and experienced personal and financial success
- She has seen and experienced personal and financial failure
- She has relearned many things and persisted
- She is sexy and classic

By establishing reference point 1, working women can learn what characteristics they like, admire, and want to develop in themselves. This reference point gives the working woman "time direction," an idea of how she wants to develop and spend her work, home, and personal time.

What qualities do most women list as characteristics they aspire to have? When asked to list their responses under the heading "The Way I'd Like to Be," the top five characteristics for women under age fifty were:

- High earning
- Physically fit
- Well educated
- Beautiful
- Patient

The top five characteristics for women over age fifty were:

- Healthy in mind, body, and spirit
- Financially secure
- Quality and loving relationships
- Time to do the things they want to do
- Someone to have fun and enjoy life with

Reference Point 2: What If You Were Moving?

What would you want to do or accomplish if you had only three months before moving to another state? With whom would you want to spend your time?

This reference point not only helps you clarify what you want to accomplish, but it helps you maintain a sense of perspective on those days when you can't seem to get anything worthwhile done. Janet, a marketing director for a small manufacturing business, recently had to take time from work to take her eleven-year-old son to the doctor—the child had a severe case of the flu. She spent an hour and a half waiting to see the doctor. Several weeks later, Janet took more time from work because she wanted to see her son perform in a class play. "I rushed back to the office frazzled and had little time left to get work done. I just remember thinking, 'If this was my last day to live, did I waste my time this afternoon?' Somehow, I calmed down and had to admit to myself that I was glad that I had taken the time to take my child to the doctor and to see his performance. It made me realize that even though I enjoy my job, my children make life worthwhile. The most important thing in my life is being with my family and sharing their experiences. That realization helps me keep my hectic life in perspective."

Working through reference point 2 helps working women realize how they want to spend their home and personal time—not out of guilt, but as a reflection of their priorities. The Traditional Homemaker, the Transitional Woman, and the Achieving Woman feel the same way: the quality of relationships is important. All three want to spend more time with their families and increase their personal time.

The Traditional Homemaker is more aware of her priorities than the other types. The Transitional Woman and the Achieving Woman are usually too busy doing to be aware.

Nancy decided to stay home with her four children while they were young. "I want to go to work after my children are in school. I don't want to miss them grow up. I can't believe my oldest is almost twelve years old. Another two years and the baby will be in school. I'm sure it'll whiz by."

Reference Point 3: What If You Won the Lottery?

Working women have a tendency to think that if they did not have to earn money, they would not work. This may be true. But what would you do if money was not the reason for working? What if you won the lottery and became financially independent? Make a list of things you would like to do, accomplish, and spend your time on if money were not an issue.

The Traditional Homemaker will probably wish to remain unemployed but take more vacations with her significant other and children and purchase more or newer material possessions. She probably will wish for more time to do the things she and the family enjoy. The Transitional Woman will find that half of her peers would stay home; the other half would continue working, but at a career where they felt more appreciated. She, like the Traditional Homemaker, would take more vacations and buy more material possessions. She would place greater emphasis on enjoying what she was doing. The Achieving Woman may find that she would keep most things just as they are and wish for more time to do everything else.

What does this mean to the working woman? In most cases it is *not* the money that determines who you want to be and what you want out of life; rather, these things are determined by *how much time you have.* Rather than feeling guilty for working or not working outside the home, it is healthier and more accurate to perceive money as a commodity and time as an asset.

Psychologists tell us that work creates purpose and worth in our lives but inactivity creates restlessness, boredom, and sometimes depression.

Though most of us would want to change our way of life if we won the lottery, this reference point allows us to understand the need for activity and focus on those activities that are most meaningful.

Sandy, an Achieving Woman, says: "If I won the lottery, I'd invest 90 percent, pay off the house mortgage, and buy things for the family with the rest. I'd keep on working, but I would take one day a week and do anything I want or need to do. I'd go window-shopping, condition my split ends with mayonnaise, spend a day at the beauty shop, or stay home and finish projects—but I'd definitely keep working."

Reference Point 4: Write a Speech in Your Honor

How would you like others to remember you? Imagine what you would like your parents, children, lovers, friends, and coworkers to say if they were asked to make a speech about you. What would you say if asked to describe your own accomplishments? This reference point helps put your values in order, just in case the other three have not yet done so.

When it's all said and done, how you want others to think of you now helps define who you really want to be. Knowing this will encourage you to spend time with those who are important to you. It adds to your enjoyment of life and increases your people-orientation— ultimately, the only activity that matters.

Susan, an accountant for a high school, oversees and is responsible for millions of dollars. She is newly remarried and has two sons in elementary school. She wakes up at 4:30 or 5:00 a.m. and is at work by 5:45. Susan's husband gets the children to Susan's office by 7:00. At 7:30, the school bus picks the children up at her office and takes them to school.

Susan's ten-year-old son makes TV commercials. At first, that seemed glamorous. But the glamour soon gave way to the reality of the commute. Since Susan lives in a small town, she must make a long drive to Los Angeles for auditions. She usually has less than a twenty-four-hour notice for each trip. "I don't think I'll have enough money for the boys to attend college if I don't do this now. When you *do* get commercial assignments, the pay is great. A few years of this, and I won't have to worry about their college education.

"Our commute days are long. It's all worth it when one of the children says, 'Thank you, Mom, I appreciate all you do for me.' This is the best speech in my honor that the children could say. That's a great way to be thought of."

Reference Point 5: What Would You Do With an Extra Three Hours a Week?

I love asking women this question because their eyes light up as to all the things they would like to do. It is possible to find these three extra hours after you have completed the Daily Task Sheet and totaled up the amount of time you spend on home, work, and personal activities. Once you identify where your time is going you can "see" that you can combine a few activities, such as errands with children, house chores with family members, taking family on small business trips, and other ideas to make more time. Only through effective time and life management can you achieve the freedom to give yourself the extra time and thus, the nurturing you need and want, and that experts say is so necessary.

We can alleviate stress through exercising, eating healthfully, and pampering ourselves. In addition, working women need to place their emotional, physical, and mental well-being high on their agendas so that they feel stronger physically and emotionally to take care of the many challenges and emergencies that will inevitably arise.

We all know that when we do not make the time to go grocery shopping for food, the family is not fed. Without food for the soul through personal and spiritual time, the working woman and her family are not emotionally fed.

Jennifer, a Thirty-Something Transitional Woman, would spend the "extra" time training for marathon runs; Sherry, a Twenty-Something Achieving Woman, would spend the time on herself, getting a pedicure, massage, and shopping; Randy, a Fifty-Something Achieving Woman, would spend the time reading all kinds of magazines; Suzanne, a Forty-Something Traditional Woman, would spend the time painting and fixing up her home; Vickie, a Sixty-Something Achieving Woman, would spend more time with her friends; and Sherrie, a Seventy-Plus-Something Traditional Homemaker, would take computer classes.

I can almost guarantee that most of you can find the additional three hours in a week if you look closely at a few things: 1) What do you do after dinner? 2) What errands do you do during the weekends that you could do one night after dinner, get someone else to do, or combine into one of the weekend days and keep a couple of hours free to do what you want? Before you quickly say, "No way," please take the time to fill out two weeks worth of the Daily Sheets that identifies what you are doing every thirty minutes.

Reducing the High Price of Stress

Doctors tell us that anxiety, which produces stress, plays a major role in illness. Stress is a factor in causing cancer, migraine headaches, asthma, arthritis, and high blood pressure—for starters. In addition, stress wastes a tremendous amount of time. As an example, you need only remember the last time you had a tension headache. Remember how it kept you from thinking creatively or clearly, making decisions, finishing the task at hand, and handling critical or sensitive situations? And don't forget the high monetary cost of anxiety. Medications and doctors cost money, and employee illness is a major expense for employers.

Lynette, a secretary and a Transitional Woman, says: "The doctor prescribed pills to settle my nerves, but it made me more nervous. I spent over $50 a month on 'anti-stress' pills. The medicine I took to relieve my tension only made it worse…I felt listless, depressed, and irritable most of the time. A friend of mine talked me into going to the gym…Now I'm an exercise junkie. I don't feel one ounce of guilt spending time at the gym, because now I spend more time feeling well and enjoying the people in my life. I now feel more control over my life."

When viewed in comparison to the cost of the problems it can preclude, "self-indulgent" behavior might be the best bargain in town. The cost of a stress-reducing manicure or massage can seem low indeed in relation to the problems stress can cause. Consider the costs—both financial and psychological—of these common stress-related occurrences:

- Accidents
- Illnesses
- Forgetfulness
- Distraction

To beat stress, Michelle, an advertising representative, treats herself to monthly facials. "I feel that I have a lot more to give other people in my life if I pay attention to what is important to me and my own needs. That's why I don't feel any guilt taking time out for 'me.' I'm able to handle all the other stuff more easily if I've nurtured myself."

Ruth, a men's clothing buyer, says, "I treat myself to weekly manicures, monthly facials, and monthly massages. If I had the money, I would have weekly everything, except swimming, for which I don't find the time. Nothing seems to calm me down more than my facials and massages. My chiropractor suggested the massages that I used to think were self-indulgent. Now, I look at them as preventive medicine. I used to feel guilty taking the time for me instead of finishing a project or spending the time with my boyfriend. I don't know about other women, but I find the time I spend on me helps me regenerate and gives me a positive frame of mind."

Terri, a Forty-Something Transitional Woman who works for a medical facility, says, "Running helps me deal with my stress. Journaling helps me fall asleep better, but there's nothing like running up a good sweat and getting tired that helps me de-stress."

Examine Prevention Costs Versus Fix-It Costs: Case Studies

The difference between the cost of *preventing* a problem and the cost of *fixing it* once it occurs is not mathematic, but geometric. Let's look at some case studies that compare these costs. I think you will agree that guilt, anxiety, and stress are extremely costly.

The Situation On one hand, you're under a lot of time-stress to complete a project at work; on the other, you feel an obligation to help your child with homework. At work, no one else has the information needed for completion; at home, your eight-year-old is bringing in Cs and Ds in math, your strong point.

The Prevention *(a)* Ask for a one-day extension on the project at work. In most cases, extensions are granted without any ill effects. However, missing a deadline has many ill effects. *(b)* Hire a tutor, be it a friend, an older child skilled in math, or a professional suggested by the school or teacher.

The Cost *(a)* A little ego. *(b)* Dinner out or a dinner made at home for the friend; a small thank-you gift or, for $2.50, a thank-you card for the friend or child; $60 an hour for the tutor.

The Fix *(a)* Make excuses about why the project is not complete, or "complete" it haphazardly. *(b)* Tutor your child without a trace of patience, because you're thinking about the work that needs to be done at your office.

The Cost *(a)* Damage to your professional reputation, an increased level of guilt and stress that will stay with you for some time, and, possibly, accumulated stress that pours over into all relationships at work and at home. This cost is prohibitive! *(b)* An increased level of guilt and stress in your relationship with your child. This cost is also prohibitive!

The Situation You've been working hard at the office, your mom needs more attention because of a recent hospital stay, and your best friend is going through a divorce.

The Prevention Take some personal time off and go window-shopping, take an aromatic bath, go for a brisk walk or run, or do anything else that will help you get your mind off everything but something you find pleasurable. After you've spent some time nurturing yourself, call, rather than visit, your mom and friend. Be prepared to let them talk while you show your support by listening.

The Cost

Window-shopping	$0.00
Scented bath salts	$0.40
Brisk walk or run	$0.00

The Fix You keep at your daily routine until you're so tired that you call in sick because your immune system is depleted.

The Real Cost Divide your monthly salary by 31, the approximate number of days in the month. This will give you your daily salary, more or less. Multiply the quotient by the number of days you are off work. Even if you have sick leave available and you are paid for this time-out, still figure the same cost.

Oh, by the way: If you missed one day, you now have eight hours less to complete your work. Remember that each sick day means one less work day.

The Situation You recently found out that you have high cholesterol and if you do not lose fifteen pounds it may become worse with the probability of extensive heart disease.

The Prevention *(a)* Start a rigorous exercise program that will be beneficial in helping to eradicate the unwanted and unhealthy weight. *(b)* Eat healthier by reading about the foods that lower cholesterol. *(c)* Learn about substitute foods that are healthier. *(d)* Purchase or rent an exercise video. *(e)* Speak with a nutritionist on foods and meals that would bring down your cholesterol.

The Cost *(a)* The cost of an exercise video or book on eating healthy and lowering cholesterol. *(b)* The cost of meeting with a nutritionist.

The Fix *(a)* Taking a cholesterol lowering drug that may interfere with other organs in the body or interfere with other drugs you may be taking. Hippocrates, the father of medicine, said several hundred years ago that all medicine is poison, it's just a matter as to balancing what you need and the ailment.

The Cost *(a)* Potential damage to other organs in the body due to drugs. *(b)* Lose out on the natural endorphins, good hormones you receive from exercising. *(c)* The personal power you feel of knowing you have more control over your health than you thought possible.

The Situation You find you're feeling anxious much of the time and it's interfering with your focus at work. In addition, you find yourself more critical with others and feel you may be in somebody else's body. You don't have time to exercise because you are falling behind with all the work you have to do, plus the added pressure of getting the children to school in the morning and you find yourself too tired at night to do anything else. Eating healthy has never been one of your strong points and so you grab whatever is nearby and fast-food restaurants are your best friend lately.

Prevention *(a)* You may need some form of help in reenergizing your body and mind. Some of this help may come in the form of acupuncture, reflexology, a healthy and rigorous exercise program, a healthy eating program, or learning relaxation techniques. *(b)* Have a complete physical with blood work done to see if there is a physical problem with your hormones, thyroid, or something else.

The Cost (*a*) Acupuncture and reflexology sessions run anywhere from $50 to $80 a session. (*b*) An exercise program does not have to cost anything if you are very disciplined and can follow routines taken from a magazine, television exercise show, etc.—otherwise you may want to join a gym, buy and follow an exercise video. (*c*) A healthy eating program can be found in several books, although the two authors that I enjoy are Dr. Andrew Weil and Dr. Christine Northrup. (*d*) A physical exam can run in the hundreds of dollars.

The Fix (*a*) Diets that set you up for failure because of the word "diet" that immediately makes you think of food you "can't have," counting calories all the time, thereby thinking of food all the time. (*b*) Ignore it and hope it will soon pass. (*c*) Take anxiety pills and any other pills that we think will give us a quick "fix" without working at it first.

The Cost (*a*) Emotional or physical burn-out or depression. (*b*) Loss of employment or clients for not doing the job necessary. (*c*) Strained relationships with family, friends, coworkers, and clients.

Guarding Your Own Time

You've heard the saying "Do that on your own time, not my time." It describes a reality that we all face: the need to focus attention.

Sometimes it is your pleasure to pay attention to someone else. Sometimes it is your duty. Other times, however, it is your right not to pay attention to another person—to concentrate instead on something that you need to accomplish or that is fulfilling to you.

Each woman must set aside time for herself, which we'll call "my time." We'll call time that can be shared with someone else "your time." Guarding "my time" can be very difficult. You know how demanding a child can be when he or she wants attention when you are reading the newspaper—a valid use for "my time."

What's the solution? First, let other people know that the time you have set aside as "my time" is very special time for you and that you would appreciate not being interrupted during a specific period. In most cases, your statement will be all it takes.

When another person violates "my time," begin by using a liberal dose of patience. If the other person continues to take advantage of "my time," state assertively that even though you can appreciate occasional interruptions, he or she has gone too far.

In some cases, it takes serious repetition to get through to others. Molly, a secretary and author, had to repeatedly tell her children she did not want to be disturbed or interrupted from 1:30 to 5:30 p.m. on Saturdays. When she remarried, she told her new husband, "You need to plan something for the children on Saturday afternoons…I won't be available."

I asked Molly if her plan worked. "It took about a month before they really knew I was serious. My husband went off to do an errand and left the children at home while I was writing in my bedroom. One of my children knocked on the door. I said my normal, 'No, it's not 5:30 yet.' Again, a knock on the bedroom door; my daughter needed me right now. Again, I said, 'No, it's not 5:30 yet.' When my husband returned from his errand, he yelled into my bedroom that Jenny had fallen from the swing and had turned an ankle.

"We all immediately went to the hospital with Jen. She was on crutches for two months."

Because we are so used to thinking that responding to others' needs is part of a woman's role, setting limits on interruptions can be difficult for everyone at first. But, as in everything, assert your rights but stay flexible. Remind yourself that you have a right to time alone, but be aware that special circumstances do occur. Once family members are secure in the knowledge that you will be there in a real emergency, they might feel secure enough to let you alone for a while.

Important Points to Remember

Learn to balance, not juggle, your time. This will help you avoid the guilt trap. To help direct your priorities, keep five major questions in mind: What type of person do you want to be; what do you want to do or accomplish and with whom do you want to do it; what would you do if money were not an issue; how do you want others to remember you; and what would you do with three extra hours a week?

Be aware of these questions during the times you feel guilty. I am confident they will not only direct you to constructive action, but help you make the transition from being guilt-ridden to being guilt-free.

Chapter Four

The Big Glitch
(When the Best-Laid Plans...)

Your day's mapped out—from jogging at 6 a.m., getting the children's breakfast and sending them off to school, to a breakfast meeting at 8 and appointments right on through a staff dinner meeting at the new hotel downtown. A jam-packed day, but you've scheduled your time realistically and have prepared in advance to avoid all possible glitches.

The jogging goes well, and your endorphins give you a lift that should carry you through the day. Then, just as you're turning into your driveway, your foot hits the sprinkler. You limp inside with a twisted ankle. Nothing serious—not enough to warrant a good war story, but enough discomfort to slow you down. Just as you're slipping into an Ace bandage (no time for ice), the phone rings. It's a colleague saying that she won't have her report finished in time for the staff meeting. Well, okay, you can handle it, but wait—from the den comes a piercing wail. You run to the rescue to find that Jimmy has dropped your ten-pound dumbbell on his foot. Now you're in real trouble, and it begins to look like a day that only Wonder Woman could salvage.

If you have no backup plans for such top-of-the-line catastrophes, you do all that any mere mortal can do. You carry your screaming child to the car; rush him and his broken toe to the emergency room; and, as soon as you can get to the phone, you ring your client. When he doesn't answer, you call the restaurant where your breakfast is scheduled and beg the hostess to explain your situation when the client arrives. A few minutes later, you dial your office, tell them what's happened, then hurry back to hold Jimmy's hand. In between these frantic moments, you try to put on a touch of makeup. You run a comb through your tousled hair and wonder if you can find someone to care for your traumatized tot later in the day.

The SWAT Team Concept

Fortunately, this scenario need not occur. All you need to eliminate the problems and make things run smoothly is a SWAT team. What is a SWAT team? It's your personal group of special backup people who fill in at home or at work when you have a real emergency. I have many examples in my files of how successful SWAT teams have worked.

A friend of mine has one close neighbor as well as a nearby relative whom she calls her SWAT team. She has an agreement to call on them in genuine emergencies only. "I do *not* impose on these people for regular child-care needs or for trivial favors," she tells me. "But it's understood that, in times of crisis, they'll come running." The neighbor, who has a need for extra cash, is well paid for her work; the relative is rewarded with special tickets to art and theater openings.

Another working woman hires a retired nurse on a standby basis. For a small fee, the nurse agrees to take care of problems as they come up. "Many times," she explains, "this lady has been a savior. I can't tell you how much lost time she has saved me."

I talked about coping with the inevitable crisis with Terry Mayo, Los Angeles's first television anchorwoman. At the time, Terry was a divorced mother with a young son.

"I've always been a very positive person and believe strongly in the power of an optimistic attitude," she told me. "But as a parent, newswoman, business owner, and just plain fallible human being, I've gained a healthy respect for Murphy's Law."

Terry believes that life is unpredictable, especially life with children.

"Several months ago," Terry said, "I had scheduled a really important interview. Just as I was about to leave, my son, Chris, locked himself in the bathroom, the dog got loose, and someone drove by and swiped the side of my car...all within fifteen minutes."

Luckily, Terry had an ace in the hole. She and Chris lived with her grandmother. Her live-in SWAT team took over almost instantly and allowed Terry to make her interview and deadline.

"I really believe in the idea of extended families," she said, "especially for single parents. I realize not everyone has a grandmother like mine, but single working mothers should really consider joining forces with an older woman, maybe someone who's widowed and lonely and needs to be needed as much as you need a warm, loving person to be there for your kids when you are away."

Linda works full time as a very busy hairdresser and colorist and has an ailing mom that she feels responsible for. It is difficult to reschedule appointments as she is solidly booked most days. She knew she had to find a creative way to help her look after her sick mom. Linda says, "I have a retired woman check on my mom for about an hour or two during the first part of the day and makes sure she's taken her medicine, that she's comfortable and doesn't need anything at the store, and makes lunch for her. She has her son look in on his grandmother after school and does his homework while visiting. He gets work done while his grandmother enjoys having him around."

How to Handle Unexpected Absences from Work

A SWAT team on the home front can go far in keeping the unscheduled time you take off from work to a minimum. The day will come, however, when some event in your personal life keeps you from making it to your job when the people at work are counting on you. Why not extend the SWAT team concept to your professional life?

Arrange for a Stand-In

Sandy, a secretary for a medium-sized firm, had a home emergency the day her boss intended to present the annual report. Sandy had no choice but to call in and say, "Sorry, I can't be there." Fortunately, however, she had a plan in place for just this sort of occasion. What Sandy did was to call in a trusted substitute, someone she knew who could handle the details. "Everything went wonderfully well," she beamed. "And at the end of the day, I sent my boss a bottle of wine with a personal note. Even now, a year later, he's still talking about what I did."

In another case, a schoolteacher I know well had to have an operation that would keep her off her feet for six weeks. "Long before I had to go in," she said, "I arranged with the school district for a trusted friend with a teaching credential to fill in for me."

During the time she was recuperating, her substitute kept her up-to-date with what was going on. As the teacher began to recover, she helped correct papers and offered advice about problems that occurred in the classroom.

Develop Personal Relationships

Arranging in advance for a substitute is fine when someone else can do your job. But what about those meetings where you simply can't send a stand-in? What about lunch with your star client, for example? Such situations are tough. In the case of restaurant meetings, it pays to develop a relationship with the management and staff at one or two particular places.

Instead of table-hopping from one trendy bistro to another, I have developed relationships with the owners and staffs of one family-owned spot and one hotel restaurant. I get more than red-carpet service. In one instance, when I was forced to be an hour late for a meeting with a client, I called the owner-hostess, whom I know well, and asked her to seat my client, extend my apologies, and start him off with a glass of vintage wine and a special appetizer. When I arrived breathlessly, nearly sixty minutes later, I found him in a corner booth being happily pampered by my friend, Marie. As you might imagine, our meeting, though off to an unavoidable late start, ended on a high note.

Go the Extra Mile to Apologize

Going the extra distance to make people happy after you've inconvenienced them is usually well worth the effort. Instead of an apologetic "I'm so sorry, but my sick child…" or "The tie-up on the freeway…" recompense the other party.

A client of mine, an attorney, had to leave a client high and dry when she received a telephone call that her daughter was about to have an emergency appendectomy. "Of course," she told me, "he understood the problem. But after I returned home, I sent my client theater tickets with a personal note of apology."

Does this approach take too much time and expense? Not if you value your job and the people you work with. Let people know in a tangible way that you've reflected on the inconvenience you caused. If you do, you will stand out from the crowd. Jane, the attorney, was recently made a partner in her firm, and Sandy just received a major promotion. Don't expect others to suffer because you do. Being considerate of others, even in the midst of your own crises, will make them see you as someone truly special and not easily replaced.

How to Set Up Your Own SWAT Team

Once panic hits, it's too late to start crying "Help!" Most of us wouldn't dream of going through life without medical and car insurance; likewise, for anyone serious about her career (not to mention her family), playing ostrich and assuming that you'll "handle whatever happens when the time comes" is both arrogant and foolish. (Take it from someone who was foolish and lost a large contract because of it.)

There are any number of possible arrangements you can make when lining up emergency help. The key, of course, is to have at least two reliable people on call before you ever need them. Only call them during a real crisis; have other arrangements for your regular child-care needs. But, it's understood that, in times of a real crisis, they will be available.

Here's how to set up your team:

Dream and list: Identify people you know and respect. Think of friends who have children the same age as yours, neighbors whom you trust with children, or coworkers who might be free to take on extra tasks during evenings or weekends. Perhaps you know a new mother who isn't ready to go back to work full-time but who would welcome earning some occasional extra dollars. Or someone who's retired or between jobs. Check with local child-care directories, and always ask a child-care provider for references. Besides hiring outsiders, a number of women, like Terry Mayo, share a home with a relative or close friend. Could you ask the friend to help if there were a crisis? Others have had good luck with au pair girls—young women from other countries who come to the United States on nine-month work visas. If you have a friend who uses an au pair, would your friend let you share the au pair in an emergency? (Hiring an au pair is often an excellent way to provide full-time child care; you may want to consider it.)

Define: Make sure team members agree on what is a true emergency. This will be covered in greater detail later in this chapter.

Divide: Take all the team members' names and organize them into categories. For example, know who you can call during a daytime crisis, a nighttime emergency, a weekend, when you're on an out-of-town trip, or when you're working late at the office.

An important digression: Only use your SWAT team when you need to and for the purpose it was intended. One abusive act will alienate that particular team member forever. Let the members of your SWAT team know, in advance, what category they fall under. And *always* thank them for their help by giving a card, flowers, movie tickets, singing telegram, balloons, a plant, dinner, or anything your budget will allow.

Don't be embarrassed to recruit team members. Chances are, you may be able to help each of them as much as they can help you. Go for it!

What Constitutes a "Real" Emergency?

From my own archives and those of a number of close friends and clients, here is a list of the ten most common day wreckers:

1. The totally sleepless night
2. A leak, freeze, or other disaster in the home
3. A medical emergency
4. A summons to court
5. The need to recover after being victimized
6. The need to pay bills *fast*
7. The need to move
8. The big deadline
9. The injury, illness, or death of a loved one
10. The forgotten meeting

The sections that follow will discuss each of these unwelcome situations.

The Totally Sleepless Night

It doesn't matter why. Maybe Jimmy was up all night with the stomach flu, or perhaps you just ended a fling with the love of your life. In any case, a night without sleep ensures a hellish next day. If you don't feel you can call in sick (even though you may feel unprecedentedly wretched), try to give yourself a break. If at all possible, take a long lunch hour, then order something to take out and eat someplace where you can catch a snooze. Tell your coworkers that you're under the weather, and see if they can lighten your load. Maybe they'll let you slip away early—after all, you'd do, or have done, the same for them. When you can, go home, make a sandwich, unplug the phone, and sleep.

"Ma, Janie's Swimming in the Basement!"

When the roof falls in at home and you can't wait until Saturday to have it repaired, try to pull off a miracle and get the repairer to come at a specified hour. (I know, it's equivalent to a parting of the Red Sea.) Otherwise, call in your SWAT team troops or, if you haven't done your homework, prevail on a neighbor to let in the repairer.

When the Pain in Your Side Is Appendicitis

If you find yourself facing emergency surgery, try to keep a cool head. (I didn't say this would be easy.) Call at least one reliable person to be your advocate while you're out of commission. Assume that you'll be a total basket case, and let him or her keep your affairs in order until you're well enough to shout orders from your bed.

A Day in Court

You were a good citizen and came forth with an unusually coherent account of an accident or crime. Now you're being rewarded by having to make an appearance in court, and you're missing valuable time at work. Make sure that all those who are losing your services are well acquainted with the reason for your absence. If possible, substantiate your explanation with a news clipping. If your absence is going to be extended, prepare for the worst (a deadlocked jury); get people to cover for you on all fronts.

You, the Victim

Your car has been totaled by a hit-and-run driver, or you come home from the movies and find that a thief has made off with everything from your stereo to your best lingerie. Besides the trauma of loss and invasion, you'll have to fill out police reports, insurance forms, and make arrangements for a new car (or negligee). All that is a day's work at least, so call in a substitute and then console yourself with the fact that your misadventure will make a great story.

You, the Culprit

You're a wizard on the job, not to mention a terrific human being. But somehow you neglected to pay those traffic tickets or utility bills, and you find yourself having to pay them in person—and immediately. (It's happened to some pretty prominent people.)

Moving Day

Moving is not exactly a full-fledged emergency; it is more of an expected crisis. Moving, even when it's from the slums to a penthouse, is a traumatic experience, and you can usually bet your paycheck that there will be a hitch or two. To minimize trauma, plan ahead. Try to move on a weekend. But if that's not possible, arrange to take a day or two off. The mistakes you'll prevent will save you time and money in the long run.

The Big Crunch

You've got a deadline and, in spite of heroic efforts, you're swamped. The best thing, of course, is to anticipate last-minute snafus and build up some "comp" time so you can finish that big report without having to pull an all-nighter or cancel important meetings. Should it come to that, call in your backups. Then bring roses to those who help you through. After all, *you* came out smelling like a rose!

The Injury, Illness, or Death of a Loved One

Do what you have to do and call in help from all sources. This is not the time to try to be the Rock of Gibraltar.

A Meeting with Whom?

You forget you scheduled a meeting with a client or someone at work. Do what you can to call in your SWAT team so you can make the appointment. If you are forced to cancel at the last minute or, worse yet, be a no-show, more than an apology is in order. Reschedule the appointment to suit the other person's convenience. Or reschedule the meeting at a restaurant, and you pick up the tab.

Important Points to Remember

Don't make the mistake of thinking that you'll be able to deal effectively with crises as they happen. Plan ahead by creating a SWAT team that can cover for you at home and at work. Make sure each SWAT team member knows exactly how you plan to use him or her, and don't abuse team members by calling on them for routine needs.

As you go along in your working life, you will find the SWAT team to be one of the finest tools in your arsenal. And, though you may not think so right now, you will find that—when used properly—you can use the team over and over again.

Chapter Five

L'Affaire:
Making Time for Love
(Married or Single)

oney, success, and power have their charms, but to most women a life without love is an incomplete one. Of all the kinds of love, Eros, or romantic love, provides an excitement unparalleled by other accomplishments. Love, like all things worth having, requires a time investment. Marriages and relationships that take a back seat to career, children, and social life tend to become stale and unrewarding.

Dr. Susan Lark says that sex is great! Most of us feel the same way, but she goes on to say that sex is good for us emotionally and physically. Dr. Lark says, "Sex burns calories and keeps your muscles and tissues in shape. Plus, an active sex life is associated with a longer life, better physical health, and a stronger sense of self-worth and potential. Simply put, sex has a huge and important effect on your physical, mental, and emotional well-being."

Planning for Romance

"I know that's what I want, and I know that's what I need, but where do I find the time for romance?" laments Georgia, an active entrepreneur. "I can't imagine having kids right now. I barely have time to be intimate with my fiancé. My business monopolizes every minute. It's amazing Steve still wants to marry me."

Most working women already have the skills they need to find time for romance. When a working woman plans a meeting, she places the date and time on her calendar. When she has a project or a deadline, she takes the time and puts in the effort to finish on schedule. When she sets goals, she does what needs to be done to reach them. The same kind of planning and effort need to go into making time for romance. If work is important to you, you work. If an activity is important to you, you do it. If romance is important to you, you plan for it.

Assess Your Current Number of Romantic Hours

As discussed in Chapter 2, chart the time you spend with your lover or thinking about your sensuality. Romantic time is personal time. Almost all working women need to increase the time they spend enjoying this activity.

Increase Romantic Time

Most women say they would love to add three romantic personal hours to their lives each week. Let's look at some ways to do this:

Three times a week, go to bed an hour early. If your normal bedtime is 9:30 p.m., go to bed at 8:30 and spend that extra time talking to your lover in person or over the phone (talking is the first part in making love), reading a steamy novel to each other, or thinking about sexual fantasies.

Each week, set up three one-hour sessions for romantic time. Allow no television, no meetings, and no work. Just as you plan to take lunch from noon to 1:00 p.m., you must plan for your romantic time. If weekday evenings are bad, try weekend evenings, afternoons, or mornings. Choose a time and see if it works. I have always believed in the cliché "Where there's a will, there's a way."

Plan three meals with your lover weekly. Try a breakfast, lunch, and dinner, or try two lunches and one dinner. However, do your best to keep the same days and times so that you establish the habit of blocking out those times on your calendar. Refuse any other commitments at those times. Out of twenty-one meals a week, coming up with three should be easy.

Ask permission to take thirty minutes extra time during one lunch hour each week. Make the time up if necessary. Your long lunch with your lover will be a wonderful entree to private time.

Treat your romantic self and your lover to three hours of time alone together. Your time could be Saturday or Sunday morning or during midafternoon, late afternoon, or evening. Plan for the children's care and pretend you're out of town—go sightseeing or for a quiet walk. Such a get-together takes little money, and you're only gone for three hours rather than an entire weekend or day.

Change your mind-set. It is important that you *believe* that your romantic self is as important as your professional or home self. I believe the romantic self is the most genuine and real of all roles.

Agree to a planned "surprise" time once a week or once a month. During this time, one partner agrees to surprise the other by planning an event. The event could be as simple as an ice-cream cone and a walk around the park or as elaborate as a weekend trip. There are two purposes to surprise time: the first is that one person tries to please the other by planning an event that both will enjoy; the second is that the responsibility for pleasing alternates from person to person.

You may also want to try springing unplanned surprise time on your partner. Without warning, try "kidnapping" your husband or lover. The results can be very exciting and a great success.

Establish holidays as romantic times. During holidays set aside a certain time when you and your lover can be alone. If you have children, arrange to have them taken care of for a few hours. This gives these days special meaning.

Once in a while, when you're both up to your ears in work, set a time to get together for a drink, coffee, or lunch. The outing will act as an escape valve. Though finding the time may seem impossible, remember: you can usually find a way to do what you really want to.

Set the mood with candles. There is something that is very calming and romantic with lit candles. I find men enjoy candles in a romantic setting as well. It says very effectively that "I'm in the mood for love tonight," which is part of the foreplay.

Spend one "romantic" hour just talking lovingly to each other while you massage and touch the other person. You go no further that evening. It sets a very effective stage for making sure you find the time for the next romantic time together which is usually sooner rather than later.

Leave a phone message for your sweetie that will not only put a smile on his face but get him a little agitated sexually. It doesn't take a stripper to know what to say—the important thing is that you leave the message. Men love this more than most women know.

Understanding Yourself

Bonnie, a psychologist, says that how a woman sees herself is directly related to how she acts in a love relationship. "In other words, if a woman feels unattractive about her face or body, she often finds it difficult to become intimately close." As this example indicates, the first step to examining our own intimate relationships is to understand the mind-set we bring to them.

In addition, women need to know what their "love needs" are. It could be validation, respect or honesty from their significant other. If these love needs are not met, this could subconsciously undermine a loving relationship. What makes these love needs so important? I believe these needs are basic in most women. What woman does not want to be seen, heard, and appreciated for who she is and what she does for her family, friends, work, and community?

What woman does not at some point want to feel as though she is "off-duty" caring and doing for others? Who will nurture her or take care of her? Tammy, a forty-something fitness instructor and avid knitter, is always knitting a scarf for others. "I was so touched," she said, "when a client knitted me a shawl. No one has ever knitted anything for me."

A Forty-Something working mother helped her ailing parent before the holidays and did not have the time to decorate the house. Her friend, with the help of the working mother's daughter, decorated the house with all her special treasures. What about making dinner for Mom once in a while since she makes dinner for the family so often?

Once again, the three types of women introduced earlier—the Traditional Homemaker, the Transitional Woman, and the Achieving Woman—offer insight into typical attitudes. See if you find your own viewpoints reflected in the next three sections.

The Traditional Homemaker

Bonnie, the psychologist, describes a problem that's common among Traditional Homemakers: "Women who stay home become dependent on family and friends for outward compliments." Bonnie believes that "the stay-at-home women often feel that life is passing them by while their working friends have it all."

The Traditional Homemaker also feels that her romantic partner may be taking her for granted since she is home much of the time, or may start to expect versus appreciate all that she does for him and the family.

The Traditional Homemaker may have a high need for validation and nurturing from her lover, reinforcing her important contributions she makes for her family and home. The other love need requires that she is validated as a sensuous and sexy woman. Many of the Traditional

Women I know love their work at home most when their family and lover show respect and love for who she is and what she does.

The Transitional Woman

The Transitional Woman has a strong awareness of her life script. Sometimes, Bonnie says, she may get caught in it. "Suppose you think your life script says 'You must be a good daughter, wife, mother, or friend first. If you're going to work, it should rank behind all other responsibilities.' You will take the time to nurture everyone else but yourself. You're caught in a cultural value system that holds the belief that you work to help the family. When a woman like this finds her work rewarding, she feels guilty. This is especially true if she can now stop working for financial reasons. She feels ambivalent about letting her newfound freedom go. She feels 'whole.' But time pressures get the best of her. She feels better as a person, but juggles her work and family life. She keeps hoping for the day when she can focus on her romantic self."

Most Transitional women have a high love need for being nurtured. They are so busy going from one thing to another, trying to get it all to work that she often forgets to take the time to nurture herself. She also has a high need to be validated as a loving and sensual woman.

The Achieving Woman

The Achieving Woman expects a lot from herself and from others, lovers not excluded. She is so busy doing that she often fails to recognize the need to love and be loved. Of the three types of women, the Achieving Woman is the most likely to be a workaholic. "Women who are workaholics prefer to work rather than do anything else," says Carol, a family therapist. "They have a tendency to go through cycles. They put a lot of effort into their work, and then they wear down or burn out, and repeat the cycle. They are susceptible to the need to nurture others during their downtime. However, they have a strong need to be nurtured themselves."

Achieving women's love needs center around being nurtured, validated as a sexy wife, and a good mother (as she usually receives plenty of validation for her independent, working career). When we have our love needs met on the home front as a wife and mother, most women report that they feel confident to forge ahead in the other parts of their lives with a feeling of being centered and enthusiastic.

Going on Dates

Earlier in this chapter, you read a list of suggestions for finding three extra hours for romantic time each week. One of the suggestions, setting up a regular time to be alone with your partner—that is, making a date—is so important that it deserves a section of its own. If you can set aside only one hour for each date, that's fine; if you can set aside more time, even better.

Begin by looking at your calendars and deciding on the time you both can set aside to be alone together. Are Tuesday afternoons between 11:30 a.m. and 12:30 p.m. good? Or would Wednesday evenings be better? If no time seems ideal, choose two and toss a coin to determine your date time. The two most important things to remember are to *set* the time and to *keep* it! No excuses—except, perhaps, hospitalization.

Jenny, a college instructor, sets aside Wednesday night for her lover. "It could be raining, snowing, or anything else, but we don't give up our night together. It's the only time I really feel I have his undivided attention."

Marjorie says that being together for only a little while "keeps my husband and me in touch with each other. I know it doesn't seem like much, but it really helps. Once in a while, we'll forgo dinner out and go to a hotel together. There's something exciting about that."

Sydney, a caterer, plans Thursday evenings for her date night with her husband. She is totally committed to this time and will not accept any catering jobs for these evenings. "David and I have been married seventeen years. When I started my catering business eight years ago, I promised myself that I would not forget my husband. I know I have lost a lot of business because of this Thursday-night date night, but I also know that it proves to my husband how important he is to me. *No amount of money can buy that.*"

Sandy, like Sydney, has discovered the fulfillment of her relationship with her husband. She has been an attorney for over fifteen years and was a pharmacist before that. Sandy has four grown children and has been married for twenty-five years. "Everyone said that I would have to work late nights and every weekend. Most of the attorneys in my office do just that. Usually I am home by 6:00 p.m., and I rarely go to the office on weekends. I'm not mega-wealthy, but I do okay. After all, how much can I eat, or how many cars can I drive, or how large of a bedroom and bathroom do I need?

"I see a lot of my fellow attorneys divorce because they let their careers take over their lives and values completely. I see how miserable they are when they work all the time and fail to make time for the people they love."

A date can consist of staying in or going out, of just holding hands or of steaming up the windows. The next sections will give you a few ideas for spending your special times together.

A Crock-Pot and Wine

Janey, a nutritionist, puts a lot of effort into making the time with her husband. "It's not easy to make a relationship work. I'm the one who plans 'special time.' If it weren't for the planning that I do, I think we would see each other only when we pass in the bathroom."

Janey and her husband enjoy stay-at-home dates, for which Janey goes to the trouble of making a home-cooked meal—or as she puts it, "a Crock-Pot-cooked meal." She adds to the occasion by bringing home a bottle of wine. They begin their special time together by enjoying dinner.

"During this time my husband puts all work away. Some of our best talks occur on these evenings. We don't answer the phone, the door, or anything else. We look forward to these times. And, once in a while, he takes over and does the planning."

Not everyone can expect to find a time at home when they can enjoy each other. This is especially true if you have children. Many working women feel that their home is not a quiet haven until 10 p.m., and then they're usually too tired to do anything except sleep. These women and their lovers need to leave the house to really enjoy their date.

An Hour or Two Out

Marjorie works at home, taking care of four children under the age of twelve. Her days are filled with crying children, cleaning, cooking, diaper changing, and afternoon chauffeuring. "When I feel particularly frazzled, my husband and I go out to dinner. I don't work, so we try to make ends meet on one salary. We don't go anywhere fancy, but it doesn't matter because we are *out* of the house. Jim likes it too because it gives him some quiet time with me."

The feeling that "I don't bring in a paycheck, therefore, we can't spend too much money," is a common one among Traditional Homemakers. The stay-at-home woman has a difficult time realizing she has far fewer expenses than the woman who works outside the home. When mother stays home, there are fewer expenses for child care, convenience foods, working clothes, and more.

Setting aside a regular time for a date is important, but never let the date become routine. Don't hesitate to go on a date at a time that's not your regular date time, and be creative about incorporating surprises and treats into the event. Sarah, a receptionist, and her husband decided to go on a special date for Valentine's Day, and her husband made it all the more special by planning a surprise for her. "For Valentine's Day this year my husband had to work, so we celebrated the next night. He got all dressed up, went outside, and rang the doorbell—my children thought he had flipped out. I answered the door, and we went out to dinner at our favorite little Japanese restaurant. He surprised me and made reservations at a hotel. He even brought the teddy he had given me the day before, [as well as] our toothbrushes, toothpaste, and other toiletries.

"We got to the room around 9:30 p.m., and he opened a bottle of champagne. It was the same champagne bottle we were going to drink on New Year's Eve, but we didn't because that turned out to be a disaster. Two of our three children were in a play that night, and one of the boys was just recovering from a bad case of the flu.

"Well, we stayed at the hotel until midnight, then went back home to spend the night with the children. When we got home at 12:30 a.m., my oldest complained he was congested and couldn't sleep. I gave him his medicine, turned on the humidifier, made some hot tea, and put a hot compress over his nose and sinuses.

"The next morning, my husband and I woke up at 9:00 a.m., left the children sleeping, and went back to the hotel room. We got home by 1:00 p.m. I felt as though we had an entire weekend—and we were only gone for nine and a half hours total!"

Sexy Times

Kerri describes the situation that results when work and responsibilities crowd out sex: "My work and my children take so much of my time. Our sex life had become boring and harried, when we got around to it." Kerri and her boyfriend of six years solved the problem by setting aside a time each week to check in to a hotel. This secret getaway helped put spice back into their relationship. And the advantage of having no distractions in their hotel room created a sexy mood that made their time together more exciting.

Kerri and her boyfriend discovered that planning was the key to sex as well as romance. When working women focus their efforts on planning for romance and sex, the results are often as successful as when they focus their efforts on an office project. Both take planning, initiative, and follow-up for best results.

Psychologists tell us that men get sexually aroused by sight, and women get sexually aroused by good communication. It makes sense to combine sight with communication. The key is to *plan* on it.

Shawna is a cosmetologist who owns her own spa and salon. She and her husband spend Friday nights making psychologists all over the world happy. She gets to her salon early on Friday mornings so she can leave about two hours earlier than on other days. "I come home, unwind a little, spend some time with the children, take them to a friend's house, and come home and get ready for the evening."

Shawna gets ready by putting on something sexy. "My husband loves to see me in negligees and teddies. Actually, I feel sexy when I'm wearing one. We make dinner together and sit and talk. We have only one rule: No touching until after dinner. Somehow this increases the excitement and yet allows us to have nice, long conversations at the dinner table. Once in a while, we break the rule.

"We play a game. We make love in a different room each time. The first time we tried our bathroom; we roared the entire time. The other room we spend a lot of time laughing in is our laundry room. You'd be surprised at how large washers and dryers can be. This is not only sexy, but it's also a lot of laughs."

Susan, who takes care of three school-aged children, has a "late-night" husband. She adjusts to his schedule so that they have some quiet time together. "I learned a long time ago that if I wanted to spend quality time with my husband, I better learn to take little catnaps during the day. Not only can I now keep up with someone who stays awake until 1:30 a.m., I take some of that time to work on several hobbies that I enjoy. It's extra quiet very late at night."

Ten Good Things

Kirsty, a thirty-something therapist, says that she asks her clients coming to see her for marital help to share ten things with the other person. "Immediately, the couple thinks of ten things they don't like about the other. I have to quickly guide them through a positive experience of writing down ten things they *do* like about the other person. The entire energy in the room shifts within five minutes."

"Thank you for…"

Every night before going to bed, thank your lover for doing or saying something that you appreciated. This exercise is twofold—first, each of you are always looking to find something good that the other person said or did for you and the other positive aspect of this exercise is that it helps to soulfully connect with your lover on a genuine level. Synthia, a Forty-Something Achieving woman says, "After a full day of taking care of people and things I look forward to sharing and exchanging something positive with my husband. I love hearing what he chose to thank me for each evening. Even though we have been married over twelve years, sometimes I am amazed by what he comes up with."

Be Present

The best gift you can give yourself or others as well as be given is quality time, an open heart, open ears, and eye contact. For the Traditional Homemaker that means not thinking about children or what needs to be done or the errands that still need to be taken care of while spending time with your lover. The Transitional Woman needs to focus on taking deep breaths and finding a calm inner place so that she can be present. And for the Achieving Woman, it may mean to turn off what is happening at work or on a large project that needs to be finished and stop to focus on taking deep breaths, slowing down, and changing gears from career work to soul work.

Sex & Health

I know how difficult it is to find time to be with your partner, but let me share a few facts about lovemaking that you already know but that may bear repeating. So, rather than just think of "the act," you may be able to integrate several things going on at once—all three types of Motivational Lifestyles will find the "integrate" approach makes sense and is a time-saver, of sorts.

According to Dr. Susan Lark (Jan 20, 2005, newsletter)

- good for bones, joints
- good for positive feelings because of endorphins
- expends calories
- extends life longevity
- emotionally connect with your own sensuality
- emotionally connect with your love partner

Now, that is what I call taking care of personal, home, and work on several levels at once.

Five Topics Not to Discuss on a Date

It is vital, during a date, that you make five subject areas off-limits: finances, children, past flames (including exes), bad decisions made in the past, and in-laws. These topics will undermine your date faster than anything else. They are emotionally fueled and anxiety driven.

I am not suggesting that you do not talk about these important issues. Just put them aside on dates. This time is just for you and your lover to share what you like about each other and your concerns, your feelings, and your love.

"After several sessions in therapy with my husband, I realized that I do still like him," says Melanie. "I knew I loved him deep down, but we always get into fights about finances. Now we discuss finances at our weekly problem-solving session. We laugh a lot more now."

Children are demanding. Disciplining children is emotionally draining, particularly as they get older. Even when two parents agree on child-rearing practices, it's difficult. When parents disagree, it's similar to an erupting volcano. "Jim and I are complete opposites when it comes to raising children," says Christie. "I am by far more strict. He just lets our teenagers get away with murder…We've come to an agreement: I discipline during the week, and he does it on the weekends. It's not perfect, but we don't spend what little time we have together fighting over the kids."

Discussing ex-sweethearts is also hard on the emotions. "No matter how much Jerry tells me he loves me, when he mentions his ex, I get all bent out of shape. We can have a perfectly nice time together until he brings up his former girlfriend. Sometimes I think I'm the most jealous person in the world, but my friends feel the same way when it happens to them."

Most couples, if they spend any time together, do not always make the correct choices or decisions. One husband says, "Joan and I have a good relationship. I must admit though, I get angry when she brings up bad decisions I've made. We've kinda worked it out. She doesn't bring up the 'old wash,' and I don't talk about my ex."

In-law jokes are for television shows and cocktail parties. The tales of in-laws are not funny when a couple argues over them. Sandy says, "We decided a long time ago not to discuss anything negative the in-laws do.

I used to get hurt when his mom would knock my cooking or housecleaning habits. Now we consciously make an effort to laugh at the in-laws' idiosyncrasies."

Making Time for the Romantic You

As working women, we know how important our personal time can be. Usually, by the time we do what we feel we have to do in the course of a day, it's time to go to bed or back to work. It is important to take your personal time and use it in any way that makes you feel happy, restful, or romantic. Making time for your romantic self is just as important as taking the time to do any other personal activity.

It is essential that working women *plan* for personal time. The Traditional Homemaker needs to know that she has earned quiet, personal time to be a woman and feel feminine, pretty, or just at peace with herself. Often, she will do everything in her power to nurture and make others feel good but cheat herself of special sensations. She feels that the description *romantic woman* does not include her.

The Transitional Woman needs to know that she also has earned personal time to be with herself and get to know herself better. These women are so busy just keeping up with everyday activities, they forget about their needs, particularly in sexual areas. Bonnie, the psychologist, says, "Women caught in the middle of wanting to stay home and wanting to go to work are hardest hit psychologically and emotionally. They literally have not made any time for themselves, romantically or otherwise."

The Achieving Woman needs to learn to slow down and keep herself on her priority list. These women focus most of their energy and momentum on their jobs and careers; they concentrate on how to do a task better, attract more clients, increase cash flow, reorganize a department, increase staff participation and output, or create a new project. They appreciate the feminine and sexy lingerie in magazines and catalogues but do not make the time to purchase these items for themselves.

Working women of all types must start a personal game plan that makes time for their romantic selves. Here are a few ideas that will help get you more in touch with your womanhood:

- Take long, luxurious baths.
- Visit stores and try on lingerie.
- Buy one sexy undergarment each month.
- Treat yourself to something that makes you feel special, pretty, or sexy.
- Rent that romantic movie you love to watch.
- Go somewhere dressy with your lover and tell him, halfway through the evening, that you're not wearing any underwear.
- Go somewhere dressy and show a little cleavage. All the models on magazine covers do it.
- Go shopping and try on sexy dresses.
- Curl up with a "sizzling" book and reread the sleazy scenes.
- Think about what you will do and what your lover will do to you tonight; get mentally prepared and the body follows.
- Listen to soft music and think about some fun times.
- Go see an X-rated movie.
- Call up a friend and go out for the evening.
- Sit around a fireplace listening to music, reading, or talking to a good friend.
- Make an appointment at the photographer's to have a "glamour" picture taken.
- Try a good cup of coffee and a good magazine.
- Wear something revealing like a low-cut top, fitted pants, or shorts while working in the garden.
- Cook or bake something in the kitchen with your negligee on.

- Take a yoga class and get in touch with your breathing and your body.
- Read a book on kama sutra sex positions and the healing energy each one contains.
- Take a shower and be very present where the suds go over your body.
- After your sensual shower, put thick lotion all over your body and slowly and deliberately massage the cream into your skin.

Any one of these tips should help you regain contact with the real you, gain perspective on your life, and provide you with the psychological resources you need to live the life you want to live.

Sometimes making time for the romantic you can take some basic restructuring. But fundamental change is possible; Candace's story is a case in point. Candace, a single woman, used to stay at the office until 6 p.m. and then go home and fix herself a quick dinner of leftovers or cottage cheese and fruit. Then she'd start working again. She and her boyfriend spent little time together. One day, Candace realized that she didn't want to spend her life alone, without the pleasures and communication of love. She told her boss that her work load was too great for one person and that she had no life outside work. They discussed what they could do to assign Candace a reasonable work load. "I knew my boss appreciated my efforts and had confidence in my ability. I took a big risk though, because I did not have another job to fall back on if he said 'quits.' I was ready for the risk. I was to the point that I needed to make a positive change in my life. I gambled and I won. I am much happier now and feel my life is more balanced."

Important Points to Remember

Working women need to restructure their thinking. They need to think of themselves and their personal needs as much, if not more, than others' needs. As psychologists note, when a woman feels good about herself, her positive attitude touches others.

There is no mystery in finding time to be with your lover. Rather, it is a matter of blocking out time, scheduling, and planning for dates that help keep the love spark alive. Women who put as much energy into scheduling time for themselves as for their lovers are winners on both fronts.

Keep your get-togethers positive and loving. Nurture your relationships, including your relationship with the romantic you. Be good to yourself. You deserve it!

Chapter Six

Creative Earning Options

P art-time work used to be a way for women to pick up a few extra dollars. It included all manner of employment, from stuffing envelopes to minding the local boutique for a few hours. But with the current (and no doubt permanent) need for more money, part-time jobs that pay minimum wage seldom warrant the effort.

Today, a woman must be creative when she assesses her earning capacity. She must evaluate many employment options—job sharing, flextime, working at home, starting a franchise, running her own business, and starting an online business to name a few—and determine which will give her the money she needs and the peace of mind she deserves. What's more, she may have to convince others that an alternate way of working is viable.

Determining Your Need for an Alternate Employment Style

Many women must meet so many demands that, to preserve their family lives and sanities, they need a work schedule that is more flexible than traditional nine-to-five employment. Working women need to understand that they will progress through different life stages. A working woman may feel compelled to job share a position after her child is born or during a later stage in life, for example. Here's how to recognize if you are a prime candidate for a different employment style:

- You are mentally and physically exhausted every day.
- You come down with colds and other viruses often.
- You are irritable all the time.
- You look forward to Friday on Monday.
- You go to bed at midnight just to keep up with the housework and wash.

If you are one of these exhausted women, the number of alternate employment options will come as a comfort to you. The next section will discuss job sharing, one of the most common alternate earning styles.

Evaluating Job Sharing

About the only viable way to nail down bona fide career-caliber employment part-time is to join forces with someone with like abilities. Then sell yourself as a package deal. In other words, share a job.

Most jobs can be flexible enough to accommodate sharing. In *Workforce 2000: Work and Workers for the 21st Century*, William B. Johnston and H. Arnold Packer reveal that "part-time, flexible, and stay-at-home jobs will increase, and total work hours per employee are likely to drop in response to the needs of women to 'integrate work and child rearing.'"

If one or more of the following statements apply to you, job sharing could be for you:

- You have a commitment to your job or career.
- You need to spend more time on personal issues and your family.
- You need time to regroup.
- After-school child care is not always available.

- You want or need to spend more time with young children.
- You want or need to work during a difficult pregnancy.

There are several types of job sharing schedules that you can discuss with your employer. One of the following case studies may give you an idea of a schedule that could work for you.

Cindy, an attorney for the public defender's office, alternates between working two days a week and three days a week. Another female attorney is at Cindy's desk on business days when Cindy is not. The two women have been taking care of their caseload in this fashion for over two and a half years. "I didn't know if this was really going to work when we first started. Everyone looked at us as if we weren't *real* attorneys, but after we started winning a few cases, very few people gave us 'the look.' I don't think this could work if my partner and I didn't speak on the phone a dozen times a day. After all, you have someone's life at stake here."

Similarly, Heidi, a court reporter with two small children, and another court reporter take turns working. Heidi works one week, and the other court reporter works the next week. "This arrangement works," Heidi says, "because I finish my cases at home if I have to. My boss thought I was nuts when I first suggested this four years ago. There weren't a lot of court reporters available then, so I don't think he had much of a choice. But he's never regretted the decision."

Laura, a Fifty-Something executive secretary who wants to spend more time with her retired husband, works flextime with one other secretary. The biggest potential glitch, says Laura, is "we have to make sure we leave specific notes and a paper trail to follow-up from day to day. I try to work three days one week and alternate to two the other week. We have been doing this job sharing for over four years—it works or I think we would be history by now."

Assessing the Potential for Flextime

Susan, an accountant, gets to work at 7:00 a.m., takes a thirty-minute lunch break, and leaves the office at 3:30—one and a half hours before employees who work a traditional schedule. "I put in the same amount of hours as everyone else, and I'm home when the kids arrive. My boss has offered me a raise because he is pleased with my performance."

Susan's work schedule is a classic example of flextime, a system of working that allows an employee to choose, within limits, the hours spent at work.

Another common form of flextime allows employees to work fewer days a week. Municipal-court judges have developed a 4–10 program, which means the judges work four days a week for ten hours a day. This program provides judges time to spend with their families or to pursue other activities.

As the next section will discuss, flextime offers advantages to employers as well as solving problems for employees. Nevertheless, those who propose flextime or other alternate work styles may have to do a lot of convincing to get others to go along.

The Internet and Flextime

The Internet has allowed industries that previously needed employees in the office to do their work, competently and professionally, at their home office. This new Internet work style has found employees happier with their work because their schedule allows them to be involved in challenging work and be able to attend children's day events or take care of a sick child or parent.

Two of my clients are lawyers and they work three days from home and two days in the office. These Achieving Women admit that they would have to give up their work if it weren't for the ingenious ways of the Internet. Ronnie, a Thirty-Something and mother of three says, "I don't know what I would do if it weren't for being able to stay in contact with the office and my clients through email, Internet research, intra-office email memos, and the cell phone." Hannah, a Forty-Something mother of two Achieving Woman says, "I thought my career was over when my husband and I decided that I would stay home with the children. I go into the office one and a half days a week and the rest of the time I'm working from my 'makeshift' office in the front room. I actually changed my law field and now I do divorces. It is so rewarding and I find I have the time to talk to my clients on the phone, especially on my cell phone when I'm out of the office."

Ally, a Thirty-Something and mother of three young children says, "I don't want to go back to teaching, but I not only want to make my own money, I want to do something I'm interested in." Ally started a baby clothes business online. "It is so great to be able to check any orders that have come in when the kids are napping or when I check it during the late morning and late afternoon. I feel that I have it all, even though I do feel crushed with the amount of time I don't seem to have for both the business and the children, but I don't feel guilty about not being home with them, especially when they're this young," says Ally.

Nancy, a Fifty-Something woman with two children in college decided she wanted to change to a new career with a less hectic schedule, so she turned to an Internet-based business. "In some ways," says Nancy, "I'm turning my hobby into a real business now. What I really love about this change is that I don't really feel like it's work because I enjoy finding antique china and selling it. When I actually count the amount of hours that I work on this business, it's a lot, but it just doesn't seem so time-crunching as my other career was.

Chris, a Twenty-Something Transitional Woman says, "I really value my time and that's why I have started a side Internet business while I'm working at a job that is okay, but wouldn't want to stay here for much longer."

Convincing an Employer

Studies show that job sharing, flextime, and other options that make an employee's time more flexible (these options will be discussed later in this chapter) benefit the employer. If you find yourself having to convince your employer to experiment with an alternate employment style, make sure you mention the points that follow.

Alternative employment:

- Increases productivity
- Increases loyalty
- Results in less absenteeism
- Is a business's social responsibility
- Allows, in the case of job sharing, the business to tap the creative juices of more than one mind

Finding Other Ways to Lighten the Job Load

In addition to changing your work schedule, you may be able to improve the quality of your life by changing your vacation schedule and child-care arrangements.

Comp Days and Personal Days

More time off can give you the breathing space you need to feel human again. Some employers are receptive to granting time off in lieu of over-time pay. Such time off is called compensatory time, or "comp" time.

Jenny found that comp time helped her remove much of the time-pressure that was stressing her. Jenny's job takes her traveling six weeks out of the year. With her employer she has worked out a plan that allows her to spend two comp days at home after a week-long trip. "These two extra days help me feel grounded again. The comp time helps me deal with jet lag, groceries, housework, and I'm able to play with my baby for two straight days. I usually check with the office when I'm on comp days. If I have to return business calls, I do it from home. I love my job, but there's also a domestic side to me. These extra days make it work."

Sarah's job doesn't require travel, but she finds there are a lot of peaks and valleys in her activity level at her job. For instance, the company frequently has one or two rush jobs a month, and these jobs sometimes require twelve-hour days for three or four days. Then everything returns to normal for a few days—until another rush order comes in. After a few months of this, Sarah approached her employer, explained the stress caused by this kind of schedule, and suggested she be allowed a comp day after one or two of these particularly busy periods. Her boss agreed. "Before," Sarah says, "I hated the extra work load. Now, since I know I'm going to get some extra time off, I really look forward to the extra work."

Increasing the number of personal days you are allotted can have the same effect as increasing the number of comp days. I have worked with several companies over the years and suggested that they give one personal day per month to each employee. The departments that use this approach have had higher morale, 36 percent higher productivity, and far less employee absenteeism. The company that implements this plan both shows and tells its employees how important they are to the business, and shows how the company views personal and family needs. Jon, a systems analyst, says, "We have seen a complete turnaround in morale since we started this program three years ago. In fact, we're thinking of adding one more day each month. Our main competitor locally has just begun the 'personal day a month' program. They'll flip when they find out we've decided to give two days."

Some companies are reluctant to try this, since, on the surface, one day a month represents another two weeks of vacation per employee per year. To convince any company you work for that increasing the number of personal days makes sense, you will need to present a convincing argument. Try using the sort of argument that Janet, an insurance adjuster, used.

Janet had a particularly heavy work load. As a result, she found herself becoming tired and discouraged. What she needed, she decided, was some additional time off each month. After she made her request, her boss turned her down flat. Janet then began to keep records of the work she was expected to complete…and the amount she was actually able to finish on schedule. After a couple of months of this, she re-approached the boss. She asked him to try an experiment. Give me a personal day off for two months, she said, and then look at the output. If it didn't go up, she wouldn't ask again.

"Somehow," Janet said, "that extra day a month relaxed me. It also gave me a new perspective on work. I came back after that first vacation day and increased my production by 6 percent. The second month, it was almost 15 percent. Armed with this, I convinced the company to not only give *me* this extra time, but all of the other adjusters as well. Now the company says it will never go back to the other system."

If you want extra vacation or personal days, approach the matter as Janet did. First, think about your job for a few days to see if you feel that an extra day off would increase your production. Keep records of what you are doing now, work up a convincing argument, and approach your boss with it. Don't ask for a permanent change; ask for a trial period. If he or she agrees, document what happens and make sure the boss knows the result. If the boss disagrees, rework your approach and try again in a few months.

If the company you work for can't give you one personal day per month with pay, ask for half a day per month or a half or full day every other month. See if you can create a reasonable plan that will enable you to come back to work refreshed and in a good frame of mind.

Child Care

More and more, prospective employees ask their employers-to-be what type of child care they offer. When the competition for employees is stiff, the company that offers child care will be the one that wins the talent.

The Child Care Action Campaign, a New York City-based coalition of leaders in the child-care field, found that "of five thousand workers with young children at five Midwestern corporations, 48 percent of the women and 25 percent of the men felt their worries about their children made their work time less productive."

According to John Fernandez, author of *Child Care and Corporate Productivity,* "Caring for a sick child led 82 percent of the women surveyed to miss work more than six times during the previous year. For men, the figure was 58 percent." It is estimated that businesses lose up to $3 billion each year due to child care-related absences.

Working at a Home Office

If your job does not require you to be at the office every day, you may want to negotiate an arrangement that lets you work one day a week at a home office. Naomi has a demanding job, and she had just given birth to her second baby. "When I had Chelsea (my second baby), working five days a week put an extra strain on me and my marriage. I love my job, and I know I'd be bored at home full-time. I asked my boss if I could work away from the office on Wednesdays. I don't get as much work done at home that I would at the office, but my spirits are better and I feel I have a better handle on my life."

Rebecca, who has fewer distractions at home than Naomi, found she could get more done by working outside the office than in it. Four days out of five, Rebecca writes reports for her boss. This requires her complete concentration, but at the office her fellow employees kept coming in to consult with her; the boss herself kept interrupting. As a result, Rebecca had trouble getting anything done at the office. To solve this problem, Rebecca suggested that she spend at least one day a week working at home—preferably, two days. Reluctantly her boss agreed to try the idea for at least a week or two. "Since I wasn't constantly starting and stopping, my production jumped immediately," Rebecca said. "I finished a report that first day that would normally have taken three days at the office."

Vickie, a successful Sixty-Something Achieving Realtor, works from her home office. She only goes into the office to write up agreements. She says, "I'm more motivated from my home office. It gives me freedom during the day. I frequently put in ten-hour days though." She goes on to say, "The phone makes me anxious when several calls are coming in at once. But, I've learned to keep a positive attitude. That's something I have control over."

Opening a Franchise

Franchising is an option that is helping many women build more flexibility into their schedules. Buying an existing franchise business or concept eliminates many of the problems of starting a business from scratch. Your service or product has a track record, and the franchisor can offer you operational techniques, advertising, marketing, and other excellent benefits. However, a stumbling block for many women is the initial franchise fee and start-up capital needed. In addition, the franchisee must pay royalties—a percentage of gross sales—to the franchisor on a regular basis.

Starting Your Own Business

The Center for Women's Business Research finds that 10.6 million firms are at least 50 percent owned by a woman or women. Forty-eight percent, nearly half, of all privately-held firms are at least 50 percent owned by a woman. It is estimated that between 1997 and 2004, the growth rate in the number of women-owned firms was nearly twice that of all firms (17 percent vs. 9 percent), employment expanded at twice the rate of all firms (24 percent vs. 12 percent), and estimated revenues kept pace with all firms (39 percent vs. 34 percent). Women-owned businesses will spend an estimated $546 billion annually on salaries and benefits ($492 billion on salaries and $54 billion for employee benefits—health, retirement, and insurance).

More and more women start their own businesses, and they do so for myriad reasons. Freedom and personal fulfillment are two of the primary reasons, according to a recent MasterCard survey.

In addition, women want to be decision makers, have more flexible work schedules, change careers, and start something from scratch to see if their efforts can make it successful. Women have started businesses in every industry, from bookkeeping to high tech. Access to the resources on the Internet has helped make these transitions easier. Personally, I would like to see more women start their own businesses.

The increase in outsourcing offers opportunities for women who own small businesses. For large businesses to downsize and stay profitable, they are contracting for work that was previously done in-house. IBM, for example, eliminated its real estate department and contracted with an outside real estate firm. Many businesses are outsourcing their data processing, advertising, and bookkeeping departments. For the female entrepreneur who wants to start her own business, outsourcing is an important trend to note.

Women are much more likely than men to seek out assistance from other business owners, or use trade associations to make contacts. While 28 percent of women-owned businesses surveyed by American Express and NAWBO (National Association of Women Business Owners), NYC indicated they used trade associations to build their revenues, just 15 percent of men-owned businesses utilized this resource. In addition, women listed "word of mouth" as the number one method they use to develop leads for increasing business, followed closely by "contacting friends or colleagues who own a non-competing business."

Let's look at several job categories and see the potential each offers to a woman with the qualifications, experience, and motivation.

Accountant

An accounting business can be started with little capital. An adding machine, pencils, and a computer would make a good start. Small-business owners are usually in need of accounting services.

Vera was let go after her company started to downsize. "Everyone was sad to see me go, because they liked my work. I thought if my boss thought I was doing a good job, maybe he would be willing to hire me by the hour and not pay benefits and worker's compensation. It worked. I started with ten hours a week, and now I have a part-time employee helping me out during tax season."

Sales Representative

Most businesses could use a good sales representative to show and sell services or products. Working strictly on commission, around your hours, is like having your own business.

Public Relations Specialist

You need a two-line phone system and a computer and printer to get started. Most business owners need effective public relations but are too busy to do it themselves.

Edith worked for a large firm as a public relations representative until her second child was born. "I didn't know if I was coming or going after Cindy's birth. I couldn't think of anything but diapers and rashes. I had to take off a lot of time because my newborn was allergic to almost everything. I decided to start a public relations firm on my own turf and on my own terms."

Provider of Seminars and Training

Suppose a woman has significant knowledge and expertise in a particular field. Why shouldn't she charge a fee to share what she knows? The fields of finance and management present many opportunities for a provider of seminars and training.

Donna sold her tow truck company after owning it for fifteen years. She now gives seminars in a variety of subject areas: proper dress for business, telephone techniques, leadership development in middle management, and developing relationships with bankers. "A lot of these things I had to learn from the seat of my pants," she said.

Editor

A dictionary, red pencils, and experience in producing manuscripts for businesses or publishers would start this business. All types of publishers are overwhelmed with written material. You can edit this material to meet publisher's standards and needs. You can also help authors who don't have a clue as to how to handle their writing.

Diana was a senior editor at a large publishing house until she was laid off. "My former publishing company hired me piecemeal to read manuscripts. It took me two years of editing would-be writers before I was making my old salary. I didn't have much in the way of self-esteem for the first few years, but it all worked out...finally."

Speech Therapist

Start with the required certification and education and a telephone. Add a working knowledge of Spanish or some other language, and you are even more of a drawing card. Studies indicate that more and more children enter school with speech difficulties, so a business providing speech therapy could offer an enterprising woman a bright future.

Secretary

Good secretaries are priceless. With a secondhand computer, paper, pen, and a lot of guts, many women start their own secretarial businesses and contract out to several companies, particularly small businesses.

Elaine, an executive secretary for six years, says, "I got a good deal on a used computer and printer. I started moonlighting after hours at my old bosses' firm and gradually had enough of my own clients that I could leave my full-time job. I make $200 more a month, and I'm able to spend more time with my eighteen-month-old baby. I'm a much happier person to be around."

Customer Relations Representative

Businesses say they have good relations with their customers, but most customers will tell you different. Startup equipment for a customer relations business would be strong interpersonal skills and the ability to recognize customer dissatisfaction.

While working full-time as a doctor's assistant, Sylvia went back to school at night to take psychology and business classes. She changed careers to become a customer relations representative for a health professionals company. "In the medical profession, patients are either happy or unhappy about their treatment. It's my job to keep the happy ones happy and to find the real reason behind an unhappy patient. I do this as an independent contractor."

Personal Coach

What are you really good at? What do people say about what you do or how you do things that would be helpful for others? Women are very skilled and talented in several areas. Could you be a personal coach for organizing the house, office, garage? If you write really well, what about becoming a writing coach? Have you excelled in sales? What about becoming a personal sales coach? The list is endless. I believe we all need personal coaches to get to the next level of expertise in our industry.

Housecleaner

Bingo! One of the main trends for the new century is convenience and service. And, with over half the working population being female, you can bet there are a lot of houses out there that need cleaning. You don't like housework? That's okay. You keep the books and train your staff to do the cleaning. You think it's beneath you? My parents came to this country as immigrants after World War II. They were without family, money, or training. My mom cleaned houses just to make ends meet. You would never believe my mom ever lifted a finger if you met her.

The only start-up tools you'll need are cleaning supplies and good ol' elbow grease.

Freelancer

The freelancer works per project. This is perfect for the woman who wants to keep up her expertise and not work full-time. Danny, a Thirty-Something Traditional Homemaker says, "I have been very fortunate with my freelance work. It has allowed me time to write my own book, work for a *Fortune* 500 company as an editor of their business newsletter, and be able to do light traveling for stories. I would like to keep this up when I get married and have children as well."

Consultant

Chances are very good that you have acquired expertise in one if not several areas and you can put this knowledge to help others in business or at home. I appreciate consultants, as they are focused on helping in a particular area, give you excellent ideas, keep you focused on your goals, and then leave you alone. You don't have to pay all the extra costs, keeping them on salary during the ebb and flow of your business cycle. In the long run, I have found them to be extremely cost-effective. In the short run, they may seem pricey, but a good consultant is worth their time, energy, and direction in gold.

Organizer

We have accumulated so much "stuff" today, from pillows to sheets and from children's toys to adult computer and software toys. What do you do with it all? For most of us, it takes up too much space and as a result we feel overwhelmed in its presence. Why don't we just throw out what we don't need and give it to someone or a family who would love to have it? Because we don't seem to find the time to do this. Thus there is a universal need to get organized and simplify our lives. Our "stuff" is placing more pressure on us than we realize.

I was having coffee at my favorite watering hole when I saw an ad for an organizer: "Three hour closet declutter and organization. Color coding, etc. $120 (Save $45), call Vicki."

Digital Video/Photo/Film

Granted, I live in Southern California, but the need for professional videographers to do weddings, bar mitzvahs, birthdays, funerals, holidays, people's biographies, and business meetings and seminars has made this career real and in demand. Dana, a Fifty-Something with four children says, "I was always the one to capture pictures, and later video of the family and friends. That is how I got so interested in becoming a videographer. It was my hobby and then when my third child went off to college, I just needed a change so I turned to my hobby and I make more than I was making as an executive secretary."

Digital Handywoman

So many of us can use computer help, whether it's in the form of one-on-one training (which is my personal favorite), on-site service, installation or upgrades, wireless networking, Internet pointers, digital photos, digital music, or tech-buying advice. I just ran across a new magazine, billed as the first consumer electronics magazine written especially for women, called *CE Lifestyles*. If you enjoy keeping up with the latest technology gadgets and enjoy integrating these systems and have patience educating others to use them, this may be an ideal career for you.

Graphic Artist

Businesses constantly develop and change logos, brochures, stationery, flyers, and other collateral material; need new designs for packaging; and require signs and other professional-looking graphics. If you have the training and experience, going into business for yourself could be the thing for you.

Computer Consultant

Women who have had extensive computer training in their work and have been laid off, want more flexible hours, or want to make more money for themselves can offer their computer skills to temporary agencies and other businesses.

Provider of Children's Parties

Parents, preschools, and children's groups are always looking for ways to keep children entertained. What about developing fun and educational programs as a means of making money? Could you create a puppet show around the alphabet for preschoolers? Or develop an environmental theme for children in elementary school? If your interests and experience are in music, dance, or art, you may have the skill to start your own kid-entertainment business.

All the businesses described here have a low start-up budget and require:

- Networking with other business people in related and unrelated fields
- Being involved in activities in the local business community
- Asking existing clients for new clients
- Becoming known in the community by participating in community organizations, functions, churches, and so on
- Servicing your existing clients on a continual basis
- Becoming a member of professional groups
- Marketing your business 365 days a year, every year

Most of the careers I have listed require a good amount of marketing to take place before these businesses can sustain a livelihood. However, with the advent of the Internet, it is so much easier today to "plug in" with others around the country to offer something of these services.

Learn from Publications

The books and pamphlets that follow will be helpful if you are considering starting your own business.

Employees: How to Find and Pay Them, by the Small Business Administration. Washington, D.C.: Small Business Administration, Office of Business Development. This eighteen-page publication provides information about the basics: interviewing, pay, temporary services, and more.

www.sba.gov

Succeeding in Small Business: The 101 Toughest Problems and How to Solve Them, by Jane Applegate. New York: NAL/ Button, a division of Penguin USA, 1992. This book tells how to turn your skills into a business and describes the difficult problems the author and her clients have confronted.

Understanding Cash Flow, by the Small Business Administration. Washington, D.C.: Small Business Administration, Office of Business Development. This resource is a ten-page pamphlet that discusses the elements of cash flow.

www.sba.gov

Useful Web Resources for Women in Business:

Business.com

www.business.com/directory/small_business/women-owned_business/

For a long list of links to sites that can help women-owned business, go to this site. Among the more unusual offerings: sites on franchises, women in technology, and women's B2B connections between North America and Asia.

Office of Small and Disadvantaged Business Utilization

www.va.gov/osdbu/links/woblinks.htm

Despite its name, this Virginia state government website has a list of sites for women-owned businesses. It's not as extensive as business.com, but it's a helpful reference.

WomanOwned

www.womanowned.com

WomanOwned began in 1998, and since then it says it has helped hundreds of thousands of women. It offers information on starting a business, growing it, developing contacts, and much more, as well as access to business tools and resources. A good all-in-one-site.

BlueSuitMom.com

www.blueSuitMom.com

BlueSuitMom.com offers a range of advice on business topics from professional organizations to image to emotional wellness. It also lets you find other women's companies easily.

Working Woman Central
www.workingwomancentral.com
This website offers resources and services for working women to save time, save money, and increase health and energy.

Center for Women's Business Research
www.nfwbo.org
This is the clearinghouse for information about women's changing role in business.

American Express
www.10.americanexpress.com/sif/cda/page/0,1641,6656,00.asp
This web page for women has links for trade shows, recruiting, and startup funds.

Nurture Your Business in an Incubator Office

The so-called incubator office, or office suite, is a business environment designed to help the owners of small businesses keep operating costs low. Incubator offices provide office space and access to basic business services, which all incubator occupants share. For example, owners of different businesses in an incubator office might share a receptionist, an answering service, a copier, a fax machine, and computers. Incubator office environments may be privately owned and run for profit or sponsored by a nonprofit group. Such nonprofit groups include economic development agencies, neighborhood revitalization groups, colleges, and chambers of commerce.

Share an Office

To cut costs, find an office that pleases you and bring in one or two other people to share the space and the expenses. You don't need compatible personalities; you just need different schedules. One woman, a

Traditional Homemaker, wanted to write. She wrote in the office in the mornings, while her children were in school. Another woman, also a Traditional Homemaker, wanted to paint. She put her daughter in afternoon kindergarten and painted at the office from 1:30 p.m. until 3:30. The third office partner, an Achieving Woman, worked full-time during the day as a college professor. After 6:00 p.m., she conducted a private therapy practice in the office the writer and the painter used during the day. This arrangement lasted for three and a half years.

Important Points to Remember

Job sharing or flextime may be the working woman's answer to the need for a more flexible work schedule. Other options for creating alternate work styles include working at home, increasing time off by arranging for comp time or personal days, buying a franchise, or starting your own business.

You are a prime candidate for a different employment style if you're exhausted daily, have constant bouts with viruses, are constantly irritable, wish for Friday on Monday, and get to bed past midnight just to keep up with housework.

Be creative when you evaluate your options. Decide on a flexible work schedule that works for you and do what you need to do to make it a reality.

Chapter Seven

Taking Control of
Your Schedule
(Before Someone Else Does)

Without plans, reflection, and careful judgment, most goals would never be accomplished, and our lives would be chaos. Without well-planned schedules, most days would be hectic, and our lives would feel out of control.

Newsday in New York commissioned me to write in "Viewpoint" an op-ed piece, entitled "Hail to the Chief." They wanted my perspective of what I thought of President Bush's time schedule. President George W. Bush has a "short" workday (in at 7:15 a.m., out by 6 p.m., often with breaks for exercise). That may be short indeed for a president, though it's right in line with the classic time-management advice of Holiday Inn founder Kemmons Wilson: "Work only a half a day, it makes no difference which half." But is nearly twelve hours of work really too short? And what does this whole discussion say for the rest of us—from moms to mega-managers—who put in such days?

It *is* possible for the CEO of the United States, and others for that matter, to keep "shorter" work days and still be profitable, performance-driven, and balanced in work and family life. In fact, it's not the hours you work that are crucial to success at all in business (even presidential business); it's staying focused on fundamentals and quality.

The fundamentals of time are the same for everyone. Rabbi Kalman Packouz describes it this way: "What if you had a special bank account where every morning you were credited with $86,400 with just one caveat—you had to spend it all daily or lose it. What would you do? Believe it or not, you do have a special bank account, called the Bank of Time." Each day, you have exactly 86,400 seconds, just as President Bush, Bill Gates, and Warren Buffett do. What you don't invest wisely is written off each night. You can collect dividends, but you can not go into overdraft.

Let's look at some ways that will prevent you from going into overdraft. The symptoms of "time overdraft" include sleep deprivation, anxiety, falling behind at work, home, and with family, and cardiovascular problems that include heart attacks, hypertension, angina, and migraines, not to mention a lowered immune system.

Using a Monthly Calendar to Avoid Schedule Overloads

With everything you need to do, it is no wonder that you tend to overload your schedule and often feel overwhelmed. Allowing time to prepare for deadlines, track heavily scheduled days, and stay aware of your energy level can help keep days manageable and well organized and help you develop a feeling of control. Remember, however, that an occasional crazy day is inevitable—when your child's last basketball game, your best friend's birthday party, and an important organizational meeting fall within thirty minutes of each other.

The best tool for avoiding schedule overloads is the month-at-a-glance calendar. There isn't much in life that is absolute. However, I am absolutely certain that it is time to throw away your daily or weekly calendar and replace it with a monthly one. The best size in terms of handling, flexibility, and functionality is approximately eight and a half by nine inches when closed; it opens to approximately seventeen by nine inches. Or, you can use your computer monthly calendar, PDA, or handheld computer. The most important thing to remember is that you can see a month-at-a-glance.

Other calendars are annoyances because they allow you to focus on only one day or week at a time. This is one of the problems I have with using a PDA to schedule my month. It doesn't allow for an all inclusive way to pre and post-plan your month so that you see specifically everything that is going on.

The monthly calendar allows the working woman to plan for and focus on a month at a time. Let's explore the advantages of the month-at-a-glance calendar more fully.

When using this calendar, the working woman doesn't need to shuffle pages or digitally go back and forth to view the upcoming week. She can therefore plan any number of activities for the entire month. By viewing the month-at-a-glance calendar, she can plan to keep the afternoon or entire day before a deadline clear of appointments so that she has enough time for last-minute preparations. In addition, with one glance, the working woman can decide to plan some downtime during a particularly busy week.

I remember when my eleven-year-old son, David, was browsing through my month-at-a-glance calendar in my office one evening as he was waiting for me to help him learn his lines for *Snow White and the Seven Dwarfs*. He said, "Mom, you are very, very, very…" I thought he was going to say *busy*, but instead he finished the sentence, "…well organized." My eleven-year-old son was able to perceive the difference between being busy and well organized, and, once you start using a month-at-a-glance calendar, you will too—and will appreciate the change that difference makes in your life.

The first part of this chapter will discuss five ways for making the best use of your month-at-a-glance calendar:

- Take your calendar everywhere.
- Circle important dates in red.
- Keep time open before and after a trip.
- Divide each day into three parts.
- Schedule timeouts.

Take Your Calendar Everywhere

Carry the following three items with you at all times, except social functions: your month-at-a-glance calendar or PDA; a notepad encased in a leather carrying case; and your business cards, preferably in a gold or silver-plated card case.

The calendar tells others that you are organized and in control of your life, and it keeps you from overloading your schedule. The notepad says that you are responsible, and the business cards state that you are professional. Making such an impression is a surefire way to help you make career advances, both in the corporate world and in the small-business market.

Circle Important Dates in Red or Spot your PDA

Circle in red the dates of deadlines, speeches, presentations, and similar activities. By distinguishing these dates clearly, you can keep from overloading yourself before and after them.

For example, if I have a speech scheduled for the fourteenth of a certain month, I circle the number "14" in red. I know that I should not plan appointments or out-of-town seminars for two full days before the speech and one full day after it. If you're using your PDA or computer calendar, use your alarm to remind you or place a dot on the date so that you know that the fourteenth holds special significance as a deadline, etc.

The reason I plan my schedule this way is so that I have plenty of time to think, create, change, or modify my speech. When minor emergencies come up, which they inevitably do, I am in a much better frame of mind to take care of them. I keep the day after a speech clear because I need some downtime to rest and get reenergized. I have found that I love to give speeches, but they take a lot of energy.

I also circle important family dates—like birthdays and anniversaries—since I'm the one who usually prepares the accompanying parties.

Keep Time Open Before and After a Trip

It's inevitable that the day before you leave town for a vacation, conference, or business trip, you try to cram a whole week's worth of work into one day. I think it's the working woman's code of ethics.

After all, you have wash to do, the house needs to be cleaned, the children's lunches made, and all your papers filed. Such directives come from the same area in the brain that says you have to clean the house before the cleaning lady comes.

Keep the day before your trip clear so that you can take care of last-minute details. No matter how well you plan your time, last-minute tasks will crop up both at work and at home. To think this won't happen only sets you up for last-minute pressures, a big headache at the end of the day, and second thoughts about leaving.

Also, keep the day of your return and the day after it free. This will allow you to take care of business at hand, and it will help you ease into the flow of events. Sharon, an accountant, does not plan any appointments the day she returns to the office. "The only thing I plan on my return to the office after being gone for more than one day is to open mail and return calls from the days I was not in the office. I don't attend my regularly scheduled Rotary meeting if it lands on the same day as my first day into the office. Somehow, the interruption of the meeting gets me further off kilter.

"When I learned I wasn't going to complete anything that first day I'm back, I started to relax and take the day more casually. The funny thing is…I started getting more accomplished just by opening and filing my mail and returning all my calls. At the end of the day, I feel as though I have accomplished a lot."

Divide Each Day into Three Parts

Take each day space on the calendar and mentally divide it into three imaginary parts: upper third, middle third, and lower third. The upper third of the calendar space is for noting appointments that occur any time from 7:00 a.m. to noon. The middle third is for noting appointments from noon to 4:30 p.m. The lower third calendar space is for noting appointments from 4:30 through the evening.

By dividing the day into thirds, the working woman can quickly view her day and determine if she has a heavy morning, afternoon, or evening. This information will help determine if she should schedule more appointments or time for quiet concentration. If I have a busy afternoon (that is, if the middle third of the calendar space is crowded), then I try to keep my mornings clear so that I have time to do what needs to be done in the office.

Libby, a human resources specialist, plans to see her clients in the afternoon. She spends the morning preparing for appointments and doing any other office work she needs to do. She also keeps Monday, Wednesday, and Friday evenings clear for her family. "I just need to take a quick glance at my calendar to know if I should schedule something in on a certain day or wait until another day to make the appointment or lunch date. This is especially helpful when I'm on the phone. I can give an answer about a certain date or time within seconds of looking at my calendar."

Schedule Timeouts

A marketing consultant and part-time writer schedules from 11:45 a.m. to 1:30 p.m. as a timeout for herself. "I used to go out to lunch with friends and clients. I now get together with friends in the evening and clients at breakfast. I schedule an occasional lunch with clients that can't make any other time. Blocking out the time on my calendar between 11:45 and 1:30 gives me a chance to exercise, shower, and dress in the same amount of time that I used to have lunch appointments. After eating lunch, I used to feel sluggish. Now, I am completely refreshed, and I am ready to go when I get to my office."

Let's pull together all the tips presented so far in this chapter:

- Buy a month-at-a-glance calendar or use the online monthly calendar.
- Take the calendar wherever you go, except social functions.
- Take a notepad to all business functions.
- Always have business cards with you.
- Keep the day before and the day after a trip unplanned.
- Divide each calendar day into imaginary thirds. Note morning appointments in the upper third of the space, afternoon appointments in the middle third, and evening appointments in the lower third.
- Start *now!*

By looking at her calendar, the working woman can tell how she spends her time and if the time mix is compatible with her motivational style. She can also determine if the day, week, or month was used to bring her closer to her goals or if her activities took her further away from them.

Let's go through the steps to determine if you are reaching your goals or if you are spending most of your time on busywork.

Using Your Calendar to Balance Your Time

When a working woman sees how she is spending her time, she may well be motivated to change her time use. Based on this theory, I have developed a method of time analysis that uses a calendar and colors.

The only necessary equipment is your month-at-a-glance calendar and three colored pencils or pens—yellow, green, and red. Here's how it works.

Professionally Speaking

First, go through the last week and underline in yellow all notations about activities that led you in a positive direction professionally. For example, underline notations about preparing for a presentation, a meeting for breakfast or lunch with a client or prospective client, reading up on a professional topic, meeting with staff starting a project, or planning time.

On the Home Front

Underline in green all notations about activities related to home goals. These would include notes about calling a cleaning service to clean your home, starting a laundry assembly line at home with other family members, visiting a child's teacher, going to lunch with a family member, taking a child to the doctor for a six-month checkup, or anything that keeps you in tune with your family life.

On the Personal Side

Finally, underline in red all the weekly activities that helped you get closer to your personal goals: notes about exercise; a timeout; a visit with friends; or massage, manicure, or hair appointments.

Make Time to Eat

Forget to eat? Taking the time to eat a healthy and well-balanced meal is an effective time management tool. If you do not take the time to eat a healthy, well-balanced meal, how do you expect to keep a healthy and well-balanced schedule? Making time to eat breakfast, lunch, and dinner will:

- Keep your energy up. Have you tried to be alert and enthusiastic at work when you're tired?
- Help with focus and concentration. Have you ever tried to concentrate when you're starving?
- Help keep extra pounds at bay. Have you ever eaten high-calorie junk food because you're so hungry?
- Help keep you healthy. Not feeling well and going to the doctor takes time, energy, and money.

If you're not convinced yet, let me share two more ideas with you:

- Studies have shown that children who eat breakfast do better in school. My youngest child, Daniel, became an excellent student his third year in high school when I started making him breakfast that included scrambled eggs with salmon, pancakes, and orange juice every morning.
- Studies have shown that eating healthy foods keeps the risk factor down for certain cancers.

Breakfast Ideas

Research shows that the most important meal of the day is breakfast and yet that is perhaps the working woman's most chaotic time of the day.

Let me share some easy, quick, and healthy protein breakfasts that will give you and your children fuel for the day. All of these breakfast ideas take five minutes or less to make! I promise!

- Poach an egg in simmering water for three minutes, drain and place on half a toasted piece of wheat bread or English muffin. Top with salsa if you wish. Out the door you go…
- Make a two egg (one egg yolk and two egg whites) omelet and stuff with canned or left-over asparagus spears. Out the door you go…
- Scramble two eggs with fresh chives and serve over one cup of fresh baby spinach leaves. Out the door you go…

- Combine a half cup low-fat yogurt with a half cup of any berries and two tablespoons of low-fat granola. Out the door you go…
- Scramble eggs with packaged smoked salmon. Add tomatoes the last few seconds, if you wish. Out the door you go…
- In a blender, puree a half cup low-fat yogurt, one fourth orange juice, and three ice cubes. Or replace the ice cubes with one fourth cup organic soy milk. You can also include a few pieces of whatever fruit you have on hand. Out the door you go…
- Fill one fourth of a cantaloupe melon with one fourth cup low-fat cottage cheese. Out the door you go…
- Combine one fourth cup low-fat cottage cheese with strawberries and raspberries. Out the door you go…
- Spread a light dusting of peanut butter on wheat toast. Out the door you go…
- Make a dozen hard-boiled eggs the night before and grab one or two in addition to the yogurt or cottage cheese combos. Out the door you go…

(Taken from the cookbook, *The De-Stress Diva in the Kitchen: 30–45–60 Minute Menus Cookbook* by Ruth Klein)

Integrate or Suffocate™

Managing your time is spending your days with quality time, quality relationships, and quality goals in several areas of your life: health, personal, family, work, spiritual, community, and money. The question I often ask myself is, "How can I make this work? How can I bridge many areas of my life in each twenty-four hour period to make them more effective and joyful rather than stressful and guilt-ridden?" I have found that one solution is what I refer to as Integrate or Suffocate.

To "Integrate" is to combine the many roles of your life and your activities. It is the intention of making a smooth, harmonious, and joyful experience for yourself as well as your loved ones by combining these different areas. It is a way of living your values and moving forward in reaching your goals. It is being present and making conscious choices.

Women feel "Suffocated" when we plan and do for everyone but ourselves. By Integrating the different hats that you wear and moving forward towards your goal as you live your values is a strong feeling of empowerment and motivation to keep Integrating. It is *not* multi-tasking. I believe we do ourselves, the tasks we're working on and the people around us a disservice when we multi-task. When you multi-task it is usually difficult to be present. It is easier to make mistakes, miss the entire experience, and push your stress overload buttons when you multi-task.

You know multitasking is not a positive experience when:

Work You're waiting on your cell phone while your landline is ringing and you're checking email while listening to a podcast on your computer.

Home You want to spend quality time with your family but you find yourself answering your cell phone during dinner or you take personal time off from work to clean your house but are bombarded by calls, interruptions, and find yourself doing very little of what you took the personal day to do.

Personal You take a walk outside to exercise and talk on your cell phone for most of the trip.

You may want to ask yourself a few questions.

1. Were you present for each task?
2. Did the tasks or behaviors bring you relaxation or joy?
3. Did your work, family, or yourself benefit in quality performance and results?

If the answer is no to these questions, then you are probably in the anxiety-driven and time-pressured multitasking role of mindlessly doing tasks rather than the Integrate or Suffocate behavior mode.

Integrate or Suffocate™ Moments

Ronnie, a Forty-Something part-time attorney and mother of four children says, "I don't take my personal time to clean the house, the children's rooms and fold the laundry—I get my children involved and we talk and laugh through the entire cleaning and folding sessions. The best part of this is that the children are a little more careful now in leaving clothes and toys strewn around—they pick up after themselves because they know it will take less time to clean later."

Nancy, an Achieving mother of two keeps one weekend day open for family and doesn't run errands on that day. She says, "I bring my children along as I do errands after school and this has become quality time with them. It gives me a chance to withhold from errands and buying on Sundays. While in the car, I encourage my children to share what is going on in their lives and I try to listen more than I talk. It's amazing what I have found out about their time at school, peer pressure, and the like. I am making a conscious effort not to talk on my cell at this time."

Terri, a Traditional Homemaker, and one of the few women I know that irons many of her family's clothes says, "I used to iron when the children weren't around and I hated it—now with my new mantra 'Integrate or Suffocate,' I do the ironing while I test the children for school. I actually enjoy ironing now—I don't see it as a boring, 'have to' chore anymore. I see it as spending time with my kids. The added benefit is that it has freed up my time which I love."

Dawn, a Thirty-Something mother of a four-year old, says, "I now eat breakfast in the mornings. I boil a couple of eggs when I'm preparing dinner the night before and then my son and I have hard-boiled eggs, wheat toast, and orange juice for breakfast now. I have always had a weight problem and I find I'm not starving by 10:00 a.m. Plus, I have made breakfast a conscious choice for quality time for my son. He loves breakfast time with Mom, and so do I."

Sylvia, an Achieving Woman, has two children in college. She made calls to find a project near one of her children's college. She makes it a point to visit her son every month and continue her business relationship nearby. She says, "I could do some of the work by phone, but I have made a commitment to see my son monthly and quite honestly, being in person with my clients is always a little better than chatting with them by phone."

Here are more ideas:

- Exercise while watching a morning news show or any television show. You can do stretches, lift weights, tummy crunches, use a torso machine, or a stationary bike.
- Exercise while you learn a new language by listening to songs in that language.
- Research reveals that three ten-minute walks taken at different times of the day are as effective at relieving tension and anxiety as one thirty-minute walk. To keep stress levels under control, take a quick ten-minute walk before work, take a ten-minute stroll at lunchtime, and then finish your day with a brisk power walk around the block when you get home.
- Exercise is part of your work day. A regular exercise routine acts as though you were talking to a brainstorming buddy. Exercise will help you de-stress and think of ways to creatively handle situations or complex events. One caveat: do not talk on your cell phone while exercising if you want to get its complete benefit.

Taking Advantage of the MINUTES

How can you take advantage of your minutes without being controlled by the clock? Time management, or life management, is *not* about saving seconds and minutes cleaning the bathrooms and the kitchen faster. I believe that mind-set only makes you more anxious because you are trying to beat the clock, which will never happen. Rather, what can you do when you have one, five, ten, twenty minutes open between appointments, waiting for a child to get into the car, or consciously taking the five or ten minutes to do the following:

Do You Have One Minute?

- Read a favorite, uplifting quote everyday.
- Close your eyes and connect with your inner spirit, power of purpose, focus, health, love, and creativity.
- Have an imaginary jump rope at your desk and jump rope, starting with one foot, then two feet and then the other foot and repeat for the whole minute. This is a great way to build up strong bones and get your blood circulated and oxygen to the brain for better concentration and focus.
- Say daily Positive Mantras, including one for mind, one for body, and one for your spirit.
- Think positive, loving thoughts and send them out to the universe. It will help you de-stress and get centered.
- Shut your eyes and breathe deeply for one whole minute.
- Fill a glass of water and drink it.

Do You Have Five Minutes?

- Read a few pages of an inspiring book or prayer or meditation.
- Stretch legs, arms, shoulders, neck, hands, and take deep breaths.
- Look at your calendar and get familiar with your day and schedule—perhaps you need to reschedule so that you alleviate unnecessary stress.
- Return a call (keep it to five minutes).
- Make a call to a loved one and say "I love you" (keep it to five minutes).
- Email a person you have not been in contact with and say "hi" and "miss you."

- Take your vitamins.
- Do kegel exercises, squats, and lunges while talking on the phone.
- Clean up email and delete spam.
- Call your significant other and say "I love you—I was thinking of you."
- Call one of your children after school to say the same thing. Those few minutes go a long way in establishing and reaffirming a loving bond between you and your child.
- Make yourself a veggie juice. This is the recipe I use, but you can modify it if you wish (takes five minutes to make *and* clean up):

In a juicer, juice

- three organic carrots
- one stalk organic celery
- large handful of fresh organic spinach
- one organic gala apple

It's delicious and helps you towards reaching the nine fruits/veggies a day goal the Cancer Society recommends.

- Do sit ups for five minutes.
- Write a "thank you" card and mail it.

Do You Have Ten Minutes?

- Clean out your purse or briefcase or both.
- Add a few names to your database.
- Clean the bathroom mirror and sink.
- Return several calls.
- Return several emails—ten minutes only!
- Gather the information you need to start a new project, including a call if necessary for more information.
- Drop off "extra food" to a neighborhood friend, child, sibling, or widow if you're going out of town and you still have delicious food leftover from dinner.

- Clean out your top desk drawer.
- Read a few pages of the book, *The Automatic Millionaire,* by David Bach or any other money book.
- File papers that have stacked up on your desk (keep it to ten minutes).
- Exercise using stairs and couches in your home or office, patio, or grassy area outside.

Do you Have Twenty Minutes?

- Make a hearty and healthy asparagus and cauliflower soup, warm up some bread, a cup of hot green tea and you just made a delicious lunch or dinner (taken from *The De-Stress Diva in the Kitchen* by Ruth Klein).

Asparagus and Cauliflower Soup
Preparation Time: Ten minutes
Cooking time: Ten minutes

- 8 scallions, including green tops
- 1 tsp. olive oil
- Half a cauliflower head
- 4 Cups of vegetable broth
- ½ tsp. salt
- ¼ tsp. pepper

Snap off cut end of asparagus stalks and discard. Sauté scallions in 1 tsp. olive oil. Put all ingredients in large pot and cook over medium heat until tender, about 10 minutes. Pureé at least ¾ of the soup in blender, then add to original mixture, stirring well.

- Take a warm, relaxing bath and remember to light the candles, even during the day.
- Update your checkbook.
- Return calls or emails.
- Take care of any charge dispute over the phone, since they will keep you on the phone for half that time.

Restructure Your Time to Fit Your Personality

When she analyzed her calendar, Sarah, an attorney and an Achieving Woman, found that she was spending more time on home activities than on personal areas. "I knew I felt completely overwhelmed; I was staying at the office late at night and worked almost all weekends just to maintain at work. I feel like a rag doll each morning. After I analyzed where my time was going, I did something about it. I hired a courier service to do all my home errands. Someone from the service returns an unwanted gift, pays an overdue bill in person, or delivers personal gifts. I don't know why I didn't think of this earlier, because our firm uses a courier to take and pick up legal briefs all the time. It's far less expensive than the time it would take me to do it.

"I also set up a carpool system with my children's friends' parents. They take and I pick up from soccer and basketball practice. I still try to make as many games as I can. I now get weekly massages…it's less expensive in money and time and more effective than the chiropractor. Plus, it feels better."

Sarah recently analyzed her calendar again and found that she is now spending far less time on home errands. She works in the office only one day each weekend, she spends time with her family on Sundays, and she has started an exercise program—she walks every morning. "I still have a lot to do, but I don't feel as ragged or angry. I can't believe what a little restructuring can do."

By analyzing her calendar, Jeanie, a Traditional Homemaker with four active children, found that she was spending almost 85 percent of her time on the home front but had very little personal time. "I gave up baking cookies for each classroom party. That was really hard—my children don't care, but I liked doing it because the house smelled so good. It's the same smell that I remember from when I was growing up, but my mom says she would *never* chauffeur her children around the way I do. No wonder she always had the time to bake."

Kristan, a Transitional Woman, found she spent most of her time working. "I used to take work home almost every night and got the children in bed as quickly as I could so I could finish my office job. I usually ended up feeling frustrated because I couldn't spend enough time with my family."

Twelve weeks after analyzing her activities, Kristan accepted a lateral career move that required less responsibility and fewer after-hour meetings. "I still work a lot, but I don't have to rush my kids to bed anymore. I spend ten to fifteen minutes with each child at bed-time. I wish I had more time with them, but this is an enjoyable time for all of us. We all have warmer feelings towards each other, and there's not nearly as much fussing."

Important Points to Remember

There are several ways to avoid overloading your schedule. Think "Time Quality" and use a month-at-a-glance calendar. With one glance you can decide to plan downtime during a particularly busy week. A month-at-a-glance calendar keeps you well organized rather than busy.

Take your calendar or PDA everywhere (except dressy social functions). Circle important dates in red or set your alarm. This signals the need to schedule time between activities.

Keep the day before and after a trip unplanned. This helps ease your schedule and lowers your anxiety. Divide each day of your calendar into three parts: morning, afternoon, and evening. Write appointment times in the appropriate space so the calendar can give you a visual signal to warn you about over- or under-booking.

Block out time, in advance, to use for personal activities. And, most importantly, find out where you're spending time by analyzing your calendar. You will feel in control when your schedule fits your personality and lifestyle. It's worth the effort.

Chapter Eight

Beating Stress by Breaking the Rules

S tress is responsible for a myriad of problems ranging from depression to headaches to a sagging libido. In addition to an overloaded schedule, boredom ranks high on the list of the symptoms of stress.

It never hurts to fight stress with a little healthy "rebellion" once in a while. By rebellion I simply mean doing something that represents a distinct break from your regular schedule. As an employee or employer, build up a store of compensatory time, or "comp" time—that is, time off that you take without pay to compensate you for extra time spent at work. A store of comp time will allow you to take occasional mental-health days. You could use your afternoon off to catch a matinee or special sale, enjoy a midweek romantic getaway with a lover, or take a class that teaches belly dancing or the art of striptease.

After interviewing hundreds of women over the years, I have come to the conclusion that 80 percent of stress comes from self-induced time-pressures: by being late because of poor scheduling, by not allowing enough time to complete work or pursue personal interests, and by not allowing enough time to spend with family and friends.

The other 20 percent is "good" stress. Experts agree that good stress—which arises from the right amount of challenge—can increase your energy level, productivity, and creativity. The optimum amount of stress is different for each person.

How to Spend Time to Save Time

It's easy for working women to overdo and over commit. When you feel overwhelmed and stressed, your body stops working properly. It goes into overdrive and shuts down creativity. Physiologically, our bodies cannot work properly under extreme stress and tension. It is as worthless to spend hours working on a project without a rest as it is to work under tension. In both cases, you waste time and spin your wheels. Certainly, you have worked on a project with a bad tension headache and realized the next day that your work was far from good or properly completed.

In these instances, it would have been far wiser—in time, expense, and professional self-esteem—to walk away from the task at hand and walk around the block, do twenty jumping jacks, or leave for the afternoon.

In other words, you need to spend time on yourself in order to save time on your task. Here are several more suggestions for going about this:

- Take half a day or a full day off when you're feeling overwhelmed. As long as you find a replacement and get your work completed, most employers do not mind. Be honest; tell him or her you need a mental-health day. Make sure this does not happen too often.

Joann asked for a "personal" day off two days after returning from a business trip. "I just needed some time to catch my breath. I felt over-whelmed and lost. I slept in until 8:30 a.m., took a long bath, and just stayed home. That one day off recharged my energy level."

- Leave the office when you are feeling stressed. Staying in a stress-ful situation without any relief only exacerbates the situation. Take a walk or listen to relaxing music for ten minutes with your eyes shut. Think of pleasant thoughts.

Susan, a medical doctor, takes at least thirty minutes at the end of the day to "just sit and change gears from work to home. When I enter the door to my home, I try to keep all of the office activities out of my head. Besides being a doctor, I'm also a mom."

- If you're a morning person, wake up an hour earlier every morning; if you're a night person, stay up an hour later. Meditate, listen to music, read the paper with a cup of tea or coffee, take a walk, or do anything else that is completely for *you* and is stress reducing.

Janet wakes up at 5:30 a.m. so that she can read the paper and sip a cup of coffee before she wakes the rest of the household. Also, she spends some of this time reading meditative commentary. "This time in the morning is my favorite time of day. It gives me a reference point for the rest of the day. It helps give me faith that what I plan to accomplish each day is worthwhile and has a purpose."

Jill, a realtor, takes two "spa" days a month. She arbitrarily marks off two days together for what she refers to as her spa days. "I figure I can stay at home and go to a spa for services. I find it has been a great de-stressor for me and by the time the two days are over, I can't wait to get back to work—my motivation and focus is back on."

Long-Term Stress Versus Short-Term Stress

Our physiology is such that, in the face of danger, our hormonal level changes so we can either fight or flee in an instant. Being in this state for extended periods is dangerous because it causes the immune system to work overtime and, eventually, break down.

Medical researchers and doctors believe that this breakdown of the immune system is the culprit in many illnesses: certain types of cancer, gastrointestinal problems, skin irritations, recurring viruses, arthritis, migraine headaches, and more.

It is far easier, healthier, and less expensive to take the time and reverse the situations that cause you stress than to try to work in spite of them.

I know that the urge to continue working can be strong, even though you know your productivity is dwindling. As I sit here writing this chapter, I have an intense urge to continue writing—even though my back is giving out and my cold is getting worse. How do I go about leaving my work for tomorrow when I really want to ignore my body and keep going?

I talk to myself and say, "Stop what you're doing, you're on work overload. *Stop!*" (It works, honest!)

Traditional Stress-Busters

Stress-busters are activities you can undertake to stop the upward spiral of stress. The three traditional stress-busters are:
- A hot bath
- Window shopping
- Exercise

Take a Hot Bath

Almost every evening I dim the bathroom lights, lock my bedroom and bathroom door, light a fragrant candle, and take a hot bath with Epsom salt. When my children were young, they knew this was my quiet time and that I was not to be disturbed. My baths consistently run about twenty minutes, and I immerse my entire body up to my neck. I consciously let go of anything negative that happened during the day and try hard not to think about anything special. This sets the stage for a peaceful night's rest.

Window Shop

Carrie stays home and takes care of three children. I asked her how she keeps the stress down. "My husband will come home during lunch, and I will go out and window shop. I love to look at window displays and the color combinations they use. I also know what styles are coming up. It's like reading a fashion magazine on a large three-dimensional scale. If my husband can't come home, I hire a babysitter for two hours."

Exercise

Janet sits at her desk most of the day. Stress from sitting as well as managing twenty-five people in her department can take its toll. Janet handles stress by walking around her building several times a day. "It's become a joke. When someone is trying to reach me by phone and I can't be found, my secretary says 'she's strolling the grounds'. I started walking by happenstance. A coworker and I had some extra time at lunch before going back to the office, and we decided to walk around the block. I remember feeling so good after doing this that I kept it up. Now you can find me putting on my tennis shoes and walking downstairs several times a day."

Creative Stress-Busters

In addition to the traditional stress-busters, consider the tips in the list that follows. Each suggestion involves activity that is more mental than physical and may call for creativity or an attitude change.

- Change the situation.
- Let go!
- Learn to live with what you cannot change.
- Take time to play.
- Trust your intuition and decisions.
- Use weekends to re-energize and build fond memories.
- Be patient.
- Live now.

- Avoid labeling.
- Stay positive.
- Build and maintain traditions.
- Examine your choices.
- Progressive relaxation.

Change the Situation

In many cases, you do not have the power to make decisions that will change policy, coworkers, or anything else. However, there are situations that you can change or modify by developing and substantiating your ideas. This is not an easy way to make changes, but patience and persistence are the key.

Eleanor worked in the accounting department at an engineering firm for two years. She found a particular procedure most stressful. "I told the head accountant that we backtrack using this particular form, but the company did nothing. I then took the matter into my own hands. I revised the form to my specifications and turned it in. The head accountant asked, 'What the hell is this?' After I showed him how it works, he said we could try it if everyone wanted to." With a smile Eleanor said, "Two weeks later everyone in the department was using the E-form." (E for *Eleanor.*)

Let Go!

Letting go of negative thoughts is not an easy task by anyone's standards. Laura, a Transitional Woman, has a difficult time leaving the house messy in the morning. "There's no way I can get the kids off to school and be at the office by 8 a.m. and keep my house tidy. Every morning I got angry with the kids on the way to school. I arrived at the office grumpy. I finally decided to just let the house go. Now, the kids straighten up while I make dinner. We're all a lot happier," smiles Laura. "I learned that the kids and my husband didn't care about the untidy house; I did. I'm still a good person even if my dishes are in the sink and washed clothes are sitting on the sofa in the front room."

Learn to Live with What You Cannot Change

There are times when nothing you do can change or modify a situation. Nancy is a full-time mom with four children. She has rheumatoid arthritis and never knows when her shoulder or leg joints will give out. She would like to go to work outside the home, but doesn't know exactly what to do. Because her husband is seldom home, all child care responsibilities lie with her. "I can't think about 'what if,' because I'm too busy doing what I have to do. But I'm going to go back to school when the baby is in preschool. I will then take different classes to determine what field I like. I know I can't make any changes now, but it doesn't mean I can't plan for the future."

Take Time to Play

The Traditional Homemaker feels she must spend playtime with the family, not in playing to benefit only herself. The Transitional Woman feels she can't take time to play, because there just isn't any time left between work and family responsibilities.

The Achieving Woman feels she needs to be doing something all the time and that the something needs to have a purpose. She views "unproductive" time as wasted.

The Traditional Homemaker needs to set aside time when the children are at school or napping. She can spend that time taking a relaxing bath, reading, working in the garden (if she enjoys it), or doing anything else that relaxes her. The Transitional Woman needs to tell herself she deserves some time off just for herself. When she is less stressed, the entire family will be less stressed. The Achieving Woman must realize that taking the time to play and reenergize will make her more productive in the long run. Her creative juices will flow better when she is relaxed. She must learn that to relax is not wasteful and to incorporate this fact into her belief system.

Trust Your Intuition and Decisions

I feel that a woman's intuition is one of her strongest attributes. A woman's intuition is the final jury to most good decisions. Never trust someone else's choices if you feel they are not for you. Jon Kabat-Zinn, PhD, author of *Full Catastrophe Living*, says:

"Trust your intuition and your own authority, even if you make some mistakes along the way. Then you get into the habit of looking inside yourself for guidance. If something doesn't feel right to you, honor your feelings."

Use Weekends to Reenergize and Build Fond Memories

Life, the Time Inc. newspaper supplement, commissioned the Great American Weekend Survey asking adults how they feel after the weekend. Young adults (ages eighteen to twenty-four) were exhausted (51 percent) after the weekend and Fifty-Somethings were recharged (51 percent). The phone survey was conducted in March and gives a review of how stressed we have made our weekends with shopping, chores, and family activities. What can you do?

Traditional Homemakers feel that weekends are for family get-togethers. However, watching soccer and baseball games, unless you truly enjoy them, are not reenergizing activities. To reenergize herself, Nancy tries to go on a family picnic one weekend day each week. "I enjoy watching the kids play in the park. I'm away from the house so I can't do any housework. It's definitely a special time for me and the kids."

Transitional Women feel that weekends are for errands. Now that Janet has learned to use weekends for rejuvenation, she takes Saturday completely off. "I sleep in till 8 a.m., lounge around the house playing with plants or reading the paper. Each child may ask a friend over

Saturdays after 12 p.m., or they can go over to a friend's house. The only stipulation is that they need to get their own rides—the chauffeur is not available on Saturdays, only Sunday through Friday."

Achieving Women feel that weekends are for getting more work done. The trick is to get these women relaxed and show them how positive relaxation is for the body and mind.

I was working seven days a week, five on marketing and public relations and two on writing. Any way you cut it, it came out to seven days a week. I justified this intense body and mind workout because of my writing deadlines. As a result of my weekend work marathons, I found that I was not as creative on Monday, my brainstorming day, nor was I feeling physically relaxed.

I now take Friday night and Saturdays off. I sleep in and then go out to breakfast *by myself;* read the paper; and come home an hour and a half later, feeling extremely refreshed.

Be Patient

People and events unfold in their own time. Most things in life occur with time, persistence, and a focus. Our fast-paced society in conjunction with new technological advances—such as fax machines, modems, faster computers and printers, and car phones—cause more stress and keep us from learning to be patient. Losing weight, done properly, takes time. After you start weight lifting, it takes time before you see muscle definition.

My impatience to get things done drove me to lengthen my work day by making 7 a.m. breakfast meetings. I was consistently working eleven-hour days. I could feel the long hours bringing down my immunity. This became especially clear when I developed an inner-ear imbalance that affected my equilibrium and made me dizzy. I thought I had brain cancer. My body was giving me a clear signal about the error of my impatient ways. Even after I made the decision to sleep more, walk in the mornings, and set up only two early breakfast meetings a week, it took me three weeks to make the goal a reality.

According to Jon Kabat-Zinn, "To be patient is simply to be completely open to each moment, accepting it in its fullness, knowing that, like the butterfly, things can unfold only in their own time."

Live Now

The only time you *really* have is *now*. It is important to be aware of what is going on around you at each moment. As I sit here writing under a deadline, I am aware of the luscious greenery outside, my healthy family, and the dirty house I call home. Somehow the deadline is not as pressing or as important.

Ann lived in the fast lane, as far as her job was concerned. She traveled over a week each month on business-related meetings, worked hard on making a second marriage with stepchildren work, and planned to start her own business in the future. When I visited with Ann concerning the development of seminars, we would quickly get our work done and share secrets about the future.

Not long after she had shared an idea for a new business with me, she was hospitalized and diagnosed with liver cancer. She was one of those positive types who flew out of town for treatments and kept planning her future. Nine months later, she left me with fond memories and her grandchildren with two dollhouses she had made from scratch. Her company hired three people to do the work Ann had done. I often think of her and wonder if she would have started her new business if she could have seen into the future.

In other words, the future is uncertain, the past is over, and the only real thing we have is *now*. This concept helps keep priorities in shape. It helps you stay aware of your surroundings and of what is truly important today.

Jon Kabat-Zinn says it best: "Awareness, insight, and health will ripen if you pay attention to and honor all the moments you live."

Avoid Labeling

It is very easy to label yourself, other people, and actions as good or bad. This attitude can be self-defeating. "I would go through the whole day saying how 'good' or 'bad' things were. If I missed a backup case at work, I would say how bad things were," comments Tracey, a court reporter. "I started to become aware of what I said to myself…and was amazed. So much of what I saw was negative, from the behavior of my two-year-old daughter to what my boyfriend wore at social gatherings. I work very hard at being less judgmental. It not only causes me less tension, but my relationship with my daughter and boyfriend have improved."

Stay Positive

Staying positive under stress and time pressures is easier said than done. It takes a conscious effort to think positively.

Susan, the doctor, says, "I have three choices on how I deal with a situation that doesn't go the way I expect: I can be upset, smile, or walk away. In most cases I choose to smile. Quite honestly, it takes less effort."

Build & Maintain Traditions

I have found that adults, as well as children, love and appreciate traditions. They become somewhat of a ritual that bring to us a level of safety and security. In a world that can be chaotic, it gives us stability to know that we can "count" on turkey for Thanksgiving, a Christmas tree at Christmas, lights on the Menorah at Hanukkah, and others.

An Achieving Woman says, "My adult children and I meet in Hawaii for a week every summer. It gives us a chance to be all together and enjoy each other's company."

My family went to a summer family camp for over twenty years. My children would have disowned us if we didn't go each year. We now meet in Lake Tahoe in the summer.

Examine Your Choices

Let's look at some choices a woman named Laura has in regard to working and keeping her home tidy. "I went through all the choices. I could stay home, have a clean house, and no money. I could hire a cleaning lady, but then the house would only be clean for one or two days afterwards. (I tried this for four years.) I could work part-time, but I couldn't find a good-paying job part-time. Or, I could go to work at a job I liked and not look back when I left in the mornings. After considering all my choices, I picked the last one."

Progressive Relaxation

Plan to spend ten to twenty minutes relaxing your muscles. For example, start with your hands and make a tight fist for a few seconds and then release and relax your hands; then you tighten your feet and relax; legs, lower back, stomach, chest, shoulders, neck, head, and facial muscles. After the progressive tensing and relaxing of muscles, you will be very relaxed and your stress will have left.

Low-Cost Tips for Reestablishing Yourself

The old cliché "A stitch in time saves nine" can be converted to a working woman's cliché: "Taking personal time saves you money and stress down the line."

You may have noticed a common theme in the traditional stress-busting tips and the stress-busters that take creativity. The common theme is to take time for yourself. In the midst of all you have to accomplish, do things to remind you that you are more than a task-accomplishing machine; reestablish yourself as a human being. This can mean taking an action that frees you to do something you enjoy or giving yourself a treat. Taking time to reestablish yourself doesn't necessarily mean spending a lot of money. And, as we have discussed, what little you do spend will be a good investment in terms of your health and productivity.

The list that follows presents tips for reestablishing yourself. In many ways, I consider these actions musts for saving self and money.

- Treat yourself to a house helper at least once a month. This house helper can be your sitter, a teenager, or a janitorial service. Go for whatever your priorities and budget will allow. (Figured in terms of your hourly wage, hiring help will probably be cheaper than hiring yourself to do the same work.)
- Treat yourself to a gardener at least once a month. (It's cheaper than going to the doctor with back pains.) Again, the gardener can be a teenager or a friend who needs a little extra money.
- Treat yourself to pretty undergarments once in a while. (They're cheaper than a whole new outfit.)
- Treat yourself to a minimum of one hour per week of playtime. (It's cheaper than taking sick leave from work.)
- Treat yourself to new lipstick. (It's cheaper than a complete makeover.)
- Treat yourself to a new pair of earrings or a scarf. (It's cheaper than an outfit or shoes.)
- Treat yourself to an at-home hair-conditioning program. (It takes less time to condition your hair than to cut it off and wait for it to grow back.)
- Treat yourself to eating healthy, energy-packed foods. (You can eat healthy food in the same amount of time it takes to eat unhealthy food—the difference is in making a conscious choice.)
- Treat yourself to sleep. (It usually takes twice as long to do something when you're tired.)

- Treat yourself to a massage.
- Treat yourself to doing something you find creative and fun.
- Treat yourself to exercise.
- Treat yourself for time to cook or bake for fun. (Most women I know enjoy cooking or baking when they have the time to do it.)
- Treat yourself by doing nothing.
- Treat yourself by being present with your children.
- Treat yourself by watching comedies.
- Treat yourself by reading inspirational and motivational books or stories.
- Treat yourself to inspirational movies, true stories.
- Treat yourself to meaningful and healthy sex.
- Treat yourself by taking one day at a time, *positively*. (It's cheaper than being tied up with a tension headache.)
- Treat yourself kindly, the way you want others to treat you. (Respect begets respect.)

Important Points to Remember

Most stress comes from self-induced time-pressures that result from poor scheduling. Part of effective time management is the realization that you need to spend time on yourself in order to save time on tasks. Listen to your body for stress signals and respond to them. To decrease stress, change the situation, if possible; let go of negative thoughts; learn to live with the things you cannot change; learn to take time to play; trust your intuition and decisions; use weekends for reenergizing and building fond memories; be patient; live *now;* avoid labeling; stay positive; build and maintain traditions; decide on choices; use progressive relaxation; and regularly treat yourself.

Chapter Nine

Crisis and Challenge: Opportunities for Growth

There is no such thing as a life without crises and challenges; how we *respond* to them is what makes the difference. By taking a positive rather than a negative approach, even the most formidable disasters and tasks can often be countered by a vital thrust in a new direction.

Crises, mistakes, and misdirection are not fatal. Indeed, much good can come of them if only we can respond constructively. The key to responding constructively is staying flexible—that is, not letting the temporary setback freeze us into inaction or despair. To do this, we must be able to distinguish the problem from our perception of the problem. This chapter will suggest ideas, attitude changes, and techniques that can help turn what looks like a negative situation into a positive one.

Recovering from Mistakes

Mundane and transient snafus such as having two appointments booked for the same time, missing a flight, staining a suit at a critical moment, forgetting the name of an important person, inadvertently hurting someone's feelings, and handling minor rejections *can* have a noncrisis ending. Everyday snafus and mistakes can turn into learning experiences and opportunities.

Bobbie has a very busy family therapy practice. "I once scheduled a husband and wife going through a divorce at my office at the same time. Both parties still felt wounded and vulnerable. I apologized for my gross negligence. We started laughing in the waiting room. Believe it or not, my 'mistake' was a turning point for them therapeutically. They stopped seeing each other as monsters."

Like Bobbie, Krista was able to profit from a mistake. "I went out to lunch with a new client and his girlfriend. Two people at different times walked up to the table to say hi to me. I introduced my client but forgot his girlfriend's name both times. I apologized and we laughed it off. I used this awkward situation as a funny way to open my conversations with my client. I'd call him and say, 'Hi, this is Krista. What was your name again?' To this day, I can't remember her name."

Confront the "Whoops!"

Mistakes happen! In fact, I guarantee that you will have to pay taxes, make mistakes, and, eventually, die.

Most situations can be fixed after a mistake. We do damage when the mistake goes on for a long time—when we do not confront it or take action to correct it.

Apologize, but do not feel indebted for the rest of your life. There's an old Jewish proverb: "Don't waste good agony."

Different types of women react differently to their own mistakes. The Traditional Homemaker feels especially upset by her mistakes, since she believes that she should know better or that her female counterpart who works outside the home wouldn't have let the mistake happen. The Transitional Woman feels guilty about making mistakes, often thinking that if she weren't so torn between all the hats she wears, mistakes would not happen. The Achieving Woman moves ahead fast, without taking many breaths in between activities. She knows that mistakes will happen, and she takes action when they do.

Go with the Flow

All women must learn to go with the flow when mistakes happen. Rather than perceiving a mistake as a monstrous catastrophe, accept it and go on. It is common for women to dwell on their mistakes and view them as failures. Janet says, "I know I'm going a mile a minute, if not faster, and I know that I am going to make some mistakes…big ones and little ones. I have to remember to look at my mistakes not as failures, but as growth…it sure is hard to do sometimes."

Nelson Boswell said, "The difference between greatness and mediocrity is often how an individual views a mistake." Sarah, a friend of mine, has a propensity for snagging her hose or staining her clothes at critical moments. "I feel horrible when I do this. I think everyone is looking at me and thinking, "What a slob." I have a high-profile career, and it's necessary to look presentable at all times…I don't have a lot of extra suits to bring to the office. Anyway, I would need to change shoes, hose, and whatever. Instead, I find that it takes far less space and is a lot cheaper to buy pins and stick 'em on the stains. I have little ones and large ones with silver and gold backgrounds. I laugh inside when someone comments on my pins or tells me how together I look." Sarah adds a whole new meaning to the concept of dressing fashionably!

This too is meant to be

Carl Jung coined the term "synchronicity" for when unexplainable events happen and we can not explain it by cause and effect, yet the events are nonetheless mysteriously linked in meaning. When these kinds of chance events occur, many times we are so busy we explain it by luck or chance.

I believe it comes from grace, a higher source, and is a Magic Moment. Try a fun experiment for two weeks. Operate on the assumption that everything that happens in your day is not accidental. Honor your hunches. Follow your urges, listen to the lyrics of a song, and notice the movies you want to see. Notice everything that is drawn to you in the next two weeks. Be receptive and alert to what life brings you.

A friend of mine, Teresa, is a busy professional who broke her arm while going down a wet ramp. It just so happens that she also found out when she went to the doctor that osteoporosis was setting in too quickly for her age. Was it just "chance" that she broke her arm?

Another friend, Yvonne, wanted to sell her house rental. She just "happened" to go over to the house to talk to the renter when a woman knocked on the door and asked if the house was for sale. There was no For Sale sign outside. The realtor had "sat" on getting one placed in the yard. Yvonne was in escrow the following day selling the house to this woman.

You are in the Performance Zone when...
- Things begin to happen effortlessly and you feel energy flowing throughout your body.
- You take time every day to think and plan *before* you start your day.
- You spend a minimum of one hour daily just for you. This can be broken down into ten or twenty minute intervals throughout the day.
- You learn to partner with others and delegate.
- You don't try to reinvent the wheel all the time.
- Your values, emotions, and attitudes are in sync with your lifestyle.
- You realize that it only takes one person—you—to make a difference for many.
- You respect your physical energy through healthy doses of sleep and exercise.
- You understand the most important time is now—because that is all you really have.
- You know that life is a package worth unwrapping.
- You realize your best move right now is forward.

Freeing Ourselves from Misperceptions

Facing a crisis or meeting a challenge may take all the energy we have. Yet many of us sap our energy by worrying, being angry or impatient, or avoiding the problem. To avoid wasting energy in this way, incorporate these ideas into your approach:

- Think of time as a neutral concept.
- Avoid "should-driven" behavior.
- Take action despite your perceptions of the situation.

Think of Time as a Neutral Concept

Time, or at least the concept of time, is neutral. Time begins to have meaning because of our frame of mind. Cathie, a stockbroker, discusses how the context affects her perception of time. "On vacation, time may revolve around naps and 'what are we doing for dinner?' questions. I seem to be obsessed with what I'm eating at mealtimes when I'm on vacation, but don't have that need when I'm home working.

"When I'm reading a novel, I lose all concept of time, but when I'm up against a deadline, it seems my heart beats with the tick of the clock. I can't believe how slowly time goes by when I'm waiting for a question to be answered, and how fast it goes when I'm working on a project."

When you're waiting at a doctor's office or waiting for a client, time takes on new perceived value. We look at these situations as "time-pressures" or "time-wasters" that bring stress into our lives. If we can just remember that time, in itself, has no value, we can avoid wasting energy on being emotional about our perceptions.

Avoid "Should-Driven" Behavior

If allowed, women let their feelings of "should" and "should not" govern their behavior. The Traditional Homemaker feels she "should" be preparing home-cooked meals, since she doesn't "work" and has so much "free" time. The Transitional Woman feels she has too much to do but "should" still be an ever-attentive wife and mother. The Achieving Woman feels that, to reach her goals, she "should" be more involved in work and home functions.

Should-driven behavior is another energy waster. If a goal is not important to *you*, then do not let it haunt you. Do not let other people's values, or your perception of them, determine how you use your resources.

Take Action Despite Perceptions

This step is the second part of freeing yourself from should-driven behavior. Suppose you determine that you are being haunted by a "should." Furthermore, suppose you determine that the "should" is attached to a goal that you'd like to accomplish but that seems out of your reach. The key, at this point, is to take action despite your perception of the impossibility of the task.

This philosophy is part of the New Action-Oriented therapy, which was developed by Japanese therapists Mirita and Naikan. They claim that taking action despite your perceptions of a situation helps you get done what you want to get done. A typical conversation with a New Action-Oriented therapist might go something like this:

"I really should spend more time working on reports."
"No, just do it."
"I need to make more of a commitment to spend time with my family and friends."
"No, just do it."
"I should be able to organize my life better."
"No, just do it."

You get the idea. The Japanese therapists suggest that, through discipline and a pragmatic approach to life, a person can address deep-seated inner feelings and achieve goals.

Understanding Our Behavior

The way we perceive our time-pressures is a product of our values, both individually and socially. Since these perceptions are deeply rooted in our past and culture, they may be difficult to track down. In other words, it may be hard to understand why we're reacting to a problem the way we are. Once we understand ourselves, it is often easier to abandon unproductive approaches and try new ones that will work.

To help women understand their reactions to crises and challenges, I suggest an analysis I call the feel it/behave it approach. The woman divides a page of a yellow legal pad into two columns. At the top of the left-hand column, she writes "Feelings"; at the top of the right-hand column, she writes "Behavior." Linda, a dining room hostess for a resort hotel, tried the analysis and found that it helped her discover why she was having trouble achieving her goal of spending more time with her children.

"I found that I didn't want to spend time with my older children, because, under the 'Feelings' column, I wrote: 'They are always talking about themselves, and when I say something about my day, they seem uninterested.' I feel neglected at home."

Under "Behavior" Linda wrote: "I don't mind the extra-long hours I spend at work. I'd rather be working. When I work I feel better because people listen to me. I'm somebody."

Linda recognized and accepted what she was doing and started taking the time to speak and have enjoyable time with each child once a day. She found that when she gave her undivided attention to her teens, then they would do the same for her. "Now that I see why I was avoiding them, we now have some of our best talks."

Ginny wants a job with more responsibility, but she does not go on any job interviews. She was asked to interview with two companies, but she declined both requests. When she analyzed her behavior by using the feel it—behave it approach, her two columns looked like this:

Feelings	Behavior
I am bored by my job. I am afraid that more responsibility at work would mean longer hours away from my family. A new job would mean I wouldn't have any time with them.	I find excuses for not going to job interviews even though they could lead to more money and the chance to use my skills.

Think of an uncomfortable situation that you would like to change. Write the problem at the top of the page. Under "Feelings," write down your feelings in the situation. Are you angry, disgusted, bored, guilty, fearful, ambivalent, rejected, neglected? Write down all your emotions. Under "Behavior," write down your actual behavior in this specific situation—what you actually do or don't do. Perhaps you want to organize time better but say yes to everyone. Perhaps you want to start a family, but it's never the "right" time.

You will find that the way you feel has a direct impact on the way you behave.

Living in the Present

Living in the present rather than living in the past helps to keep life issues in perspective. When our perceptions are kept within the confines of a reality check, then the concept of time remains neutral and we can use our energy constructively.

Use Reality Checks to Maintain Perspective

When we're in the mood for rock music, we turn the radio dial to a rock station. When we're in the mood for classical music, we know to turn the dial to that kind of station. If we are in the mood for oldies, we need to turn the dial again.

When we're in a crisis situation, we must use a reality check to turn the dial on our thoughts. A reality check can change negative and anxious thoughts into positive thoughts.

Dana took a day off to spend time with her father, who was recuperating from a routine hospital procedure. "When I first arrived at the hospital, I felt rushed, nervous, and frustrated that my dad chose that day for the exam. By midafternoon I needed to get out of this depressing place. I realized how fortunate I was to be able to walk out of here at any time. I don't *have* to be here because of a medical problem. Whenever I have a crisis situation, I just remember how closed in and depressing the hospital was, and I snap out of it."

"I remember when my little one had the croup," says Cindy, a medical assistant. "The doctor told me that children with croup sound worse than they are, but it can be dangerous. I have never heard anything so wretched in my life. I told myself that, if he gets better, I will never take anything but life-and-death issues so seriously again. It's been a year now, and I've *almost* kept my promise."

In times of crisis, use the points that follow as reality checks.

- Ask yourself, What is the worst thing that can happen? If the answer is not a life-or-death matter, turn the dial. Turning the dial keeps your perspective in the present, the here and now.

- Immediately think of two of life's blessings. When you feel a slight smile on your face, you'll know you have turned the dial.
- Ask, "Can this 'crisis' turn into learning?" If the answer is yes, turn the dial.
- Ask, "Will time make things better?" If the answer is yes, turn the dial. Even the most tragic of cases eventually gets better with time.
- If the "crisis" helps you feel humble, turn the dial. Golda Meir, Israel's fourth prime minister, said: "Don't be humble, you're not that great."

Planning Life as a Whole

If you look at a clock, you see that the face is divided into twelve major and sixty minor parts. It is the perception of these parts that makes some women obsessed with time. The obsession causes stress. Remember, the whole is greater than the sum of its ticking.

Rather than looking at time in increments—fifteen minutes, for example—look at time as a whole: a whole life. When you have only thirty minutes to complete the errands, the task becomes stressful. If the errands have not been done as part of a whole life, they take on a whole different perspective.

Susan Helper, a medical doctor, says, "I only have so many hours in my day. I have to divide these precious hours with my practice, my family, and my friends. If I look at each day and what I need to accomplish, I would go off the deep end. I try to keep my life in balance by not worrying if I don't accomplish everything today, because in the scheme of things I have longer than twenty-four hours to do it all."

I asked Susan what happens when she has to go to the hospital to see a patient and her son wants to read to her. "I obviously have to take care of my patient, not because the patient is more important than my children, but because the patient needs me right now. I feel it's important for children to know that they can't decide when they do and do not want to be with their parents. It's realistic to teach them that you can't have what you want when you want it at all times, and that they have to give something up once in a while also.

"It is important to plan life as a whole, rather than plan time with every click of the clock. The real question becomes, 'What do you want to do with your life—what do you want to accomplish as a whole?'" Susan wants to be an excellent medical doctor and to enjoy the other parts of her life—husband, children, friends. Looking at the whole helps her to put daily tasks in proper perspective. It can do the same for you and allow you to claim the lifestyle you *want,* rather than the tasks you have to do.

Two techniques can help you look at time and life as a whole:

1. Ask yourself, Is it absolutely necessary to do this *now?*
2. Make a daily to-do list.

Ask If It Is Absolutely Necessary Now

Lorraine is the owner of a small business. She must take care of the business and her family each day. "Some days my list of things to do is so long it depresses me. I start out motivated, but usually I can't finish it all in one day. I keep asking myself if I *have* to do this now, or can it wait for later in the day or possibly the next day? I still get a lot done, but not everything I want to. I have learned to distinguish between what I have to do *now* and what I can do later."

Make a Daily To-Do List

To make a to-do list, use one or two sheets of a legal pad, PDA, or computer to-do list. At the top of the sheet, write the day and date. At the top left margin, under the date, write "People to Call." Include phone numbers in *front* of the names. One of the biggest deterrents to making or returning calls quickly is having to look up the numbers.

About one third down the sheet, write "Things to Do." This is where you list what needs to be done for work, home, or yourself. Write the due date in front of your task. This helps you see its immediacy.

In the last third of the page, write "Places to Go." List the destinations in order. But be flexible—number five may become number one tomorrow. Number four may become number two because it's closer to the last stop than you previously thought.

Your to-do list should look something like this:

 DAILY TO-DO LIST

Wednesday, March 11, 2006

People to Call or Email:
> 324-4687—Jim Drake/Oilfield Services/seminar update
> 323-4241—Carla Clips/Maintenance of office
> 800-336-1233—Reservation for the weekend of March 23–24
> Cynthia: Cynthia@hotwires.com

Things to Do:
> TODAY—Fax article to clients TODAY—Summarize meeting
> March 13—Dr. Shipley's proposal
> March 14—Office meeting and presentation
> April 9—Gather information and send to seminar members
> Internet Research—Business reports for trends

Places to Go:
> 1—Cleaners
> 2—Post office
> 3—Pick up film for attorney's brochure
> 4—Drop off basket to Jon's client

When you've completed a task, make a plus sign from the dash that precedes each task. This will keep your list organized and neat, and it is faster than scratching things out. To find unfinished tasks, you need only look for the dash. If you're using your computer to-do list, simply delete completed items.

At this point, ask yourself again whether it is absolutely necessary to do the task now. If you can keep these "parts" of your day in perspective, you can begin to get closer to what you want from life.

Think of these incremental tasks as vehicles to get you where you want to go—not as destinations in themselves. Nothing worth achieving is ever done quickly.

Enjoy the activities on the way to achieving your goals, just as you would enjoy the sights and tastes on the way to your vacation spot. Once you've reached your destination, you can decide on a new vacation spot for next year—in other words, one goal will follow another. Enjoy the sights!

Staying Flexible

To stay mentally flexible, don't push it! Even if you don't finish tasks as soon as you like, don't strain. "I make the most mistakes when I feel pinched for time," says Sarah, a medical transcriber. "The doctors I work for would rather have the files a day later than have mistakes. The only time that doesn't work is when they must be in court. I realized that's only 5 percent of the medical cases. I used to push hard 95 percent of the time and make many errors. I now work on court cases first, leaving everything else until later. What a difference it makes."

Also, remember that it's okay to change directions midway through a project. "Every year collecting all the information I need to give my accountant for taxes is excruciating. It's like pulling teeth," says Jane. "I'll do as much as my patience endures, and then I go do another job for a while. It helps keep me from going nuts."

A classic tip for maintaining mental flexibility is going for a walk to clear your head. "My best ideas come when I'm by myself and walking around the neighborhood," says Janet. "Ideas just come. Often, new ways of dealing with an old problem pop up."

By staying flexible, you can avoid being frozen by the enormity of a crisis or challenge. Janet, currently a director of business services for a school district, faced a big challenge when she decided to go back to school to get her bachelor's degree. Her husband, a law enforcement officer, had variable hours. "My life could not revolve around my husband. If it did, I'd have a great excuse not to go back to school." Janet has two children. What looked like an insurmountable task on the surface turned out to be a lesson in flexibility. "My seven-year-old daughter, fourteen-year-old son, and I would have dinner in the college dining commons, or I would bring a sandwich from home and we would have dinner on the grass outside my class. My son would spend the evening in the library where they had audio equipment, and do his homework. My seven-year-old would sometimes go with her brother or would come to class with me. Many nights my daughter slept in my arms while I listened and took class notes. We would get home around 9 p.m. We'd take baths, pick up some clutter…I made a choice between being a good student and having a clean house…clothes were on the sofa ready to be folded. Bedtime was 10 p.m.

"I had to give up sleep in order to do what I needed to do. I trained myself to wake up at 3 a.m. and study until 5, when I started to get ready for work and woke the children for school."

Janet now has her master's degree in education counseling and personnel services. Asked how she kept going, she muses, "I had to learn flexibility and not let the little things get in my way. I believe I had a force surrounding me that would protect me—I *owned* it. Getting my degree was worth the effort. I needed to do it. I believe education provides choices for me…Without choices, I have nothing…I had a good, stable, secure job before, but I still needed to do this."

Janet confides that "there are women out there who are afraid to achieve. I have seen what happens to women who don't go after what they want, who can't be flexible with their time and their life. I told myself 'I'll never let that happen to me.' I've seen the bitterness and stagnation…caused mostly because they won't flow with what's happening to them at the time."

Important Points to Remember

Life brings crises and challenges. The way you *respond* to them determines the quality of your days and the quality of your life. Crisis and challenge bring opportunity.

When deciding what tasks or errands need to be done, you must stay flexible and look at the whole. Enjoy the process of getting where you want to go in life.

Decide what is absolutely necessary to do *now*. When a situation occurs that you *perceive* as a crisis, use reality checks to gain perspective and go with the flow as much as possible.

Chapter Ten

Home Sweet Home, Inc.
(The Pros and Cons of
Working at Home)

Knock-knock!

"Who's there?"

I t doesn't matter. If you work at home, any interruption is a time-killer. Time management presents special challenges for the woman with a home office. Neighborhood mothers cheerfully volunteer your services (you are home, after all), friends assume that your "flexible" hours justify phone calls and visits during your work day, and the pile of dishes in the sink is screaming, "Wash me!"

With a few home-office-management principles, you can put in a productive work day in far fewer hours than the traditional business timetable requires. You can learn to block out the endless list of interruptions and distractions that can—and usually do—occur on the home front.

The TEN Biggest Time-Wasters in the Home Office

When asked to list the top ten home-office time-busters, the working women I surveyed responded with this list, which cites items in order of most distraction:

1. The need to clean the house
2. The telephone or visitors
3. The need to check email
4. The need to do the wash or ironing
5. The need "to nosh"
6. The lack of information
7. The feeling of isolation
8. The need to run errands
9. The need to dress to see a client
10. Transition time

Let's look at each one of these time-wasters and discuss how other working women handle them. Take bits and pieces from each idea to develop your own way of handling these problems. As in everything in this book, you need to pick and choose what works best with you.

The Need to Clean the House

Before they can start working in their home offices, working women feel they *need* to have a clean house. The Traditional Homemaker feels that her work comes second. Therefore, the house must be clean before she can start on "her" work: a home job, paying the bills, her hobby, and so forth.

The Transitional Woman working at home also feels the need to have a clean and organized home. She views her income as supplemental; her real job is home and family. The fact that the Transitional Woman actually enjoys her work, in most cases, plays a secondary role.

The Achieving Woman who works at a home office can't wait to get started. But, being a perfectionist at heart, the need to have a clean and organized house is in the back of her mind, even though she may be able to ignore it.

Susan McKee, a public relations specialist, said, "I decided that my home would be both neat and clean. I realized, of course, that as a full-time professional there was not enough time to accomplish both. So I decided to keep my home neat myself while working harder to earn enough money to hire someone else to keep it clean."

Working women often perceive a clean home and a neat home in different ways. Jenny, a home-office working woman, says, "A clean home is spotless—bathroom sinks and mirrors shiny, all ironing up-to-date. A neat home is basically where things are picked up off the floor; beds are kinda made; dishes are neatly stacked in the sink; and dirty clothes are placed in different piles, ready to be washed."

A House Helper: A Great Invention

Most working women interviewed prefer a clean home, but accept a neat one. The Traditional Homemaker and Transitional Woman often think about having a house cleaner come in once or twice a month, but only a few follow through and hire one. The Achieving Woman usually hires someone to help clean the house once a week. She does the chores on the other days.

I want to suggest ways for you to have a house helper, no matter how much you make. A house helper can be a neighbor you trade off with once a week or once a month; a teenager you pay minimum wage; an older child; an aunt; and/or, in some cases, a full-fledged housekeeper.

Tina, a Traditional Homemaker, works twenty hours a week. When she works, she has a hard time keeping up with just the basic cleaning. Tina found, however, that her next-door neighbor didn't mind cleaning—what her neighbor hated was grocery shopping. The result was a beneficial trade-off for both of them. Tina shops for both families on Saturday, and her neighbor cleans Tina's house three hours a week. This works out fine for both of them.

I have a friend who hires a janitorial service three times a year to clean house and wash windows. There are, however, other ways to solve this problem.

Bedroom Plus One

Cindy, a home-office mom, makes her three children responsible for their bedrooms plus one other room. These rooms need to be neat. If not, the children can't play outside, watch television, or talk on the phone. "They're responsible for whatever needs to be done in their rooms. For example, nine-year-old Claire has to keep his room neat, but this month takes care of the smaller bathroom, too. He washes the sink basin and cleans the mirror daily. He also makes sure there are neatly folded clean towels on the rack." When asked if this helps get Cindy prepared to work in her office, she quickly states, "I couldn't do it otherwise. There's only one of me. Why not use every member of the household?"

Thirty Minutes in the Morning

Gail, a realtor, straightens her house in the morning before she starts making phone calls in her home office. "I give myself thirty minutes to pick up whatever needs to be done. I take another break at noon if I'm home and wash the dishes in the sink from the night before. It doesn't take time out of my work day, and it's a good break."

Telephone Calls and Visitors

If you're going to do business from home, you need to honestly treat your work as a business. It's difficult for others to treat you seriously and professionally if you do not honestly perceive yourself as serious and professional. The telephone is one of your most important business tools. In fact, the telephone forms the basic line of communication between you and your client, and between you and more business information. As in any other type of communication, the working woman must handle it with care. Professional communication is critical to a good relationship with clients, vendors, and employees.

When you are a professional who works at home, projecting a professional image may also be important when dealing with friends and family. You may have to let them know, gently but firmly, that the fact that you are home does not mean that you are available. Let family and friends know what your business hours are. If they interrupt you during those times, suggest they call or come back later. Realize that you play a role in determining the productivity of your work time by deciding when you answer the phone or door, how you screen your calls, and who you give your phone numbers to.

A Second Line, Please

It is vital to have a business phone with its own phone number, whether that means a second home line you use only for business or use your home phone to call out and use your cell phone to receive calls. This way the caller can return your call and not get a busy signal or a "beep." Because many working women want to keep their operating costs to a minimum, they tend to use the home phone for business. After all, goes the thinking, "I can't afford a second line," or "I don't really need it." Wrong!

There's nothing more unprofessional than when your client calls you at your home office and your child answers the phone or your answering machine takes the call with a cute message left by you, your husband, or your children.

It is also essential that you have a separate line for your computer and/or fax machine. Again, it is not professional to tell the person to call you before faxing over papers or not being able to accept or make calls because you are online.

To Answer or Not to Answer

Sue, a writer, does not give out her home number. "I found, even after I published my first two books, people called to chat since I was at home. I never had a second line put in, because I rarely use this phone. I found that if I did not give out my phone number, except in rare situations, I had control of who I wanted to speak to."

Sue takes control of her work time by not answering calls when she needs to concentrate. When she takes a break from work, she'll check Caller ID to see who needs to be called first. "Every time I was on a roll, the telephone would ring, and when I first started writing I felt I had to answer it 'just in case.' Now, I don't even notice when it rings."

I asked Sue if she used an answering machine.

"No, because I can still hear who it is and then I may want to talk to them. My good friends know not to call me between 10 a.m. and 7 p.m. My long-distance friends and I email to each other."

Sharon finds that her secretarial business depends on the telephone. "I have an active social life and felt that I needed to get my own business phone. This way I know how to answer the phone, a social 'Hi' on my cell phone or a business 'Sharon here.' I also found that making this distinction made me feel more professional. I don't know if this is a consequence or not, but my secretarial business started improving right about the time I invested in this practice."

Gail, the realtor, finds that the phone is her most precious business asset. "I could save a lot of money by using an answering machine or letting my cell take messages, but I'm in the 'people' business. I personally don't like any type of answering machine.

"I invested in a twenty-four-hour answering service to receive my calls. When I am at my home office and I don't want to be disturbed, I let the answering service pick up the call. This is a good way to check on their service—how many rings before they pick up the receiver. I leave instructions with the answering service when I'm working on special projects. I could never do that with my answering machine."

Another reason working women invest in an answering service is to keep their operating costs down without hiring a full-time secretary. Cindy says, "Most of my clients think I have a secretary…it sounds professional. There's a lot of competition out there…everyone and their sister-in-law seems to be in real estate now. If I can be a little different and more personable and professional while I'm at it, why not?"

Judy, on the other hand, does all her business on her cell phone. "If there's one thing I've learned in all the years I have been doing business is that people want to get in touch with me and I need to be there to talk to them. I have no problem having them leave messages when I'm talking or in a meeting, but the fact that they have direct access to me is important."

E-who? Email

If you would like to get your day derailed, I suggest you check your email first thing in the morning. If however, you would like to stay on track for the first few hours of the day, then check your email one and a half to two hours after you start your work day. Most of my clients immediately resist this concept. When I ask them further what would really happen if they checked their email later, they pause and think for a moment and then say, "Not much, I'm just used to checking my email first thing in the morning." Here are some of the reasons for not checking email first thing in the morning:

- Other people's anxieties and "emergencies" gets transferred to you.
- It takes longer than you think to check email and get back to people, even if it's only a few.
- It takes your concentration away from things that matter most.

- There is a 99.9 percent chance that you will not miss anything if you check your email two hours later.
- After the first two hours, you are now mentally prepared to check and deal with email.
- Make sure you set up files in your email folder so that all emails from people or clients you must read first will be organized to do so without going through a cluttered in-box.

The Need to Do Wash

What do you do with the piles of wash on the floor in the laundry room after you've taken the time to sort through them? What about the comments from the family: "Where's my shirt, my thermal underwear, my PE shirt, my sweats?" After all, you *are* home and "should" be able to get a simple task like the wash done, especially if the garment doesn't need to be ironed. What do you *do* with your time anyway, working woman? If this is echoed in your home or within your mind, stop! It's important to let other family members know that you are not a laundry. Here are some ideas to redistribute the burden of laundry.

One-Day Service

Impossible? Not if you have a well-developed system. You can devise a system whereby wash becomes a family event. Cindy developed an "overnight" area in the laundry room. It is the responsibility of each family member to put the clothes he or she needs the next day in that spot. If he or she forgets to put it in the laundry room before 5 p.m. the evening before it's needed, S-O-R-R-Y.

"It helps me figure out what wash is a priority for the family. This way I don't have to yell and scream and ask for their clothes or have them whine at me in the morning for whatever it is that they need… Our mornings go so much more smoothly now," says Cindy.

Wash It and Dump It

Both Cindy and Gail put in a load of wash first thing in the morning, before going to their home offices. "I get at least four loads in a day. The first one I do first thing in the morning. At lunchtime I put the wet wash in the dryer and put a new load in the washer. Then I take an afternoon break, and repeat the cycle again after dinner. I take equal piles to the children's bedrooms. The kids are then responsible for folding, putting the clothes away, and putting the ironables back in the laundry room…. It's a great system as long as I don't go into the children's bedrooms after I dump the clean clothes there."

The Urge to Nosh

It is common for working women to nosh themselves into oblivion during their working hours at their home offices. It is a natural inclination to go to the refrigerator or pantry when they're home. This is especially true when they want to take a break or are procrastinating in starting on a project.

Fruit, Vegetables, and Gum

Marty is a pharmaceutical representative and keeps her office at home. She finds she has no problem with noshing on her "out" days, when she keeps appointments with doctors. But the days she stays at her office at home, she gets a bad case of the noshies. "I started by eating everything I could find in the pantry—handfuls of cereal, cookies, and chips. At the end of the day I felt awful. I was so stuffed, but I hadn't eaten anything nutritionally sound. I now buy loads of sugarless gum."

After going through the nosh stage, women start to gain pounds and inches where there weren't any before. Before Marty started chewing gum, she tried getting into three dressy outfits one weekend.

"None of them fit. I was horrified…I couldn't get the skirts over my hips…and I'm not fat."

Ethel, an interior designer, went through the eating stage and gained weight. She decided to do something about it. "The more I read and experienced how I felt when I ate healthy, the more I got into nutrition. My husband calls me a health nut, but I tell him I'm just a healthy eater."

I asked Ethel how she keeps her weight down and avoids the eating binge. She says she has a bag of raisins or an assortment of dry, low-sugar cereals at her drafting table. "When I'm thinking, I just absentmindedly grab for the cereal or raisins. That does the trick. The by-product is that it makes me thirsty, so I drink a lot more water now than I ever did before. I have bottled water sent to my house. Most of my breaks are to go to the bathroom."

Katherine, a reading tutor, has a routine that works for her. "I go to the gym three times a week, in the morning, and work out and lift weights for about an hour and a half each time. I come home, take a shower, get dressed, put on makeup, and work the rest of the day. I also buy diet soft drinks by the case. I'm really conscious of my weight, so I only keep healthy things in the refrigerator. I usually eat a tuna-fish sandwich for lunch. It works for me."

Shelly, a consultant who works out of her home office, loves to eat and has a lot of energy. "I could live on fresh fruit and vegetables. I love grapes, so I often have them on my desk. It's better for you than smoking, and I find I pop one in when I'm thinking about things…. I've skinned them with my teeth, I've rolled them around in my mouth, and I've sucked on them more than once or twice.

"If I'm not too tired the night before, I cut up carrots or pineapple to eat the following day. I have little packages of fresh fruit and vegetables all over in my refrigerator. I munch on dried fruit also, but I don't open the package of the dried fruit unless I don't have anything in the refrigerator."

The Lack of Information

It is a rare home office that has a complete library of resource books, and many working women feel that they cannot do a good job without them. Few working women have the time and money to develop a large library. What do you do?

Library as Office

The library can be a very good office away from home. Resource books are nearby, dozens of newspapers and magazine articles are within reach, and you're away from the telephone and refrigerator. For Linda, a freelance copyeditor, the library is her permanent office. "It's rent free. The money I save pays for supplies. Research items are available and close at hand. I have a wireless computer to connect me to the Internet—I'm set."

Many libraries provide all the essential equipment: computer, pay phone, resource material, people to speak to, and peace and quiet away from familiar sounds.

Another approach to finding good resource material is on the Internet. Once you find the sourcebooks for your industry, the information and the Internet become invaluable. However, sometimes the Internet is not enough. Dani, a Transitional Woman, a professional writer, and editor does a great deal of her research on the Internet, but says, "I still need to make trips to the university library for some of my projects. There really isn't anything like a library."

The Feeling of Isolation

Working at a home office is lonely. There's no one to talk to, get you motivated, or to exchange ideas. Breaks usually consist of noshing, cleaning, or telephone interruptions. For weeks at a time, one is a very lonely number.

Take Steps to Lessen Loneliness

To decrease loneliness:

- Start your day at a coffee shop two or three times a week. Bring some work you need to do, read the local paper, or plan your daily tasks. Surrounding yourself with people early in the day has a tendency to motivate you.
- During a break, call a friend to say hi. Keep the conversation under ten minutes. Calling friends at your convenience is a great way to stay in touch.
- Eat lunch *away* from your desk. Go to the park, another room, or treat yourself to a lunch date. If you worked outside your home, you'd most likely eat out.

Develop a Network

Having a home office requires that you stay in touch with your competition and others in your business, locally as well as nationally. It also requires that you share important information and make good decisions. What happens if there is only a staff of one—you?

To be effective in business as well as fight the debilitating sense of isolation common to those who work alone, you must develop a network. Here are some tips about getting plugged in:

- Put together a group of people in your profession or a group of other home-office workers.
- Faithfully attend state or national association conferences.
- Join and regularly attend Chamber of Commerce meetings.

- Stay abreast of community events; add your expertise in a volunteer role.
- Plan two lunches or breakfasts a week with people you enjoy and with whom you can be yourself and feel safe to share concerns and doubts.
- Write a press release to your local newspaper twice a year, just to let others know you're still out there.
- Chat online with others in your industry.
- Set up bimonthly conference calls with people in your industry to brainstorm and exchange ideas.

The Need to Run Errands

Since the major responsibility for significant others usually rests with the working woman, she is endlessly running errands. She does everything from picking up her daughter's ballet or soccer shoes, wax for the children's new braces, milk for breakfast, and cards for sick friends or clients.

To decrease the time you spend away from your desk, take inventory, stockpile, offload, and anticipate.

Take Inventory of Your Most Common Errands

On errands, where do you find yourself the most? In the dairy, produce, or bathroom department of a grocery store; the card or cold-remedy department of a drugstore; the gift area in a department store; or the library, checking out encyclopedias? After you have an idea where you spend most of your time on errands, you can take action and save a lot of time.

If you frequently find yourself in the places mentioned in the list that follows, take the recommended action.

Dairy department: Have delivered to your door your milk, eggs, orange juice, and any other items you often run out of. The increase in cost is only pennies when you compare the gas, time, and time pressure taken off you. In fact, in most cases, delivery is far cheaper if all this is taken into account.

Produce department: If you have a family that enjoys fresh produce, then buy fruit and vegetables with long lasting appeal. Buy green bananas, cranberries, apples, dates, figs, cauliflower, broccoli, carrots, celery, and zucchini, to name a few.

Card stores: Taking the time to send cards is not only thoughtful, it can be beneficial. I will more readily take the time to do something for someone who has, by sending a card, been thoughtful or appreciative.

One way to decrease the number of trips to the card store is to start your own card collection, with major emphasis in areas that are prominent in your life. Your card selections probably relate to your life stage. Are a lot of your friends getting married, having babies, getting divorced, changing careers, getting promoted, getting sick, or traveling? Remembering these occasions helps you nurture your support system at work, at home, and personally. Taking the time to nurture your networking system saves you time and energy when that support is necessary.

E-cards are lovely, but keep in mind that there isn't anything as special as a hand-written note. Pamela, an engineer says, "I'm on the computer all day and I send e-cards on occasion. I often receive a hand-written card from one of my friends and I can't tell you how special I feel when I receive it, although I love receiving e-cards too."

To keep track of birthdays and anniversaries, keep a calendar separate from your daily calendar. Since these dates come up year after year, get a date book without day or year, only month and date. You can easily make one up:

June 1 Casey Richards
    2 Jack Horne
    3 Kelly Rand

If you have a supply of cards on hand, you can simply go to your card drawer instead of the store. This method not only saves time, but your date book will help you remember important events year after year. Your friends, clients, and family will be impressed.

Cold-remedy department: If you find yourself in the cold-remedy department, keep a few extra bottles of Tylenol or Cold-Eeze in your medicine chest. I would suggest you keep vitamin C on hand also, in the form of tablets or fresh oranges.

Gift stores: Buy gifts when they're on sale. With your date book at your side, you can save time and money in choosing the right gift. The working woman often has to settle for what is left because she didn't have the time to go shopping before hand. Plus, the gift is more expensive because it is a last-ditch effort to get something. P.S.: Keep the gift wrap near the gift closet.

Another way to take care of gifts is through the Internet. Teresa, a Forty-Something fitness trainer does all her shopping online. She finds new shopping sources and stores all the time as she web surfs. "I had all my Christmas shopping done this year before Thanksgiving and it was all done online," says Teresa with a smile.

The Need to Dress to See a Client

What happens when you're pounding on the computer, getting your work taken care of, and a client needs to see you immediately? You don't sound very pleased over the phone, because you weren't planning to see any clients today; you're in a bathrobe and you have oily, unmanageable hair. Your client, on the other side of the receiver, can't see you (thank God) and perceives your unwillingness to visit as "something must be wrong." Here are some alternatives.

Wake Up and Work It
It is important for the home-based working woman to wake up, take a

shower, and get ready for work. In other words, put on your makeup, make sure your hair is the way you like it (even spritz it if you want), and get dressed in your working attire. This serves three important functions. First, you feel as if you're at work; therefore, you perform at a higher capacity. Second, at a moment's notice, you're able to visit a client or pick up something at the printer's or anywhere else. Third, getting dressed and looking good increases your self-esteem. It's a lot easier to think you're ugly, fat, or undesirable when you see yourself in a bathrobe or sweats and with messy hair most days.

Transition Time

Transitional time is the time spent doing things here and there almost unconsciously and before you know it, you've lost thirty minutes or hours by the end of the day. Women do these things almost by osmosis, not realizing they are doing them. Women think of them as "quickies." It places a whole new concept to the term "quickies." What are some of these transitional time robbers?

- Making that extra call in the morning to say "hi" to a girlfriend
- Checking email "for only a moment"—that is an oxymoron
- Quickly making the children's bed and picking up around the house
- Organizing papers and files during your high energy time
- Checking email

Important Points to Remember

Working from a home office presents special challenges. The ten most common time interruptions are the need to clean the house, the telephone or visitors, the need to check email, the need to do the wash or ironing, eating, not having enough resource material, feeling isolated, the need to run errands, the need to dress to see a client, and transitional time.

When the need to clean hits, remember that it's okay to have a neat, rather than a clean, house. The telephone and email are your friends as long as you are in control of incoming calls and your inbox. Limit in-person visits, too. Turn the need to wash into a family affair. Go ahead and nosh—just make sure you eat fruit and vegetables. Use the library as your office on days you need resource information. To offset the feeling of isolation, eat breakfast out, take outside breaks, develop a network of friends and business associates, and be aware of transitional time.

Take inventory of your most common errands. Stockpile what you need and find other ways to reduce trips, including shopping sources online. Dress professionally every day you work.

Treat yourself seriously, and others will too. Your attitude shows your clients and suppliers that you are professional and available for them.

Chapter Eleven

Mirror, Mirror, on the Desk: Organizing Your Desk to Reflect Priorities

The myth about the correlation between Mensa minds and disaster-zone desks is best left to cartoonists and dilettantes. The cold reality is that women who juggle jobs, kids, and husbands or lovers can't afford to spend precious minutes hunting for a buried memo or a misplaced love letter.

Whether at home or at the office, the condition of your working space reflects your level of professionalism and ultimately has an impact on all areas of your performance.

Clearing your desk is the first step to maintaining a business space that will help you work efficiently.

Clearing Your Desk—And Keeping It Clear

As a rule, you may have an organized desk. But every two or three weeks you get busy. Papers pile on your desk, and then you have a messy desk.

I suggest to my clients that they take their unfiled papers and stack them neatly under their desks or neatly in one area of their bookcase. Another method is to purchase a nice looking basket that comes in all colors and sizes and neatly stack your unfilled papers in the basket. I can not stress the necessary investment of purchasing manila folders, organizing containers, and labels to keep your office under physical and emotional control, even when you don't have the time to file and put them away. This "transitional organizing" step will keep you and your papers focused. When papers come through the fax or into your in-box, simply stack them on top of the others. This keeps your desk clear for the entire time it takes you to complete your task. If you have twenty minutes between appointments, then take the stack on the floor, in the bookshelf, or in the "transitional organizing" basket and file the papers in the correct spots. Lynn, an Achieving Woman nutritionist says tongue-in-cheek, "If it weren't for all my papers that I need to refer to and client files, I'd be organized."

No matter where you keep the papers, however, the key is to organize them in a way that's meaningful to you. Audrey, a schoolteacher, says, "I have so many papers to read through each day. I started two stacks of papers on my desk. One is for papers to grade, and the other is for memos. My goal is to work through at least half of each stack each day. I'm able to keep up this way."

Elaine, a secretary to four people, keeps one large stack on her desk. The papers are in order by immediacy of completion. "I keep the stack on the right side of my desk. When realtors come in to give me more work, they see how far I've progressed. It's stopped a lot of 'I need this immediately.' I only hear that when they really mean it. Otherwise, their material goes under the stack and the size of the stack lets them know when they'll get it."

Kim works at a printing business. "I keep two lists on my desk now. One is for rush jobs and the other is for normal turnaround. We get people all the time that say they need something yesterday. Everything we did had to be done immediately. I couldn't find anything on my desk. We started charging $35 for rush orders. We found that over 80 percent of the people don't really need the printing done ASAP. For the 20 percent of people that really do need it immediately, they gladly pay the extra $35. I now have an orderly desk and happier customers."

Organize the Top of the Desk

Important things go on top of your desk and stay there: a paperweight, paper clip holder with clips inside, stapler, pencil-and-pen holder, small clock, telephone, and one or two small *tchotzkes* (knickknacks). You may want to have your computer on your desk, but it is important to keep a part of your desk clear for working in a large space. Many of my clients prefer to have a side table for their computer, fax machine, and printer. It allows a clean look on their desk and helps to keep papers and distractions of "work that needs to be done" nearby, but not "in their face." Everything else goes somewhere else, including the pictures.

Pictures are wonderful and they make us feel good, but they distract us from our work. Family relationships are never routine. They are either on a high or on a low. If you glance at the picture during either peak, it will tend to take your mind away from your immediate task.

I define the word *clearance* as the ability to see a neat desk when you enter and leave your office. Clearance provides a huge feeling of satisfaction, completion, and organization. Clearance gives way to open, creative thinking.

One technique for achieving clearance is what I call the three-Ds filing system. The system uses three manila files, which are kept on top of the desk or at a side table within easy reach.

The Three-Ds Filing System

Each D in the three-Ds filing system stands for the time I must do something.

- Do it this morning.
- Do it this afternoon.
- Do it now.

I assign a file folder to each deadline, and I file papers related to each deadline in the appropriate folder.

The "do it this morning" stack needs to be done before lunch. In most cases, these papers need a signature, a quick review for errors, or a yes or no response. This work needs to be completed in the morning so that others can continue the process.

The "do it this afternoon" pile needs to be done after lunch. Again, in most cases, the work requires a small amount of time and energy. But, because it requires so little time, the tendency is to put these tasks off and the process of procrastination begins. Procrastination begets procrastination—and frustration for others.

The "do it now" papers need to be done as soon as I receive them. This stack can be kept small by keeping up with the first two Ds. Much in the "do it now" file relates to "putting out fires" resulting from delays or procrastination.

Now that the top of the desk is clear, turn your attention to the desk drawers.

Organize the Desk Drawers

Make sure your desk has at least three drawers: a center drawer and two side drawers. Turn each drawer into an organized filing area.

The Center Drawer

In the center drawer, store extra pencils and pens, ruler, stamps, and phone directories from organizations, your children's classrooms, and such. Keep a telephone file in this drawer for easy access. I use labeled manila folders to organize my papers.

The Side Drawers

Use one side drawer to store stationery, envelopes, scissors, extra change, makeup, Kleenex, and legal pads.

Use the bottom side drawer for active files. These are the files that you constantly work with. By putting them back in the same place every time, you will alleviate the need to search for them. If you find what you need quickly, you keep yourself from becoming distracted by nonessential tasks.

Use the Area Under the Desk

You can use the space under your desk for more than overflow from your desk top. Under my desk, I stack the mail that needs to go home. I keep my purse there as well as anything else that needs to go home from the office. It helps me remember to take things home.

In addition, I keep my to-do list and my errand list under my desk. This serves two functions. First, I must constantly bend down, which promotes circulation to my upper body. Second, what I need to see is easily accessible without my having to open, shut, and bump the desk drawers. (I found that when I constantly opened the drawers, I got runs in my hose.)

In addition, I keep a 50.7-ounce water container under my desk to remind me to drink and stay hydrated. Besides being out of the way, it is unlikely to spill on papers, and its location keeps me bending.

I suggest that you do *not* have a trash basket under your desk or anywhere in your office. If you like to eat fruit in your office, having the trash can nearby is asking for an office with the odor of banana peels and apple cores.

I simply throw my trash on the ground in one not-so-neat pile. When my mind wanders, I get up and throw it away *outside* my office. Sitting in one position for several hours takes its toll on the working woman's back, shoulders, wrists, and legs. The process of throwing the papers down, bending down to get them, and walking into another area gets the circulation moving.

Some days when I'm particularly antsy, I try to throw the trash into the can while taking a break in the kitchen area. I give myself two points for every "basket" I make. I've met some nice office neighbors this way. In fact, I met a client by doing this. I threw several baskets one day, and the event got me talking with a man who was waiting to see his accountant. Next thing I knew, we were exchanging cards. Two months later he became a marketing client. Moral: Some baskets are worth more points than others!

Now that you have developed a few habits that have transformed your desk into a model of organization, develop one more habit that will get each new day off to a good start.

Get Set for Tomorrow

Clear your desk before leaving your office each day. Then place whatever you must deal with first tomorrow in the middle of the desk. This will help you focus on what needs to be done as soon as you enter your office.

Focus is important for working women. Because we play so many roles, our minds can easily wander away from the task at hand. Anything that disrupts focus is what I call mind interference. By placing your priority task in the middle of your desk, you can avoid mind interference, quickly don your professional persona, and get to work.

Establishing a "Back Room"

You don't necessarily need a back room, but you do need an area that is away from your desk. This "back room" area will help keep your main work space organized and allow you to be productive. Keep dormant files, research articles, press releases, old projects, and other inactive but important papers in the back room. The copy machine also goes there.

You can establish a back room, even if your work space doesn't have one. If you don't have walls dividing the two areas, use furniture. Use a bookshelf, use a couch, or use large plants to surround the back room area. The most important element is that you should not be able to see the inactive files. You need to alleviate mind interference.

Use Bookcases for Filing

Bookcases are great for filing books, magazines, articles, or newsletters. Put articles and newsletters in labeled manila folders and file them by topic. Sarah, a Transitional Woman, says, "I do a lot of reading. I keep magazines and make copies of special articles I think I'll need in my work, in my relationships, or when I want to decide on places I want to visit eventually. I've started a good library of information."

As you find articles or addresses you want to keep, put a yellow stickie note on the proper page and write the purpose of keeping the article. This saves time; you need not leaf through the magazine, book, or article to find the information you want or why you wanted to keep it in the first place. Make directions simple: "Make a copy and file under Administration," "Make a copy and send to Janet," or "Write for more information."

Because of our wonderful technology, you can also scan the articles you want to keep and save them on your computer. Just make sure you set up specific folders and keep the material labeled and filed appropriately for easy retrieval.

Doing a Weekly Cleanup

Weekly cleanups are a must. No matter what system you use, there are times when you don't have time to file your material in its proper place. Again, simply stack the papers, folders, ads, and other material in a neat pile. The best time to file this stack is in the afternoon if you're a morning person, or in the morning if you're an afternoon person. Two things to remember: do not file Monday mornings, because filing will slow you down for the day, and do not file Friday afternoons, because you won't get it done—you'll be thinking of the weekend and you'll be tired. Other than that, go at it!

Keeping Yourself from Overdoing It

So far, you have organized your desk and created a work space to maximize your efficiency. Don't get carried away in your desire for clearance, however. The only times when your desk should be completely clear are on your first and last days of work. Other than these times, always keep these three things on your desk:

1. Your reference point
2. The active project
3. A timepiece

A reference point is an object that gives you a feeling of security. It establishes for you a familiar environment in which you can feel free to create, develop, and work. If you have more than one reference point, that's fine—just don't use photos of family or friends.

Ann's reference point, or personal *tzchotchke,* was a crystal unicorn. "The janitor moved it once, and I had the worst day. I like it right by the phone, where I can see it clearly. I know that sounds superstitious, but I can't help it."

The active project should be on your desk at all times. If you have three major projects to complete, place two to the side or under your desk. And, as mentioned earlier in this chapter, put the active file in the middle of your desk when you leave for the evening.

You must know the time to keep appointments, follow progress, and give your mind and body a break for lunch. Therefore, always keep a timepiece on your desk. If you have unlimited time for a project, turn it away from you if you want. If not, have it face you.

Important Points to Remember

Maintaining an organized desk and file system is vital to getting work done efficiently. Use your desk as your filing system—each drawer has important functions. The area under your desk, a designated place on your bookshelf or side table can play an organizational role as well.

Weekly cleanups are essential for keeping your office neat and papers placed properly. Don't clear your desk completely, however. Keep on your desk objects that impart security, task focus, and time awareness.

Be creative. Develop a filing system that works for you. Be sure the system provides efficiency, exercise, stability, and focus.

Chapter Twelve

I Think It's a Definite Maybe (A Quick Guide to Decision Making)

The decisions a working woman makes sometimes seem to have magnified importance because of the many roles she plays. For example, a decision she makes at work can affect workers up and down the hierarchy; in addition, because she is probably the family member who coordinates care for the children and home, the same decision can have an almost immediate effect on her family. Her personal time is affected as well, and the whole interplay of work, family, and self must find a new equilibrium. Working women realize how important their decisions are, and to them the need to make decisions often seems like an extra-heavy burden.

As women, we tend to have two problems with decision making. The first concerns the decisions themselves. We tend to choose what is safe; in other words, our decisions tend to support the status quo. This chapter will discuss how, in resisting change in decision making, we are sometimes wasting time and cheating ourselves. The second common decision-making problem for women is indecision. Whether disguised as procrastination, reconsideration, or what economist Pareto calls "the paralysis of analysis," indecision is a habit worth conquering. By studying your own decision-making patterns, you can become decisive; this chapter will show you how.

Resisting the Urge to Resist Change

Most working women do not like change. The Traditional Homemaker likes her life just the way it is. Routine habits and patterns give her a sense of security. She feels that if she rocks the boat, someone in the family will be adversely affected. You often hear the Traditional Homemaker say, "I'll go back to work [school] when my children are in school"; "I can't go to dance lessons—they're at night, and I don't want to leave my husband home alone"; "I'll spend more time on me when the kids have left the house—I have all my life"; and "I'll start traveling when my husband retires."

Ann, who travels half the year with her semi retired husband, says, "I stayed home and raised three children. I would only plan to do things during the day while my husband and children were gone. I kept a tiny room in the house to do my artwork. If only I knew then what I know now. I would have made the decision to rent a studio and work on my art every day."

Like the Traditional Homemaker, the Transitional Woman usually tries to put off anything that sounds like change. She says she's too busy for it: "I don't have time to do anything but raise my kids and work. I couldn't add one more appointment, meeting, or obligation to my schedule if my life depended on it."

Susan, a controller for a medium-sized business, says, "I was so locked into my schedule that my car could have made trips without me. I had set times for everything and wouldn't even consider any change."

The Achieving Woman doesn't mind changing the status quo of managing her work and priorities, providing she does not need to take time to relearn anything. She knows she can get more done if she stays with the tried-and-true methods. But are the old methods necessarily the best?

Change brings risk, it's true. But change also brings newness, freshness, and a different perspective. Great things can come of change; intellectually, most of us know this. Emotionally, however, we fight change and may not accept it unless we are forced to.

Susan, the Transitional Woman and controller, was forced to make changes when she was diagnosed with multiple sclerosis (MS). "Everything changed," she says. "I came home during lunch to rest. I put the children in an afternoon center where they learned how to work with computers, my husband and children washed the dishes every night, and we hired a cleaning lady twice a month—something I had wanted to do for years. I don't know why it took something drastic to help my life change for the better, but it did."

Shirley had always had trouble with overcommitting herself. She couldn't say no to anyone. "I didn't want anyone to be upset with me. I placed incredible expectations on myself. Sometimes I was so tired I couldn't fall asleep for hours." Shirley's life changed when she was laid off at work. "I started my own business, which I had wanted to do for years. Unless the activity dealt with my business or the kids' welfare, I said no. For the first time in my adult life, I am doing things because I want to rather than because I think I should. Once I practiced a few no's, it wasn't so hard to do. Making those decisions helped me create more time for the two areas that were most important to me at the time: my children and my business."

The moral of these stories is that you must embrace change. Eventually, change may well embrace you, so why not do it on your own terms? The sooner you make a change, the sooner you will enjoy the benefits of change, which often include a new outlook and enthusiasm for life. Developing the ability to change means developing the ability to take control of your life.

Tips for Developing a Change-Receptive Personality

Cultivating a positive attitude toward change takes work in all areas of your life. It involves doing things that make you feel less secure and self-confident and exposing yourself to new perspectives and information. The following tips outline some helpful activities that will help you grow into a woman who can not only take change in stride, but initiate it.

- Analyze your Personal Motivational Lifestyle. If the way you are using your time is out of sync with your priorities, you are probably under too much stress to accept change. Shift your time use so it matches your priorities. The burden of stress should lessen, and you will be more resilient.
- Make a goal and reward yourself when you achieve it. Achieving a goal will make you realize your power, and this will increase your belief that you can handle any change that comes along.
- Discuss fears and concerns with a trustworthy friend, a member of the clergy, or a therapist. Fears and concerns don't seem as extreme when they're out in the open. You may realize that you have more capacity to deal with all aspects of life—including change—than you thought you did.
- Try new scheduling ideas. The simple fact of doing things in a different order or in a new place can help you exercise your flexibility. If you usually go to the gym in the morning, for example, try going in the evening. You might not like it at first, but try it for one month. A long trial period will tell you if the new arrangement has any unexpected benefits. On the job, try changing meeting times around. If you usually meet at break-fast, see how meeting at a different time works. Don't fall into the trap of saying, "I can't. There's no other time that will work."

- Bring in new people. To stay open to different perspectives, talk to as many different people as you can. Surround yourself with people who have fresh ideas. This might include appointing or serving on a task force so that you can expose yourself to as many different perspectives as is practical.

Once you have seen the benefits of staying open to change, I doubt you will ever want to be any other way. Many women are stuck, however. They cannot accept or make changes because they cannot make decisions. The remainder of this chapter will discuss the psychological factors that drive decision making, and the discussion will include a section that will help you assess your own decision-making habits.

Understanding Decision-Making Patterns

As you might expect, the emotional motivations in decision making coincide closely with the three Personal Motivational Lifestyles. Not all women—not even women with the same Personal Motivational Lifestyle—handle their emotions in the same way, however. As a result, there are several distinct patterns of decision making.

Emotional Motivations

One of the primary motivators in decision making is fear. The type of fear that a woman must face bears a strong correlation to the type of woman she is.

One of the Traditional Homemaker's greatest fears is failure. She considers herself a personal failure if home and family needs are not met. Her basic premise is that she's here to provide all the necessary emotional support for her family.

In my experience, the Transitional Woman's greatest fear is success. If she spends an extended amount of time at work, she may not only get promoted, but she may have less time for her husband or children. Likewise, the single Transitional Woman does not want to get too involved with work, because she wants to be available for marriage, children, or travel.

The Achieving Woman's greatest fear is rejection, particularly in the workplace. Her fear of rejection from her work peers, clients, management, and boss drives her to overachieve. The Achieving Woman brings her need to overachieve to her relationships as well as her work. If she can't get perfection, then she perceives a problem and may opt to quit. Marriage and perfection do not go hand in hand; therefore, among the three types of women discussed in this book, Achieving Women have the highest percentage of divorces.

Patterns of Decision Making

In my work with women, I have distinguished six types of decision makers:

1. Analyzers
2. Information overloaders
3. Risk takers
4. Traumatizers
5. Fence sitters
6. Procrastinators

Each of these types of women brings a distinct psychological perspective to the decision-making process, and each type's decision-making style has an impact on the woman's time and the quality of the decision she makes.

In the sections that follow, try to see yourself. If you see that you are prey to the pitfalls of your decision-making style, make the changes that are recommended for your specific type.

The Analyzer

This woman needs to look at *all* aspects of an issue. This is helpful, to a point. There comes a time, however, when further analysis wastes time and is counterproductive.

Psychological perspective: The analyzer is afraid to make a mistake because she thinks it will make her look dumb or foolish.

Time implication: Because the analyzer spends a lot of time reworking the same information, her decision-making style can waste time.

Positive action: Make a decision based on the information and your experience. If your decision could have been better, then accept that fact and correct the decision. We learn from our mistakes, but only true leaders accept and correct their errors with pride.

The Information Overloader

The woman in this category keeps getting more and more information. She never makes it to the analysis stage, let alone the decision stage.

Psychological perspective: Being an expert is very important to this woman. She feels that if she misses one new discovery or point, she will not be perceived as the expert. She will lose status and let her colleagues down.

Time implication: Because gathering new information takes priority over decision making, this decision-making style wastes time.

Positive action: Get information from no more than seven sources. I have found that seven sources is usually a sufficient number to allow me to spot trends. After reviewing the seven sources, make the decision!

The Risk Taker

This woman makes decisions based on equal parts of information and her own gut feelings or experience. The risk taker feels that too much information is redundant and a waste of time. She feels she has the necessary arsenal to make the decision.

Psychological perspective: This woman is not afraid to take risks.

Time implication: This decision-making style wastes little time.

Positive action: If the decision is negative, change it!

The Traumatizer

This woman makes a decision and then constantly worries about it. Making the decision is not time-consuming for these women, but the complaining and rehashing afterward sap energy as well as time.

Psychological perspective: She doubts her ability to make sound decisions.

Time implication: The traumatizer wastes time worrying when she could be accomplishing her goals.

Positive action: Keep a list of your major decisions and write down their outcomes. Were most outcomes positive or negative? Chances are good that most of your outcomes were positive. This will help you gain self-confidence in your decision-making ability.

The Fence Sitter

This woman finds it excruciatingly difficult to make decisions. For every reason she finds to make one decision, she finds one that moves her to make the opposite decision. She cannot prioritize the reasons related to the decision. Her constant comment is, "On the other hand…"

Psychological perspective: The fear of making a mistake is this woman's predominant fear.

Time implication: This decision-making style is a major time-waster.

Positive action: Make a list of advantages and disadvantages. Rate each advantage or disadvantage from one to ten, according to its importance. The decision should become much clearer.

The Procrastinator

This woman waits to make decisions until it's "time." She says, "I'll make it eventually." The result is that she is forced to make a decision because time has run out, thereby lessening her feeling of responsibility. This woman rarely takes the initiative in life. She lets most things "just happen."

Psychological perspective: The procrastinator has a difficult time accepting responsibility and feels overwhelmed easily.

Time implication: The fact that the procrastinator waits until the last minute is in itself a time-waster. The procrastinator's decisions are likely to be so ill considered that further time is wasted in reworking and re-implementing them.

Positive action: Change your thinking. A forced choice is no choice.

Beating Indecision

Once you realize that decisions don't have to be perfect, you will free yourself from the paralyzing anxiety that can lead to indecision. In fact, the mistakes you make in decision making can be a source of strength for you as you approach future decisions. To explain this, I often tell women what Frank Sinatra said about painting:

> You see, the great thing about painting is that a lot of paintings don't work, and it dramatizes what happens in life. When you first start painting, and it doesn't work out, you're devastated. But you keep painting. Then you're not bothered by your mistakes. You just say, "The next time will be better." That's what happens in life. That's why I wouldn't change anything: because I made mistakes, but those mistakes taught me how to live.

Important Points to Remember

Women tend to have two problems with decision making. First, we tend to make "safe" decisions, decisions that minimize change. Second, we tend to be indecisive. To make the most of our time and our lives, we must learn to embrace change, which often brings vast benefits. By understanding our decision-making patterns, we can conquer indecisiveness.

Decision making is often based on fear. As a rule, the Traditional Homemaker fears failure, the Transitional Woman fears success, and the Achieving Woman fears rejection. These women, because of their fears, waste time with indecision.

It's taken you years to "perfect" your personal decision-making patterns. If you've made the decision to change your style, just do it.

Chapter Thirteen

The Write Stuff

E ven the best and brightest of us must sometimes admit that a short pencil is better than a long memory. Note taking and journal keeping are two invaluable tools for working women. To those who harbor an aversion to the written word: *Beware.*

As we evaluate our time-management skills, we often discover a surprising discrepancy between how we think we spend our time and how we actually fill our hours. A time log can quickly pinpoint wasted time and dispel the belief that "I don't have a spare minute!"

In this chapter, you will learn how to use starter sheets, time-log sheets, task sheets, and your calendar to discover what you need to do and how you are using your time, to organize your efforts, and to keep yourself motivated. You will also learn ways to use lists to make yourself more effective at work and at home.

Using a Starter Sheet

The mind is a fascinating computer. It's compact, portable, and has an exhaustive list of programs. For preventive maintenance of your "mental computer," you must write down important thoughts, feelings, and ideas, and stay positive. The starter sheet enables you to do all three.

To make a starter sheet, take a legal pad and write down a paragraph, preferably a page, about what you want to accomplish today and why it's important to do it today. Separate this information into work, home, and personal categories. This sheet serves two functions: it helps organize your priorities in each area, and it prepares you mentally for the day. You can do this on the computer, but there is something quite powerful about putting pen to paper.

Analyze what you've written. This lets you think about your day in an organized way. You may find that what you thought was important to do today is actually not. Or you may find that writing your tasks down relieves stress, even though you haven't done your tasks yet. The starter sheet helps combine your conscious self with your unconscious self. Writing ideas down gets you from the worry or procrastination mode into *action*.

Toni, a Transitional Woman, felt stressed. "My aunt was coming to visit for the weekend. I had a project deadline coming up, several client events in the making, children out of school for spring break, and dinner to prepare for ten the next night. And, thanks to Murphy's Law, my cleaning lady had shown up two hours late.

"I wrote down what I thought needed doing. I also noted my feelings. This relieved my stress. After I analyzed what I had written, here's what I decided to do. I would work on my project while deep-conditioning my hair, take a twenty-minute walk, then wash my hair, let it dry while working on three client files, take the children and my aunt grocery shopping midafternoon, and start our meal at 3:30 p.m.

"Somehow, it all worked. At 10:00 p.m. I fell asleep talking to my aunt, while sitting up!"

The next step, after preparing the one-page starter sheet, is to transfer the important priorities for the day onto your time-log sheet.

Using a Time-Log Sheet

Transfer the top two priorities in each category—work, home, and personal—to a new sheet titled "Time Log." The one-page starter sheet can now be used to practice shooting baskets in the trash can, or you can keep the sheets in a manila folder or three-ring binder as a journal.

Include in your time-log sheet your feelings for the day, but state them positively. For example, I recently felt dumped on at work and at home. For my time-log sheet, I turned the sad and negative feeling into a positive statement: "I choose to spend time with people who appreciate me for who I am—I have a lot to offer."

Place the positive statement at the top of the sheet, on the left.

Jana, an Achieving Woman, is in customer service. Her one-page starter sheet gave her direction for the day. "The two most important things I could do at work today were to call the media for an event our firm was doing, and fill out activity sheets for two other clients."

Here's what Jana's time log looks like:

 TIME LOG

May 15 Wednesday		
Positive Comment: Things have a way of working out—stay positive.		
Work:	*Hours Spent*	*Completed*
Priority: Make calls to media		
Priority: Prepare activity sheets for 2 clients		

TIME LOG continued

Home:	Hours Spent	Completed
Priority: Wash two loads of laundry		
Priority: Set dining-room table for Sunday brunch		
Personal:		
Priority: Take a hot bath to relax tense shoulders		
Priority: Read		

As you can see, the time log, in one glance, starts the day with a positive comment; allows you to set and follow up on daily priorities; and lets you examine the time spent at work, at home, and for personal interests. It clarifies exactly why you don't have a spare minute, if that is the case. You will notice lifestyle patterns developing. In addition, you can examine where your time-stress comes from: work, home, or personal tasks. When you understand where the stress is, you then know where and how to focus on changes.

When Jana studied the lifestyle patterns that emerged from her time-log sheet, she found she completed home projects more frequently than work projects. This knowledge gave Jana a place to focus on her time-stress.

Cathie, a Traditional Homemaker, analyzed her time log and found she was spending too much time volunteering at the hospital. "I get such a good feeling spending my time volunteering at the hospital. I saw why I didn't have any time to do anything else after reviewing my time log. I was spending twenty-five hours a week at the hospital. By the time I came home, I was too tired to start any new projects, including making easy and healthy recipes. I was just diagnosed anemic, and I need to learn new eating patterns and substitute foods that contain iron."

After looking through her time log, Lauren, a Transitional Woman, found she was spending too much time at work and not enough time at home or on personal activities. "I started a job that had seasonal peaks, during which there would be longer hours. After a seven-month 'seasonal peak,' I knew something was very wrong. I had a long talk with my boss. He hired a part-time person to do the extra work. I now work longer hours only during March and December and have more time to do things at home and for me."

Using a Task Sheet

I've devised a task sheet to organize events, review follow-up, and account for completion. The task sheet is different from the time log; the task sheet lists all the activities that need to be done to achieve the priorities listed on the time-log sheet.

Jana's time log, for example, listed her two top work priorities as calling the media and preparing activity sheets for two clients. Her task sheet would list all the activities she has to do to complete her priorities. In other words, it would list the names and numbers of specific media people and any other information she would need to complete her activities.

Jana's task sheet might look something like this:

TASK SHEET

- 325-8990 Channel 29
- 845-7905 Channel 22
- 888-7854 Radio 1620
- Email Mel, Sherri, and Robert
- 777-4567 Mercury Alert
- 753-4445 Bistro Hotel—Client 1
- Itinerary typed and faxed—Client 1
- Summary letter, Jason—Client 1
- Confirm carnival booths—Client 2
- Distribute press release—Client 2

When a task is completed, she simply puts a line through its dot. The task sheet breaks down priorities into simple activities, alleviates the stress that comes from worrying that you'll forget something, and gives you a feeling of accomplishment for the day.

You can also use your task list on your computer. Make the list of what tasks need to be done. I highly recommend that you use "customer relationship management" software such as ACT to keep your database up-to-date with names, addresses, email addresses, phone and cell phone numbers, etc. I also recommend that you keep your database minimized on your computer ready to find a number with a simple click of the mouse.

I was asked by *Self* magazine to do a time makeover for Julie Herendeen, an Achieving Woman who is a group product manager at Netscape. After looking at her time log, she says, "I was spending so much time at work and on email transactions. I came home, couldn't sleep, didn't have time to call my parents, and definitely didn't have time to meet other singles. Looking back, I was a working maniac." The first thing I had Julie do was not check her email before going to bed. Her home computer was networked into her office. We then set up two evenings a week for Julie to have dinner with friends and socialize—she scheduled these events on her calendar. We also added one weekend day a week for fun, sleep, or anything else she wanted to do that did not include work. Julie now has time to call her grandmother who is in her nineties. Says Julie, "She is my role model and she told me 'don't put too many things aside.'"

Reviewing and Rearranging Your Calendar

Look at your month-at-a-glance calendar daily and rearrange appointments if necessary. This daily review is necessary because events arise unexpectedly, a task takes longer to do than anticipated, and so on.

Once you decide on a priority, guesstimate the time you need to complete it and add thirty minutes. This additional time allows you to complete your task without rushing, gives you downtime before starting a new project, allows for any unexpected interruptions, and gives you extra time to think of what to do if a problem arises.

Sandy, an Achieving Woman, says, "Daily, I would call my next appointment and tell them, 'I'm running fifteen minutes late.' I now cushion my schedule by fifteen minutes between all appointments, meetings, and projects I'm working on. I don't fall behind as much. Occasionally, when I do, I call my next appointment *ahead* of time to say I'm running behind."

Look at your calendar several times a day, if necessary, and rearrange meetings or appointments to get your top-priority tasks completed. One day, Jackie, a Transitional Woman, needed to complete an itemized budget for the manager of the department. 'I looked at my calendar in the morning and needed to change some meetings so that I could complete the budget. I had made several of these appointments weeks earlier. But the budget took priority, so I canceled them. I have found that most people welcome the free time. I do keep high-priority appointments, though," says Jackie.

Using Lists

You are already aware of how helpful a grocery list can be. As a working woman, however, you can probably profit from expanding your use of lists. Consider how the following lists might help you be more efficient:

- Customer-satisfaction lists
- Client-file lists
- Lists for others
- Running lists
- Errand lists
- Gift lists
- Movie lists
- Outing lists

The sections that follow will discuss each type of list.

Customer-Satisfaction Lists

This type of list is a great way to keep in touch with your client and prevent miscommunication before a problem exists. If the problem is already established, the list helps you bring satisfaction.

Start a customer-satisfaction list for each client. It may seem like a lot of additional work, but once it's in place it will help you reap large social and financial dividends.

If you give customers service and satisfaction, most will be loyal. Staying in contact is one way to maintain communication, improve customer relations, and prevent problems.

Client-File Lists

Insert a sheet at the top of each client file. Even if you do not plan to work on that account, list the things that you need to do for that account. Once they're written down, you don't have to waste time on remembering them. The additional plus: it takes the stress off you if you forget what needs to be done.

Lists for Others

I list everything that I want my secretary to do each day. When she finishes a task, she puts a line through the number of the completed task. I have delegated the duties, but I maintain control and accountability. Often times I start a list and send it via email to her. I realized I was robbing my secretary's time with every email I sent her only addressing one item at a time. I now minimize the email and recapture it for every new item I want to share with her. I simply number the items and she answers each item accordingly via email as well. This method allows each of us to view the information and not disturb each other for every little item.

Why not use a list to delegate tasks to your house helper? Whether your helper comes in once a week, once a month, or not at all (I need to talk to you), start a running list of what needs to be done around the house. I went to grab a pencil that slipped out of my hand underneath a couch pillow. In addition to the pencil, I found stale popcorn! Vacuuming under the pillows became an item on my household task list. Add items to your list as you find things that need to be done around the house. The list will keep growing, I guarantee it!

Running Lists

A running list is one that you constantly add to. For example, a retail store would do well to use running lists for special orders. Rather than take the time to place several special orders per day, the retailer could add the orders on the special-order form as they come in and place the order once or twice weekly.

Lists of Errands

An errand list might be a running list. List the errands that need to be done and add to this list as you think of more errands. Don't waste time running errands every day; do your errands once or twice weekly.

You will find that you will take care of several errands at one place. The 80–20 rule says that 80 percent of your errands will occur at 20 percent of stores. In other words, if you had a list of ten items, chances are that eight of them can be completed at two different locations. By doing errands in batches, you will save time.

In addition, consider delivery service. The small delivery charge may be worth it.

You may want to keep a separate list for Saturday errands, those that can only be done on Saturday because of school or work interference. Examples include children's haircuts, clothes and shoe shopping, or extra fertilizer for the garden vegetables. As the week progresses, add errands to the Saturday list.

Gift Lists

Keeping a running list for family members, friends, and associates who "have everything" is helpful. When you're with one of these people and they mention that they would like to have something, write it down on a legal pad titled "Gifts." When the special occasion arrives, you have the ideal gift—something they wanted.

Movie Lists

It's Saturday night and you want to rent a movie, but it seems as if you've seen everything. Keep a running list of movies you didn't have time to see at the theater or a movie someone suggested that you think you would enjoy. You won't waste time or get frustrated next time you go to the video store.

Outing Lists

Start a list of vacation ideas or ideas for local weekend travel. If you read about a place you would like to visit, write it down on your running list. Include names of hotels, phone numbers, and addresses. Susan, a friend, takes her children to a large city one hundred twenty miles away once a month. She keeps a running list of places to go. She and her children look forward to this minivacation. Their last trip consisted of a children's play and church carnival complete with candy apples and face painting.

Using Legal Pads

On what should you write all your lists? I suggest using a legal pad. I started using legal pads over ten years ago. It was the only neat, large, and organized bound paper in the office. I suggest to my clients that they bring several legal pads when they have an exhibit booth at a conference and when they take notes at seminars and workshops.

Venus, an Achieving Woman, owns a beauty spa. She rented an exhibit booth during a women's conference. "Over one thousand two hundred women attended this conference. I had legal pads titled 'Makeovers,' 'SPCA Charity,' and 'Boyfriends and Husbands: Addresses.' I received hundreds of good leads."

Carrie, a Transitional Woman, is a voracious note taker. "I used to take notes on tiny scratch pads given out at seminars. I ended up turning the pages more than I took notes. Since then, I've discovered legal pads. I get a lot of information on each sheet and can take as many notes as I need. I've never gone through an entire legal pad at one seminar yet."

Cynthia, a twenty-something Achieving Woman, won't leave her home without her hand-held computer. "One of the best investments I have ever made was to purchase a hand-held computer so that I can take notes at my training sessions and add business cards as I receive them. This must save me several hours a week," she says.

Important Points to Remember

Write down on paper or in your computer what needs to be done; don't depend on your memory. Written lists save time and relieve stress. Start each day by writing down what you think needs to be done and why it needs to be done today. This one-page starter sheet helps you define your two daily top priorities in the areas of work, home, and personal tasks.

Develop your time-log sheet to help you complete your priorities. Write down the date, a positive statement reflecting what is happening in your life, two top priorities for work, home, and personal activities, and the hours spent on the tasks. Follow up on task completion. Analyze the sheet to determine the areas in which you are completing your tasks and the areas in which you are not. This will help you make lifestyle changes, if necessary.

The task sheet can organize and account for the completion of activities. The sheet deters procrastination and keeps you from feeling overwhelmed.

Use your month-at-a-glance calendar to plan each day. Change appointments and meetings, if necessary, to accommodate your top priorities.

Save time and ease stress. Write it down!

Chapter Fourteen

The Telephone, Cell Phone, & Email: Women's Best— and Worst—Friends

O f all the conveniences brought to us by Alexander G. Bell, the telephone is the most likely to become a slave master rather than a liberator. Computerized phones and cell phones with automatic dialing, and other tricks hardly compensate for habits that all but destroy our intended schedules.

For most of us, it's incoming rather than outgoing calls that need to be monitored. Obviously, a crackerjack secretary is the best solution to handling both trivial and critical calls. But for those of us who lack the luxury of a top-notch right hand, there are tactics that can eliminate the enormous number of woman-hours that are lost at the sound of the bell.

Understanding Telephone Myths

Three myths about phones hamper the efficiency of most working women. The first involves the need to answer the phone, the second involves underestimating just how much time answering the phone may take, and the third involves cell phone mania of always being connected wherever you go.

Myth 1: "It's My Job to Talk to Clients at Any Time"

"Every time I sit down to do something, the telephone rings and there goes my concentration," laments a busy stockbroker. "In particular I feel the need to accept all incoming calls." This is a frequent comment. "I'm here for my customers, so I need to accept calls."

Of course you must communicate with your clients. But thinking you must be available at all times is unrealistic and will lead to poor time management. And, as this chapter will discuss later, the best path to communication may not be a telephone conversation.

Don't burden yourself with the perceived need to be always available. The fact is, clients don't expect you to be available every time they call. After all, how often do you reach your doctor or dentist on your first try? They almost always have to call you back. And that's exactly what you need to train your clients to expect. As long as you get back to clients the same day, most will be happy. In fact, when you call back, most people will appreciate that you are busy and keep the conversation short.

Ruthie, a sales rep, doesn't answer calls between two and four in the afternoon or seven and nine in the evening. When she's in the office during those hours, the secretary answers the phone and explains that Ruthie will call them back. At home, she turns on the answering machine. "My problem," she says, "is that I can't get the paperwork done if I'm constantly interrupted. I make errors."

If you're a Traditional Homemaker whose work is at home, freeing yourself from the perceived need to answer the phone can be just as practical for you as for the woman who works away from home. You cannot be available twenty-four hours a day, even to friends and family. If you provide a way for people to let you know they called and then return calls faithfully, no reasonable person can possibly object.

Myth 2: Answering Takes Only a "Minute"

Consider the time it takes to get back into the concentration mode.

When you start a project it takes a while to get warmed up and start the ideas flowing. A phone call interrupts this process completely. When you hang up, you must start the process all over again. Writers know that the first couple of pages never flow as easily as their later work. Any interruption means they lose about thirty minutes before they can regain their concentration. If you value your train of thought and your time, don't answer the phone!

Myth 3: Cell Phones Save Time

I believe the advent of cell phones has brought about "cell phone mania." This mania consists of the mindset that we need to be available to answer our phones 24/7 and the temptation to see who's calling every time the phone rings. This pressure has caused women unnecessary stress, overcommitment, loss of concentration in work and driving, and social and relationship disconnect. This cell phone myth runs across all three Motivational Lifestyles and generations.

Unnecessary Stress: Because of this 24/7 mania, people expect us to be at their beck and call, answering the phone every time it rings. The constant "noise" of the phone ringing constantly is a stressor as well. Nomi, a realtor, says, "Sometimes the sound of this cell drives me nuts and I can't concentrate."

Overcommitment: Deni, an investor relations consultant, says, "Because I have my cell phone handy I tell my clients I will call them right back if I'm busy or on the other line and then it puts so much pressure on me later to return all the calls and keep doing what I have to do."

Loss of concentration at work: Again, any time you allow the phone to control you at work, you will not only lose your concentration every time you answer it but it will interfere with the quality of your work because of potential lack of focus and repeated interruptions.

As for driving and using your cell: I would not be opposed to a "no talk and drive" mandate, as some states are beginning to implement.

Jerry said, "I almost had a horrible accident because the driver was on their cell and I doubt if she was paying attention to the road that much."

Social and Relationship Disconnect: Whenever I go out to breakfast, lunch, or dinner and I see a parent or a friend talk on their cell phone while the other people around the table are not talking, I interpret this as a social and relationship disconnect.

Ways to Control Your Cell Phone

1. Turn your cell phone OFF until you're ready to make outbound calls or check your messages.
2. Return your calls in clusters and decide what time of day to do this.
3. Keep the cell OFF when you're driving.
4. Keep your cell OFF when you're with family, friends, at a meeting, in the theater, and out to dine.
5. Wean yourself from using your cell phone as an office when you're driving or in any of the above situations.

I am weaning myself off my cell phone. I find that I was depending on it too much. I make calls that I could easily make at the office or on a landline. I am working on using my cell only as an outbound line and everything else on a land line. It may sound obsolete, but since "cell phone downsizing" I find that my concentration is higher, my focus stronger and my need to chat while in the car only a habit. How do I do this?

1. I keep my cell phone off most of the day. I check for messages four times a day.
2. I return 50 percent of my cell messages on a land line.
3. I catch myself from calling my children to say "hi" while I'm driving.
4. I refrain from making calls to my clients in the car. I am much more present with my clients over the phone and often take notes of our conversation rather than leaving it to memory.

5. I keep my cell off in restaurants or coffee houses—I've switched to "relax mode" during this time.

Making Connections

Now that you have learned a few ways to guard yourself from unwelcome telephone interruptions, let's look at a few ways to make the most of the telephone when its use is appropriate. As mentioned, high-quality communication—not constant access—is the goal.

Why Talk?

Think about your incoming or outgoing calls. Are most of them conversational? Or do you need specific information, such as a person's name, the name of a project, a confirmation, or something else?

Voice mail industry leaders say that half of all business calls contain one-directional information. I have personally found this to be much higher, more in the 75 percent range of one-directional information. That is, someone tells another person something. In most cases, the two people don't even need to talk; one person must simply convey information.

Many people waste time because they become locked into the idea that they must speak directly to someone. If all you need to do is convey information, be creative in looking at the many ways you can do it. You can prepare a message that contains the information and leave it on an answering machine, voice mail system, or email. You can relay the message through a secretary or another third party. (Leaving messages with a third party works best when the third party knows who you are trying to communicate with and what you want to convey or need. Always let your secretary know if you are waiting for a specific person to call.)

If all you need to do is receive information, let the information provider know how he or she can leave word for you. In your message, say what the best time to leave word is and the time by which you need the information.

Choose the Best Times to Call Back

When do you find yourself least in the mood to schmooze or chat on the phone? Usually before lunch and before going home from the office. Therefore, I have found that the best times to call back and ensure a brief businesslike call are from 11:30 a.m. until noon and from 4:15 until 5:00 p.m.

Make Cluster Calls

As suggested, you do not have to be on twenty-four-hour call, as long as you return your calls within twenty-four hours. When you are ready to return calls, optimize your time by returning as many as you can at one time. I call this making cluster calls. You may choose, as I often do, to call back between 11:00 a.m. and noon and between 4:15 and 5:00 p.m.—times when people are most likely to keep conversations short. You'll need to plan and make changes for different time zones.

I find that another productive time for cluster calling is during the noon hour. I stay in my office twice a week until 12:30 p.m., making calls. You will be amazed at how many people are in their offices at this time. Many of them stay in at noon so that they can get quiet work done. They want to keep their conversations short so they can get back to work.

Remember that cluster calling doesn't have to be an at-your-desk activity. Put spare moments to use by making calls wherever you happen to be. I clip phone messages to my calendar, which I take everywhere except dressy social functions. I keep two paper clips on the calendar at all times, just for holding messages. I place the most urgent message on top, and arrange the rest of the pile in the order of priority.

I return calls as I'm waiting for my car to be washed (my time is worth more than the costs). I also make and return calls in my car before lunch. By using cluster calls to respond on the same day, working women can exhibit professionalism and alleviate stress.

Cluster Emails

I place phones and email into the same category—controlling communications. Rather than respond to emails individually, decide what times of the day you will check your email and what times of the day you will respond to your emails. This is exactly what you need to be doing with your phone communications, landline or cell.

Prevent Telephone Tag

Telephone tag is an annoying two-person sport in which one person knowingly or unknowingly calls another person when he or she is unavailable and then the second person does the same thing to the first person. These two unavailable people leave a string of telephone messages for each other. The result is the waste of valuable time and, in some cases, a lost sale, a blown deadline, or a critical misunderstanding.

Shelly, a realtor, says, "When I first started in this business, I was constantly chasing people. After I lost a few clients, I developed a new system. Now, I leave phone numbers and times with the company secretary and on my voice mail so people can reach me. I check for calls at my office at least once an hour, especially if I'm in escrow. You never know what can happen."

This section will present several ways to prevent telephone tag.

Find Out When to Call

Most days you have a natural rhythm in your schedule. You may find that you are usually in your office between 8:00 a.m. and 9:00 a.m. or between 1:30 p.m. and 2:45 p.m. Your clients' schedules have rhythms too. Ask your clients the best time to reach them, and mark it on your Rolodex file or phone file.

Use the "Twice Then Send" Approach

Leona has a full-time job and manages thirty-three rental units. She uses the "twice then send" approach. "When I call someone on the telephone two times or email them twice and I do not receive a return call or email, I send a note in the mail. They usually get it the next day. In the note I tell the person what I need and to call in the information to my office…I save myself a lot of stress doing this, plus I have a paper trail if I need one. I'm just too busy to play tag."

Don't forget that, in some cases, faxing a message may be more effective than mailing it or phoning it, providing it is not confidential material.

Use Home Phones

When I have difficulty reaching someone, I leave a message stating my home number and ask the person to call me at a specific time. I give a specific time so that the call does not interrupt our dinner hour or come so late that it will wake someone up.

The same goes for reaching the other person. I bring their home number home with me and call between 7 and 9 p.m. I often do this on Monday evenings, since this is the day I get most projects started.

Email and Call

If you do not hear back from someone via email after an amount of time or you have sent them more than one email trying to contact them without any reply, then give them a call. Because of firewalls, security software, and spam ware, it is becoming more difficult to reach people via email.

Get Placed on the Email List

When I start working with a new client, we immediately exchange emails and put each others email address on our "okay to receive emails" list. Otherwise, your email may be automatically rejected. You may want to check out spamarrest.com to help you set this up.

Stop to Visit

I have several clients who work constantly with their clients—a salon owner, an attorney, a stockbroker, a realtor, and so forth. There is a very small chance of getting them on the phone when I need to speak to them. If I am in the area and have five to ten minutes (that's approximately as long as a phone conversation would take), I stop and have a conversation face-to-face. This helps me stay in contact and be available for them, even though they have hectic schedules.

Use a Third-Party Relay

Women with children should realize that their kids can serve as third-party relays at home. Not only can they prevent telephone tag, but they can—like a secretary—create a positive impression for you and your business. All children should know how to conduct themselves responsibly on the telephone.

Don't make the mistake of thinking that clients won't call you at home. As Shelly says, "I do so many things with so many people I never know which number—home, cell or office—they're going to call. It's really not their fault, because sometimes I'm at my home during the day (for lunch and sick children)." I asked Shelly at what age she thinks children are able to relay telephone messages accurately. "As soon as they know their letters and numbers," she said. "I instruct them to repeat the names and phone numbers just in case. I'm one of those who gets very annoyed when I don't have the right information. Having the kids repeat the phone numbers alleviates the problem."

Schedule Regular Meetings

A marketing specialist I know works with two graphic designers. Telephone contact proved so difficult that she decided to hold weekly meetings with each one. Says Sue, "I need to spin on a dime with my clients—that's one of the reasons they hire me. Setting up weekly meetings with these designers ensures that we don't play telephone tag." Please do not depend on email for contact that is most effective for "in person" meetings. There just isn't a way to compare the energy and synergy that is created when people are brainstorming and creating in person.

Similarly, Tina, a sales rep, and her major supplier decided to play tennis together once a week. Afterwards, usually over iced tea, they talk business. This gives them time to order more inventory, change policies, talk about any problems, and basically regroup. "My major supplier is only in town twice a week. This time together allows me to get some good prices and up-to-date information on our business trade locally and in other locations. I have a strong suspicion that this is why we have such a good relationship, and in my business, it makes the difference between making a good living and just a living."

Leave Messages with Email Address

I suggest that you start leaving your email address at the end of your recorded voice message so that your caller can choose to get in touch with you via email. If you find that you are receiving too much unsolicited email, then scrap the idea. However, more times than not, your caller appreciates this and it prevents telephone tag. Quite honestly, I often prefer email messages over phone ones because it not only saves time, but I return the communication sooner and it reduces the amount of chitchat.

Teleconference

What a great way to stay in contact without leaving your office or home office. Valery, a Forty-Something sales rep for a publishing company says, "Before my company started weekly teleconferences, I wasted so much time traveling to and back from meetings."

Focus Day Without Phones

Please don't start to hyperventilate. I am only making a suggestion that you plan for one focus day a week without using your phone as usual. During this focus day the only time you are on the phone is if you initiate the call because it directly applies to what you are doing, or you need to call someone to pick you up for an emergency! I also suggest that you come up for "air" twice during the day; one may be in the late morning before lunch when you listen to your messages and return any urgent calls and then again at the end of the day. You may also want to check your emails at the same time, but don't get into the trap of other people's email emergencies—only respond to urgent emails.

Today it is very easy to let the phone ring and go into message mode, whether you have a secretary or not. Years ago it was not thought to be the most professional way of doing business by letting the answering machine capture the messages, but today, it is almost preferred, if not expected! Jamie, a marketing professional says, "I can't believe how my life has changed by implementing a focus day once a week. I am not as stressed during the week because I *know* I have one day a week to get good work accomplished. I actually anticipate Wednesdays (her chosen focus day). Some weeks I can't take the entire day, but I make sure to take three or four hours."

Teaching Your Secretary to Run Interference

This section is for that lucky working woman who has a secretary or a professional answering service.

The secret to making the best use of a secretary is keeping in close contact several times a day. Alert the secretary to the phone calls you want to receive. Tell him or her when you can be reached in the office and what you want them to say when you are not available.

Remember that your secretary's way of receiving calls—what the secretary says as well as the tone of the conversation—is extremely important. All incoming calls must be received warmly and competently. The feeling the secretary generates has a direct influence on how your client perceives you as a person and as a professional.

Establish these three important procedures with your secretary:

1. If someone has tried a few times to call you, apologize for the inconvenience. At this point the secretary should tell the caller that his or her message will go on top of the pile, and the secretary should follow through by putting it there and bringing it to your attention. You could also offer to give the caller her email address if she wishes to try to reach her with this avenue. However, this would only be used for specific clients.
2. Never ask the name of a caller and then put him or her on hold. The caller may feel unimportant if the call does not get through immediately.
3. Always use positive statements. Don't say, "No, she's not in the office"; say, "She's at a conference today. Is there anything I can help you with?" Another example is, "She's out of the office until noon, but I can reach her in an emergency." Other possibilities are, "She's out of town until Thursday, but she checks her messages twice a day," and, "She'll be back in the office at 2:30 this afternoon." The caller perceives a positive statement as an offer of help, not a dead end.

Two other rules of telephone conduct are as important for you as they are for your secretary:

1. Wear a smile when you pick up the phone.
2. Identify yourself. Ask how you can help the caller and follow through.

Time Management Secrets for Working Women

Use the same approach when you work with an answering machine or voice mail. Smile, be positive, ask how you can help, follow through, and stay in touch. Just as you need to check in continually with your secretary, you must continually check your machine and voice messages.

Technology is Good...Yes?

We are fortunate to live in this era with ever-improving technology at our fingertips. However, much of technology is a double-edged sword. On one hand, it saves us countless hours and stress and on the other hand it has caused us undue stress and complicates our lives and infringes upon our space, family, and quiet time. Let's look at a few of these double-edged swords and how we might resolve some of them.

Cell phones

Positive:

- Stay in contact with family and clients at a moment's notice
- Light to carry
- Ability to do several functions from one piece of light technology
- May be less expensive than a landline
- Text messaging ability to get through when air space is limited, in case of a crisis

Challenge:

- Always available and can violate private space (We spoke of these challenges earlier in the chapter)

Solution:

- Stay in control of your cell phone as we discussed earlier

PDA—Personal Digital Assistant

Positive:

- Convenient to have names, addresses, phone numbers, email addresses, and other capabilities at your fingertips

- Lightweight for traveling
- Combines a phone and computer
- Captures and writes down information that is fresh in your head
- Saves time retyping information into your computer

Challenge:
- If you lose your PDA it's gone unless you develop a system to regularly sync it with your computer
- Need a password and encryption because there are security issues with PDAs
- Technology can always go haywire
- Has limitations for use as an at-a-glance planner
- Can be expensive

Solution:
- Follow up with "end of day transition" that allows you to sync with your computer
- Use the same time management principles we discussed earlier for your PDA as you would for your phone and email

Research via Internet

Positive:
- Saves you time, money, and stress
- Research from your home or office
- Wealth of information

Challenge:
- Information overload
- Need to know how to search
- Some information not available
- Requires time to do the searches

Solution:
- Important to keep all research material organized into specifically labeled files, with paper or paperless

- Bookmark your favorite research websites
- Plan enough time to go to a library when doing research online—don't keep all your eggs in one basket. Denise, a writer and editor, says, "I love researching on the internet, but I still have to make trips to the university library more than I would like"
- Use KartOO.com—a free search engine that substantially helps you to refine your research

Important Points to Remember

The telephone can save you time, provided you are in control. It's okay not to be available for calls twenty-four hours a day; your real responsibilities are to provide a way for people to let you know they need you and to respond to messages within twenty-four hours from the time they come in.

Remember that you may not necessarily have to talk to someone directly to get a job done. Let your contacts know how and when to leave word for you. If you're the one who needs to convey information, find out the best times and means for doing it.

To respond efficiently to messages, cluster your calls and emails and make them at times and at places convenient to you. To prevent telephone or email tag, send your message by mail or fax after two tries, use home telephones, stop by, use a third-party relay, or schedule regular meetings.

The impression a client gains through telephone contact can have a powerful effect. Make sure anyone who answers your phone—you, an adult, or a child—can convey a warm, positive attitude and take messages accurately.

Remember, the telephone and email are there for your convenience. Use it wisely, and it will be your best ally.

Chapter Fifteen

Let Ginger Do It:
The Gentle Art of Delegation

No man is an island, and no woman can do it all herself. No matter how small your business or what position you may hold in an organization, knowing how and when to delegate responsibility is critical for growth and success.

Proper delegation can double a working woman's productivity, no matter where she is on the career ladder. She must divide those tasks that involve policy from those that involve the actual operation of the business. It is important to remember that effective delegation goes both up and down the business hierarchy.

This need to delegate also exists on the home front. Delegation at home allows the working woman to spend special time with "delegatees."

Understanding the Need for Control

Most working women have an obsessive need to control every aspect of their work, home, and personal activities. This need for control, which inhibits delegation, stems from two sources: fear and guilt.

Expel Fear

The Traditional Woman feels she needs to control everything that goes on in the home, particularly, or she will lose her family unit. The Transitional

Woman is busy juggling her life and, if one baton drops, she fears she will lose it all—work and family. The Achieving Woman feels that if she loses control at work, in particular, mistakes will be made and her credibility will suffer.

Give Up Guilt

Many women place unreasonable demands on themselves because they are running from guilt. They feel guilty about not being perfect, about not being able to do everything, so they redouble their efforts in every area. They try to control things to make other people happy.

The cartoon strip *Cathy* shows how feeling guilty about having a career caused one woman to redouble her efforts at being the perfect dog owner—even when her trouble was far from justified. Cathy comes home to find that her dog, Electra, has ravaged the house.

> Electra! What happened in here??!
>
> The mail is ripped up…the pillows are shredded…half of a blue suede pump is buried in the plant!!
>
> Oh, Electra…
>
> …I was gone too long today! You must have been so bored and lonely! Maybe you thought I wasn't coming back! You knew you did something bad, and you got scared and did something even worse!
>
> It was all my fault! I shouldn't have been gone so long!
>
> I'll make you a special dinner! I'll get out all your toys!! I'm so sorry my sweet, sensitive puppy!!
>
> GUILT: Dog's best friend.

Cathy's response seems extreme, but is it any more so than what real-life women put themselves through because of guilt? Consider a few typical cases.

Clare, a Traditional Homemaker, says, "Since I had a part-time job, I felt I needed to do everything. My children were busy doing homework, and my husband worked hard all day. I ran myself silly just keeping up with the housework and washing. Then one day my eleven-year-old asked me to play catch, and I said I had to do the wash. He said, 'Mom, why do you spend more time washing than playing with me?' That gave me a clue as to how to solve the problem. Both the eleven- and thirteen-year-old now help me with the wash and ironing, and I spend more time with them—including the time we spend together with the wash. All along I thought I was making them happy."

Linda, a Transitional Woman, went back to work after her first child was born. She worked part-time for a while, but she needed two full-time paychecks to run the household. "I hated to leave my baby at the time. I would run home at lunch and directly after work to see him. I didn't want to miss any firsts. I came down with a series of colds that just lingered for eight weeks. My doctor said I had to either quit work or calm down. I stayed at work because I didn't have a choice. I finally trusted my sister-in-law with the baby, and you know what? I didn't miss any firsts."

Lani, an Achieving Woman, did everything herself in her small business—including activities such as typing, accounting, and filing, which she could delegate to others. "I did everything myself because I knew where everything went and I could do it faster than someone else. The only problem was that all that work was piling up. I had no choice; I had to hire someone. I went through four temporary workers before I found a good one. I can still work faster than she can, but now I'm getting my work done, with a lot less stress."

An alarming but real thought: life would go on if you were not here!

Cultivating the Habit of Delegating

If the examples in this chapter have made you realize that you are obsessed with control, the time has come for you to learn the habit of delegating tasks to others. To do so, follow this four-step plan:

1. Decide what tasks you like to do.
2. Prioritize your tasks.
3. Double-check your priorities.
4. Ask for help.

Decide What You Like to Do

To begin to understand what you like to do, think about all your activities in a general way. A great way to review everything you do is to think about your tasks as you walk, jog, or do other exercise. After you have thought about the matter for a while, sit down with a pencil and paper.

Divide a sheet of paper into three categories—one each for work, home, and personal tasks. By category, list all the tasks you do now. As you review each task, ask yourself: does this activity uplift me, give me energy? If the answer is yes, then the activity is one you enjoy. Circle it in green.

Next decide which tasks you feel neutral about; circle them in yellow. The tasks that remain uncircled should be the tasks that you not only dislike but that drain you of energy; circle these in red.

Keep in mind that there is a difference between an activity that you simply don't like and an activity that drains you. I don't enjoy washing dishes, but the task doesn't drain my energy. I not only dislike ironing, I find that it exhausts me and makes me feel irritable. Filing papers and magazine articles also drains my energy, as do some types of errands.

Obviously, the tasks circled in red are strong candidates as jobs to be delegated to others.

Prioritize Your Tasks

Decide which tasks—at work, at home, and in your personal life—are really priority tasks for you personally. If one or more people could do the job about as well as you could and in the time available, consider letting them do it.

Sheila, an office manager at a law firm, was involved in accounting, public relations, interviewing callers, and much more. "The partners and I got together and brainstormed what each person absolutely had to do to make the firm profitable and which items could be delegated to others in the office. We felt I had to write the checks and accept all telephone interviews. We decided that I would delegate all outgoing correspondence and the ordering of supplies. This is a painful process. I hate to give control to someone else who doesn't care as much as I do. We're planning to have these brainstorming meetings once a month. I'm sure I'll let go of more responsibility, a little at a time."

Double-Check Your Priorities

The priority of a task may change from morning to afternoon. For example, if you find you are running late in completing a task and another activity needs to be completed by tomorrow, you may need to drop what you're doing and go to the task with the pressing deadline. Mary, an Achieving Woman, had three priority tasks on a recent day. She needed to develop budget strategies for two different clients, as well as make a presentation to a new client. "I didn't realize how much time I spent on one of my client's budgets. It was two o'clock, and I didn't have my proposal ready. Since I had an early-morning appointment with my proposal client, I dropped the budgets until I finished the presentation proposal. I finished one budget by late afternoon and had to finish the other one after my morning meeting."

How does establishing priorities relate to delegating tasks? Remember Lani, the small-business owner, who put off hiring help because she knew she could do the work faster than someone else? Chances are that you, like Lani, will be able to do the job you delegate faster than the person you delegate it to. In addition, assigning and explaining the job will take time. If a task has priority—if it has a pressing deadline—then doing the job yourself makes sense from a time-management standpoint. Find another activity on your task list to assign to a helper.

Ask for Help

Most women have a difficult time asking for help. We feel there must be something wrong with us if we have to delegate. After all, we're women; we can take care of *everything*.

Why do women have so much trouble asking for help? After many informal surveys, I have found five basic reasons:

1. The fear of seeming incompetent
2. A dislike of infringing on others' time
3. The fear of rejection
4. The belief that a job requires specific knowledge and experience
5. An ego involvement with the task

Before looking at some ways to ask for help at the office and at home, let's look more closely at each of these reasons.

The Fear of Seeming Incompetent

Women may feel that if they ask for help, they admit to not being in control of their work, home, or personal lives. Whether they are in control is not the real issue. The issue is women's sensitivity to others' perceptions of their capacity to be in charge.

A Dislike of Infringing

Here is another case in which women show their sensitivity to others. They may not ask someone for help for fear that the other person will say yes even though he or she means no. Women, from their past experience, know yes-saying behavior better than most. Certainly you have said yes to something that takes your time when you really wanted to say no.

The Fear of Rejection
Women seem to have an innate fear of rejection. This may explain why most women dislike making "cold calls" and prefer making "warm calls"—calling on someone they have met previously. People tend to avoid behavior that causes them to fear negative consequences. Therefore, we do not ask for help in case someone says no.

The Need for Specific Know-How
Working women are intimately involved with their tasks at work, home, and in personal activities. They know—through hard work and experience—which systems work. Being confident in this knowledge sometimes distracts them from spending their time in more efficient ways. Women need to learn that if they ask for help and the other person's process is different from theirs and the end result is the same, it's okay.

Ego Involvement
A specific task may embody a woman's femininity, productiveness, or some other characteristic intrinsic to her ego. As a result, it is difficult to let go of that task. Carrie, a Transitional Woman, loved making her children's school lunches. "I made sure they had lettuce in their sandwiches, fresh fruit, and fruit juice. The hours of my new job made it difficult for me to continue. My husband took over, and I don't feel their lunches are as nutritious now."

Seeing What's Possible
Once you have discovered the freedom of asking for help, you will find yourself developing new ways to organize and manage tasks. Consider the creative approaches that Sydney and Karen developed. Sydney, a

sales representative for a large corporation, says, "I hate to make confirmation calls. I asked my secretary to do this for me, and I proofread her letters. It works out well for both of us."

Karen, an Achieving Woman, started laundry-folding parties for her family on Mondays and Thursdays after dinner. "The entire family sits on the floor in the living room and plays word games as we fold. We actually have a good time. My six-year-old, who finds the matching socks, asked if we could play the game on Saturdays."

Enjoying the Benefits

You may already have discovered a fringe benefit of learning to delegate work. In the process of distinguishing the tasks that drain you of energy, you also discovered the tasks that energize you. You can use this understanding to revitalize yourself regularly and in stressful times, when you especially need a lift.

Jenny, who writes nonfiction articles, explains how she uses one of her revitalizing activities. "When I'm at a standstill with my writing or I just don't feel like writing yet, I'll go out in the garden and weed or pinch back my herbs. It gets me going again."

Karen, a medical transcriber, takes walks around the office building. "I take four or five walks each day. Before I started walking, I would straighten out desk drawers, straighten paper clips, and other piddly things. I spent too much time straightening. Walking is a good way to help me with my diet, too—I drink more water."

Susan, a Traditional Homemaker, plays piano when she needs to be reenergized. "I don't play too well, but well enough to play hit tunes. Playing piano is just enough to take my mind off worries."

Kathleen, a Transitional Woman, says, "I started taking walks with the family, including the dog, after dinner. We clear off the table but don't do the dishes until after our walk. It's a good way to get refocused with the family after being gone all day."

Preventing a Relapse

Being obsessive about control is so much of a habit for most of us that we are all in danger of forgetting to ask for help. Three major symptoms can warn you that you are trying to do too much. These symptoms are procrastination, the feeling of burnout, and depression.

Procrastination

We've all done it—put off something until later. Besides not getting done what needs to be done, procrastination leads to the feeling of being overwhelmed. We keep putting off tasks, and the pile of tasks mounts. This feeling paralyzes us from getting our work done.

Burnout

The word *burnout* comes from mechanical engineering, where it refers to damage caused by improper use. If you have been using yourself improperly by not asking for help, you have no energy. You feel as though you can hardly move your body, and your mind is just as sluggish. Prioritizing becomes very difficult.

Depression

Depression is characterized by a lack of energy and the feeling that nothing is worthwhile. Depression causes inactivity and moodiness, which reinforce the depression. The depressed person feels that work and life don't matter. If depression is chronic, the sufferer should seek help from a doctor, member of the clergy, or counselor. Counseling can help a depressed person make changes that will reflect his or her priorities and, in so doing, reinvest life with meaning.

If your procrastination, burnout, and depression are simple symptoms of overload, however, you can get yourself back on the track by delegating what you can and then doing something for *you*. The list that follows presents fifteen ideas for self-nurturing:

1. Take a morning off from work.
2. Treat yourself to a Saturday at a salon.
3. Tell the family you're off-duty for dinner and dishes for a couple of evenings.
4. Cuddle up with a good book and a cup of herbal tea.
5. Go out with a fun friend for the evening.
6. Take a two-hour lunch occasionally.
7. Have your makeup redone.
8. Say no to any more responsibility.
9. Treat yourself to a facial.
10. Spend a long, leisurely time in a bath; light aromatic candles.
11. Take off an hour early from work, tell the family you'll be home after eight, and do something fun.
12. Spend an entire weekend doing things you enjoy—no cleaning or errands.
13. Hire someone to clean, iron, and do a few errands twice a month.
14. Look at your calendar ahead of time and reschedule appointments during a busy day or week.
15. Save $10 a week for six months and take a trip out of town overnight.

You *deserve* to do any one or all of these stress-reducing activities. If you don't treat yourself well, how can you expect others to do so? Remember, procrastination, burnout, and depression take more time and money in the long run than any of the fifteen ideas from the preceding list.

Important Points to Remember

Working women need to give up the obsessive need for control. The Traditional Homemaker feels she needs to control because she fears losing her family; the Transitional Woman because she fears losing everything; and the Achieving Woman because she fears losing credibility.

To discover the tasks you can delegate at work and at home, list all your activities, discover the ones that energize or drain you, double-check your priorities, and ask for help.

Be aware of three symptoms of trying to do too much: procrastination, burnout, and depression. To prevent these symptoms, delegate work and do something you enjoy. Whatever it takes, do it.

Not only do you deserve a life with less time-stress, but preventing overload is less costly—financially and mentally—than curing the symptoms it can cause.

Chapter Sixteen

A Seven-Letter Word: Waiting

Traffic congestion, doctors' offices, ballet rehearsals, soccer practices, clients' reception rooms, and being put on hold. What do all of these activities have in common? The need to wait. Learning to use the valuable time spent waiting is essential to effective time management. Waiting time does not have to be wasted time.

The thing that often keeps women from making use of odd bits of time is the lack of a critical tool or information. They don't have an address, paper, or Aunt Sally's sizes, for example. This chapter will discuss how to organize the trunk of your car so that you always have what you need. The chapter will also present many ideas for discovering the productivity of waiting time.

Using Your Car as an Office and Kitchen on Wheels

Susan is a full-time accountant and has two children, one of whom is on call as an actor in commercials. Susan carries a hip buzzer and takes a two-hour drive for each audition, callback, and taping session. Susan's car trunk is as important as the engine. She says, "I pick Phil up from school, and off we go. On several occasions, I have one or two added outfits for him, depending on the type of audition. He's dirty from school, so I have a hair dryer, underwear, shoes, shirts, and pants in the trunk. He just dresses in the back seat."

What about satisfying his hunger pangs? "I keep carton drinks, granola bars, and other dry food in the car trunk at all times. I found out the hard way not to use canned drinks. I also keep a lot of educational tapes, music, and stories in the trunk. One trip I get to choose what we listen to, the next trip my son chooses. Sometimes I bring my second son along. While Phil auditions, Brian and I spend some quiet time together. I actually look forward to this, even though my friends think I'm nuts. Otherwise, I'd be cooking and cleaning the house. This way I spend more time with my children."

Vera, an account representative, has three children in orthodontics. "One child always seems to chew on something and messes up her braces and needs to go to the doctor's office. Have you ever been inside an orthodontist's office in the afternoon? There are so many kids. I plan my child's appointment for early mornings, which helps a great deal, but I still have to wait. I spend the time, usually around forty-five minutes to an hour, doing PR with a client or nearby supplier. I keep several company coffee cups in the car trunk. Our customers love them because there is a different saying on each one.

"Lucky for me, the office of one of my suppliers is nearby. I call him a couple of days before the orthodontist's appointment so I can arrange to talk with him and drop off another coffee cup. I'm convinced this is why we have such a good working relationship."

Divide your car trunk in half. In one half, store work-related equipment, such as the expanding file folders I'll discuss next. In the other half, pack family-related necessities. This division helps to keep the trunk organized and neat.

Develop a Mobile Filing System

I suggest that my clients buy three small expanding file folders. They cost under $6 each and can be used year after year. These files are worth their weight in gold. Label your folder to divide it into several segments: a segment for thank-you cards, children's birthday cards, adult birthday cards, all-occasion cards, scissors, tape, ribbon, wrapping paper, paper clips, and anything else you deem important.

The second expanding file folder holds reading material. Index it by topic: romance, sex, career, hobby, finances, parenting, and so on.

The third folder contains the active list: names, addresses, phone numbers, and other important information about clients, babysitters, doctors, close friends, the cleaning lady, and your hair dresser, to name a few. As long as the active list is in your trunk, you'll never have to make an extra trip home or to the office to get basic information. You can also have this information in your PDA or cell phone.

However, the folder should contain more than names, addresses, and phone and fax numbers. Using one five by seven card for each client, write down the last contact, whether in writing or in person, that you had with each client. Use this information to check whether you sent the birthday card or whatever. Don't depend on your memory for everything. Also list what you gave the client, if anything, at your last visit. You can also keep up with these contacts using any number of customer-relationship software, such as ACT.

Ann, an account executive for a stationery store, is rarely in her office. "I keep a filing box in the passenger's seat of my car and call clients on the road. I even fax information to them from someone else's office. When I first started I planned my calls before leaving the office. Well, I soon found that my planning was in vain. Many of my prospective and existing clients couldn't see me, or I had to change times and didn't have their numbers with me. Now that I've developed a system, I see more customers and fit in a little play time on the side."

Your mobile filing system allows you to call, fax, write, or visit any person you're actively involved with, so that waiting time turns into positive action.

Or, you can use a PDA—an easy method to keep your database in one simple, lightweight piece of equipment.

Using Waiting Time

With your car properly equipped, you're ready to be constructive wherever you find yourself. Try these suggestions next time.

Write Thank-You Notes

Writing thank-you notes often ends up on the bottom of the working woman's priority list. Yet this is a fairly simple task in terms of brainpower and time. Nancy, who has four children, does a great deal of waiting, transporting, and waiting again. "People always ask how I find the time to send thank-yous. Little do they know that I wait a third of my day," laments Nancy. "If I'm waiting for my girls at ballet and there's a card shop near, I march straight over and buy some cards. This wait time is the only real peace and quiet I get, except when the babies are napping."

If you want to positively impress your friends, clients, suppliers, and babysitters, write thank-yous. It does not take much time to write a quick note, especially when you're waiting, and the effort reaps an abundance in return. Very few people take the time to thank someone for their time or efforts. But when you do, these people will continue to be helpful and save you time in the long run.

For example, I have taken the time to nurture my relationship with the staff in my children's orthodontists' office. As a result, the staff accommodates me by scheduling the children for late-afternoon appointments. The children rarely wait over five minutes to get in (the two orthodontists have over three thousand patients).

At work, I have spent time nurturing my printer. As a result, I receive completed printing projects days earlier than I would otherwise.

I suggest that my clients write one thank-you note a day. Working women have more than one person to thank each day: there's the sitter, for going that extra mile; the grandparent who came to the rescue unexpectedly or expectedly; the significant other who helped in some way; the client who suggested your name as a speaker; the supplier who corrected a mistake; the media, for showing up at an event; the printer who produced your newsletter within two days; and the customer who brought in a new customer.

To be able to write notes "in the field," you must have cards on hand. Keep attractive cards, with the insides blank, in your car trunk. Second, as you think of the person you want to thank, congratulate, or send a note "just because," write his or her name and address on an envelope. Third, slip the card (unwritten) under the envelope flap. Carry the cards in your month-at-a-glance calendar. (Remember, you always bring your calendar everywhere except social events.) As you wait for someone to return a call or for lunch, a child, a doctor, or a client, fill in the card. Drop your cards in the mailbox on your trip home. Sending cards is a great marketing and customer-relations gesture. A person's gut reaction to a handwritten note is always surprise and then appreciation.

Talk and Shop

Andrea owns a women's clothing store. She actively promotes her store while she waits at her children's tennis events. "Recently, waiting for my boys to finish their tennis lesson, I struck up a conversation with the woman next to me. The woman was very thin. She told me she had difficulty finding clothes in her size. She had been in my store but couldn't find anything to fit. Well, something was wrong because we specialize in small sizes. I apologized for the lack of proper service and set up an appointment. She is now one of my best customers. Plus, we're good friends to boot."

My husband and I go out to dinner at a neighborhood restaurant once a week. The restaurant is in a shopping center. We put our names on the waiting list and then go midweek grocery shopping for milk, orange juice, fruit, and other basics.

Buy Gifts

People get married, have babies, recover from surgery, move out of town, get a year older, and celebrate Bar and Bat Mitzvahs, to list a few. These events usually call for gifts. While you're waiting for a child or client, get your gift buying out of the way. Sue says, "Valentine's Day is one of my favorite holidays. I have a Valentine's area in my hall closet. The week before Valentine's, I wrap several gifts and place them in the car trunk. This saves me from rushing to buy gifts. Since they're already wrapped and in the trunk, I get them to the right people on time. In addition, I sometimes preorder candies and cookies and have them delivered."

When it comes to gift buying, catalogues can be a great help. In addition, you can do your catalogue browsing during waiting time. Getting your holiday shopping squared away will probably be much more satisfying to you than leafing through the old sports magazines at the dentist's office. I keep no more than three catalogues. I ask my husband and children to look through them and initial the items they like. I do my holiday shopping two months before I need to. I also choose gifts for other family and friends this way. No long holiday lines to wait in!

Glenna, a full-time stockbroker, does her shopping when she's out of town for pleasure or on business. "It's about the only time I have to shop. If I see something at a good price, I'll buy two or three. That way, I have the gifts I need for a wedding, housewarming, or whatever. I take advantage of wedding registries. I order the gift by phone and dictate the card's message."

Teresa, a fitness coach and author, docs all her shopping, banking, travel plans, and more online. "The Internet has broadened my world so much. My trip to Paris was all planned via the Internet. My daughter college applications, health records completed online. I didn't talk to a human being through the whole process," Teresa says with a wide smile. She goes on to say, "I completed all my Christmas shopping by Thanksgiving and most of it was done online."

Return Phone Calls

What happens when you're not in your office very often and you need to return ten calls per day between working, transporting children, fitting in errands, and housecleaning?

Jennifer, involved in telemarketing for her company, spends her day on the phone. She returns calls by using home numbers after work. For example, if someone conducts a home business, she knows she can use the home phone number to reach her contact in the evening. "If I'm waiting for one of my children after work, I'll call the home numbers and usually reach the people I need to talk to. This works for me."

Marty, a pharmaceutical salesperson, calls on doctors. "They don't have much time to talk to me to begin with, and many times I have a certain time frame to return their calls—in between patients. I write the times next to my sales sheet and try to call them at those times. I might be getting my hair cut and have to excuse myself for five minutes so that I can reach the doctor at a specific time to either set up an appointment or to drop off sample drugs."

Important Points to Remember

Waiting can be a positive opportunity for working women. Turn your car trunk into an office-kitchen on wheels. In one half, store work-related equipment; in the other, pack family-related necessities. Develop a mobile filing system using three expanding file folders. In the first, keep cards, paper clips, and gift-wrapping equipment. In the second, keep reading material, indexed by topic. In the third, file names, addresses, and phone numbers of active clients and important others. Or, just bring along your PDA with your database.

Write thank-you notes to clients, suppliers, acquaintances, friends, and family. Keep cards with blank insides (for handwritten comments) at your office and in your car trunk.

Use waiting time to return phone calls. There is only one of you—let everything else wait!

Chapter Seventeen

I'm Committed:
But to What?

The combination of a woman's talents, special interests, and everyday responsibilities put a heavy burden on her to make choices. What happens when someone asks a working woman to participate on the board of directors, help her son's first-grade room mother, be the assistant coach of the soccer team, or simply make dinner for a friend who is coming home from the hospital? Overload!

Working women need to use and enjoy their talents rather than be burdened by them. They must learn to make the best choices at the moment and not commit to those activities that take away from their special interests. Women need to avoid the overcommitment crunch.

This chapter will discuss how to avoid overcommitment by making expedient choices that coincide with your personal values and how to keep a positive attitude in the midst of it all.

Considering Choice

Life is a buffet of choices—some good for you, others not. Before examining the techniques of choice making, consider three issues that women often forget in regard to their choices: freedom, education, and priorities.

Realize Your Freedom to Choose

Women have the freedom to make decisions and choices. You can choose where you want to work, what interests you will pursue, and which school programs you will participate in. Sometimes women forget they have this freedom and the fact that, sometimes, the freedom to choose means the freedom to say no.

Choose Education

The best choices are educated choices. Therefore, take every opportunity you can to broaden yourself. In some places you can complete your college degree from your television set or computer. Correspondence courses are another way of furthering education. Take evening classes; attend informal discussions; or expand your outlook through library research, reading, and spending time with people you think have something to teach you. As my dad frequently says, "No one can take away your education, and only you can get it."

Set Priorities

Therapists say that working women have too many choices and that this situation causes us frustration and anxiety. To avoid frustration and anxiety, you must decide what is important to you at the moment and make the choices that support what you think is important. In short, you must set priorities. Setting priorities has been a focus throughout this book, and it will be the key in implementing the choice-making techniques outlined in this chapter.

Making the Choice to Avoid Overcommitment

To keep a rein on commitments, you must:

- Set priorities
- Feel free to reschedule
- Prepare

Set Priorities

What is important to you? Stop now and make a list. When someone asks you to do something, determine whether the job is in keeping with what's on your list. Say no to anything that isn't. Remember, however, that priorities change with your life stage. Daily priorities change as well.

Susan, a marketing director, says, "I plan every day, but I keep spontaneity at the forefront. My child is top priority, and I have to be able to drop things. I've always been a single mom. I divorced when I was pregnant with Misty. My daughter told me she was in a guitar recital the night before the program, and I had to reorganize the next day so I could be there. When I got there, the recital had been rescheduled for the following day.

"It's not unusual for me to schedule dinner meetings with clients at 7 p.m. so that dinner and homework are already done. My personal time is another major priority. My eight-year-old daughter goes to bed at 8 p.m. People ask me why bedtime is so early, particularly during the summer. I tell them I need quiet time for myself—I don't feel selfish. Occasionally, I leave Misty at the babysitter on Friday afternoon and pick her up Monday morning. We both seem to enjoy the time off from each other. The remainder of the week we spend special time together. I've set aside my real-estate career until she gets older. Plus, I love my present job and don't feel the need to change now."

A college diploma is one of Stephanie's top priorities. "I worked out a schedule that lets me work full-time and go back to college. I should have my degree in five more years. If an activity doesn't bring me closer to finishing my degree or work, I say no."

Lani, a freelance bookkeeper, also follows through on her priorities. "My relationship with my husband is a top priority. I have learned over the years that when we're doing well together, the entire family does better. He called Wednesday afternoon, during tax season, and wanted to know if I could take Thursday off. It caught me off guard, but I rescheduled two appointments with clients (without telling them the reason). We had a great time together, and it gave me a much-needed breather."

Sue, a medical doctor, says, "I prioritize *every day*. I try to limit the external pressures, including the number of committees I serve on. I avoid evening meetings, and I resigned as chief of staff at a local hospital when I became pregnant with my third child.

"I love my profession, but I made it a point to cut back. I leave my office between 4:00 or 4:30 p.m. and arrive home before my husband comes in at 6:30. Even though I work through lunch, I have fewer office hours than I used to, but I've made that choice. I figured this out after my second child was born. I was always rushing and found myself angry and stressed out. It took a real effort on my part to make the changes. If I have a patient who is extremely demanding, I'll refer them. They would be better served by someone else."

Susan, a school district accountant, is Jewish and feels strongly about Friday-night dinners. "I don't have to get up or leave early from work on Friday to prepare this meal. I buy the chicken, season it, and freeze it Thursday night. I put it in the Crock-Pot when it's frozen Friday morning, and have the chicken ready by dinner. I make bread Thursday night, put it in a glass bowl, and store it in the refrigerator. I take it out in the morning and punch it down. Then I put plastic wrap around it and punch it down again at 4:00 p.m.—the kids throw the dough in the loaf pan and let it rise one more time. I enjoy cooking, and I'm not going to give it up Friday nights—the house smells good. The tone of the evening is special."

Nancy, a mother of four who suffers from rheumatoid arthritis, has adjusted her life to match her priorities. "Otherwise, I'd go nuts. I've set my priorities, and I'm not waiting for anything or anyone anymore. I used to wait to buy clothes or get a sitter. I got my guitar restrung—I was waiting on that, too. When the kids say, 'Mom, will you play "Chopsticks" with me?' I now say 'Yes' instead of 'Later.' I'm going on my cruise, even though my husband can't go. I guess I've made living right now a top priority."

Feel Free to Reschedule

Most clients, family, and friends don't get upset with you if you need to reschedule a meeting, appointment, or an activity. A person usually gets upset when you do not call *ahead* to reschedule or you cancel at the last minute.

Susan has to reschedule her patients when there's an emergency at the hospital. "I've had to ask my patients if they could come in tomorrow morning. Most of them have not minded."

"I have so much going on at work," says Janet, "that I have to occasionally reschedule management meetings. I've learned that most people welcome the date change, because they are behind schedule as well."

Judy works full-time and does anything she can to prevent canceling a scheduled activity. "I hate to cancel something I committed to earlier. I have learned that I don't use the word *cancel*. To cancel something is 'flighty.' I *reschedule*. I started doing this after someone I admired professionally rescheduled an appointment with me twice."

Prepare to Work Effectively

Once you have made a commitment, the best way to keep it within the bounds of the schedule you've established is to work effectively. This means approaching your work efficiently as well as preparing a backup plan in case something unexpected happens.

Candace, a staff manager, keeps files on her clients. "I've worked out a system whereby each file has an 'action sheet.' That's the first thing you see when you open the file. I list everything I have to do for this client and check items off as I go along. It's a great way to delegate some aspects of the job and still keep control."

"Because of my arthritis," says Nancy, "I double or quadruple the recipe of everything I make. Yesterday, for example, I couldn't cook. I went to our large freezer, a must, and just warmed something up.

"I always quadruple the recipe for pancakes. The children take the pancakes out of the freezer in the mornings and put them in the microwave. I know they've had a good breakfast, and they're out the door."

Sometimes working effectively means not doing too much work. Here's an idea for entertaining: Yes, go ahead and entertain at your home if you like. But, make sure you have at least one main dish and one hot appetizer "catered." Many supermarkets today have freshly prepared food. You can pick up these items at a local deli or have a friend (who enjoys cooking) do it for a fee (offer to watch her children one evening or weekend). You spend a minimum of time in the kitchen and get applauded for your delicious dinner. Hire your child or a high school student to clean up. It's worth the $30.

Dealing with Overcommitment

Sometimes, despite our best efforts to avoid overcommitment, we find our calendars crammed and our energy stretched to the breaking point. What then? This is the time for another round of choice making—we must make the right choice for that moment. This is also the time for a sense of humor.

Make the Right Choice at the Moment

You have your day planned, but you find yourself running behind. You have much more to accomplish. What do you do? You decide which client, activity, or meeting you need to do *at this moment*. You must constantly ask yourself, "What is the most important thing I have to do *at this moment,*" and then do it. Reschedule or delegate everything else. Susan says, "The key to managing my time is organization and being able to change at a moment's notice. I've always had that mindset. It's simply survival. I grew up to be accountable. I make choices—they may not be the right ones, but I make them.

"If I'm hit with that tidal wave when all three kids ask something of me, I try to meet the most necessary demands. If the others don't get done, they don't get done. This is reality. The children have a right to make demands, and I have the right to say yes or no."

In the course of reevaluating your priorities on the fly, you may discover that many of the activities that were important to you in the past have outlived their usefulness.

Jennifer, for instance, always baked cookies for her children's class events, even though she no longer enjoyed it. For her, this habit had outlived its usefulness.

For four years Lori held Monday-morning meetings with her staff. One of her employees suggested they meet in the afternoon on Mondays, allowing everyone to get into the swing of things. "The afternoon meetings turned out to be extremely productive. I was setting the early meetings out of habit," Lori said, "not because they were productive. I don't hold early Monday morning meetings anymore, even with suppliers. I need the time to get involved with what I'm doing."

Review the things you do each day at work, at home, and in your personal life. Eliminate activities that no longer seem important.

Maintain a Sense of Humor

A sense of humor is a wonderful way to temper the feelings of anger, frustration, and anxiety that usually accompany overcommitment.

Janet, a single working mom, uses humor to keep her perspective. "Every night my daughter and I spend twenty to thirty minutes reading to each other. If she's angry with me or she's had a particularly difficult day, I'll read something humorous to her. When I'm having a tough day, I ask her to read to me—a motivational book or poems. It has a calming effect, and it keeps me in close contact with her."

Most "terrible" vacations, unbearable meetings, and uncomfortable work, home, and personal situations end up being humorous as time passes and the more you share them with others.

Susan, a medical doctor, knows the value of humor. "I try to put on a happy face and have a sense of humor. Let me give you an example. We were invited to another couple's house for Thanksgiving dinner. We received a call just before we sat down. The host, who's a surgeon, another guest who's a surgeon, and myself, the internist, had to leave the dinner. My husband ended up carving the dinner for himself and four children. It wasn't funny at the time, but that Thanksgiving has become a humorous family story."

Jeanie says, "I get so confused and overwhelmed by chaos. I have to keep things in control or I feel like I'm frozen in my footsteps. I've come up with OOPS—Organize, Organize again, Prepare, and Smile. The smiling part is probably the most important."

Humor is what saves Nancy on difficult days. "You have to have humor in life, especially with children. When I have absolutely had it, I hum the same Hawaiian song and I tell the kids I'm in Hawaii. It's my way of signaling that I need time alone. I used to get angry and yell. Now I use this approach, and the kids start laughing."

Protecting Yourself from Going Crazy

This chapter has already discussed maintaining a sense of humor as one technique for dealing with overcommitment. There are other tips you can use to bolster your personal resilience in the face of overcommitment. Some involve developing a resilient attitude; others involve bolstering your outside resources. The list that follows summarizes these tips. (You'll note that maintaining a sense of humor is so important that it appears again.)

- Keep a positive attitude.
- Get enough sleep.
- Laugh a lot.
- Surround yourself with a support system.
- Maintain your perspective.
- Develop a peaceful refuge.

Keep a Positive Attitude

It takes more energy to deal with a negative frame of mind than with a positive one. When time-pressures occur, stay positive and do something about them. My attorney friend takes fifteen minutes each day to sit quietly with her eyes shut. "I, personally, think of positive things: a trip to the ocean, a healthy body, a positive outcome in a trial…anything that makes me feel calm and peaceful."

Get Enough Sleep

Studies show that a good night's sleep helps the body act and the mind think effectively. How many hours do you need to feel truly rested? Here's a rule of thumb: if you feel tired first thing in the morning, then set eight hours of sleep as a priority. It's a great way to say no to evening meetings.

Laugh a Lot

The working women I interviewed who have a good grip on their sanity laugh a lot. They're able to laugh at their stressful lives and at the unbelievable situations they find themselves in. I attended a funeral for a forty-five-year-old man. His best friend told an off-color joke at the service. About 80 percent of the people laughed, and the other 20 percent didn't know how to respond. The best part was that the widow was laughing.

Surround Yourself with a Support System

This is extremely important. I have seen dreams shattered and relationships broken because women have not developed a support system. Nurture those relationships that make you feel good, positive, and confident. Stay away from people that make you feel inadequate and negative. It's hard to do if these negative people are family members. But tell them in a non-defensive way how their actions make you feel. If this doesn't work, seek a clergyman or a therapist. You cannot change anyone, but you *can* change your behavior and attitude. The change you make will change others' behavior and attitude toward you. Stay positive, laugh a lot, and be persistent. With these qualities your odds will be better than those you'd find in Las Vegas.

Maintain Perspective

When time-pressures and events start tumbling, maintain perspective. What is the *worst* thing that could happen? If death is not on your list, relax. Remember, mistakes happen. It's what you *do* after the mistake that matters. If you have to reschedule appointments, then do it. If you have to be taken to the emergency room, you'd have to reschedule— why wait? Reschedule now.

Develop a Peaceful Refuge

Every working woman needs a place that's hers. This place makes her feel safe from everything else. For many women, it's their home. For others, it's one special room. Georgia bought a wicker love seat, lamp, and small table, and placed them in the corner of her bedroom. "It's my space," she says. "I go there to think, read, or just take a nap."

Simplify

Look at your clothes, shoes, jackets, boots, scarves and anything else in your closet. Start to downsize and simplify your wardrobe. You will be amazed at how many more outfits you will creatively put together when you let go of several items.

Then, move to the next area that you would like to simplify and let go. Ginny, a Transitional Woman, says, "I made a commitment to myself to simplify and clean out one area of the house each weekend for four weeks. I started in my closet, then in my bathroom with cosmetics, then in the kitchen and then in the hall closet with towels and bed sheets. I can't tell you how less burdened I felt."

Important Points to Remember

You have many talents and special interests that increase the chance of your overcommitting yourself. To keep your commitments and responsibilities in check, do only those activities that are consistent with what you deem important.

As you go through your daily plans, keep a sense of humor. When situations become particularly difficult, look for the humor. Chances are good that you'll find a chuckle somewhere in the craziness.

Remember to reschedule, rather than cancel. Make the change as soon as you realize it needs to be done. The more notice you give, the better the result.

Prepare as much as you can at work, at home, and personally.

When you're feeling the time crunch, ask yourself, "What is the most important thing I have to do *at this moment?*" Then do it. Reschedule or delegate everything else. In addition, if you find yourself performing the same tasks and activities that you did several years ago, ask yourself, "Has this activity outlived its usefulness?"

There are six basic ways to protect yourself from going crazy: keep a positive attitude, get enough sleep, laugh a lot, surround yourself with a support system, keep your perspective, develop a peaceful refuge, and simplify.

Priorities help you live the life you want. Choices keep you focused on your priorities.

Chapter Eighteen

Meetings: Running Them and Attending Them

Formal meetings are often the products of mindless routine and frequently get bogged down in a pattern of "touching mountaintops" rather than dealing with important issues. Such ineffectiveness wastes both time and money. Working women must learn to use meetings effectively, whether they are running them or attending them. This means knowing how to prepare for and contribute to meetings and how to communicate clearly. Clear communication calls for an understanding of body language—your own and that of others. Clear communication can save hours of apologies, frustration, wasted effort, and stress.

Keeping Meetings Short

Meetings play a vital part in business. However, it is important not to get "meetinged out." One way to prevent this is to keep all meetings to fifty-five minutes or less. If a therapist uses the fifty-five-minute hour to discuss intimate details of feelings and interactions, then the working woman can accomplish a lot in the same amount of time.

A brainstorming meeting is the exception to the rule of the fifty-five-minute meeting. Brainstorming meetings usually take several hours. By bouncing ideas back and forth, participants encourage spontaneity and creativity. Many companies, departments, associations, and groups brainstorm once or twice a year to foster new input, hash out problems, create new products or procedures, and plan.

As long as the purpose of the meeting is not brainstorming, you have a role—as the leader of the meeting or as a participant—in ensuring that it is short and effective.

Control the Meeting as the Leader

Make the most of any meeting you are in charge of by following these suggestions:

- Distribute an agenda.
- Plan to start on the quarter hour.
- Start on time.
- Wait no longer than ten minutes for participants.

Distribute an Agenda

An agenda includes the date and time of a scheduled meeting, the goal of the meeting, what will be discussed, and blank space for note taking. Every meeting should have an agenda, and the agenda should be distributed in advance, so participants can gather their thoughts and any other needed information.

The agenda is an active part of any meeting. It is not only important to follow along, but also to interact, whether you are the leader or a participant. As an idea comes to mind, write it down. If you object to something discussed, write down your feelings or any modification that you can suggest.

Keep clean copies of meeting agendas filed in a three-ring binder for easy reference and accountability. This prepares you to lead a future meeting or allows you to make a copy for an absent participant.

Mary, a business consultant, constantly uses agendas. "I wouldn't think of going to see a client and not have an agenda ready. This way, everyone knows the purpose of the meeting. I also have better control; I can move the meeting along if it goes off on a tangent. I constantly say, 'Let's move along to the next item.' I have even had meetings where I've written 'Brainstorming' under 'Agenda.' It gets the message across clearly and quickly."

Plan Quarter-Hour Starts

Start meetings at 8:15 a.m. (if people attending are morning high-energy people) or 3:45 p.m. (for afternoon high-energy attendees). Starting at 8:15 in the morning allows you to get moving without wasting another fifteen minutes waiting until 8:30. Starting at 3:45 means that participants will have enough time after the meeting to go back to their offices and organize for the next day. Sandy, an office manager, says, "I like having informational meetings at 3:45 in the afternoon. We never go past 4:30, and we get all the questions answered. I still have time to get back to my desk and make a few calls."

Start on Time

Start the meeting on time, even if not everyone has arrived. Some women feel uncomfortable starting with only half the members present. You may feel uneasy the first few times, but after that chances are good that your members will be there on schedule. Most of us do not like entering a room late.

Wait Only Ten Minutes

If you schedule a meeting and no one shows, wait ten minutes—that's all. You will show people that you are punctual and that you respect your time and want others to do the same. Again, this has to happen only once.

If the meeting is at a restaurant, ask the host or hostess to tell the latecomers that you left after waiting ten minutes past the starting time.

Liza Jo, a sales rep, works her schedule around this ten-minute rule. "I don't care who it is. If they're more than ten minutes late to meet me, I'm history. If they call to let me know they will be late, I either wait ten minutes more or reschedule the appointment. This may seem a bit harsh, but time is one of my most valuable assets. The old saying 'Time is money' couldn't be truer in what I do. Since I've set this rule, I see nearly twice as many people a day as before. They know I act this way, and most of my customers are very punctual."

Control the Meeting as a Participant

Keeping a meeting effective is easier if you're the leader than if you're a participant. However, there are ways you, as a participant, can help control the action.

- Ask for an agenda in advance and do your homework.
- Arrive early.
- Set time limits.
- Close out topics when closure is called for.
- Ask and answer questions.
- Volunteer to get information.
- Listen, listen, listen.
- Be aware of body language.
- Attend regular meetings faithfully.

By acting on the preceding suggestions, you will be noticed and respected as a meeting participant.

Ask for an Agenda

Encourage the meeting leader to plan ahead by asking for an agenda before the meeting. Read the agenda and think about what you have to contribute to each item. If necessary, do a little research. Be prepared to cite resources, provide examples, or hand out articles that support your points.

Arrive Early

Network with participants before the meeting. By chatting, prepare them for the topics that are to be discussed and get a feeling for the best way to present your ideas.

Set a Time Limit

You can't tell the boss when to end a meeting, but you can put a time limit in the leader's mind. When you come in, tell the leader that you have an important call coming at a specific time and ask if he or she thinks the meeting will be over by then. This keeps the leader in control but lets him or her know how much time you have.

If a meeting has gone past an hour, I have had good results by calling the leader afterward and expressing my concern. I explain my desire to stay for the entire meeting and outline my schedule constraints. Is it possible to keep the next meeting to an hour? The most common response is "My intent was to keep it to an hour. I know people are busy. I'll try to get the information presented within the hour next time. Thanks for calling."

Close Out Topics

If someone goes on and on about a pet topic, sometimes you can close it out by summing up what's been said and then stating, "If that issue has been addressed, perhaps we need to go on to something else."

Another way to provide closure on a topic is to suggest forming a task force. A task force can study all sides of an issue at length and make recommendations that will allow participants to settle the matter quickly at a future meeting.

Ask and Answer Questions

Experts say that most of the action in a typical meeting occurs in the last twenty minutes. To use meeting time to its fullest, ask and answer questions throughout the meeting; get the discussion going and keep it going. Someone has to start. And, chances are, the earlier you start discussion, the earlier the meeting will end.

Volunteer to Get Information

During most meetings the participants decide to contact someone or do some research. Don't let action come to a standstill as everyone waits for a volunteer to do the job. Volunteer to do the job yourself. Volunteer to do only *one* thing at each meeting, however.

Listen, Listen, Listen

By listening carefully, you will not waste the group's time by asking needless questions or introducing a topic that is not appropriate to the context. In addition, you will be able to tell when someone else goes off the track and tactfully bring the discussion back to where it belongs. Another benefit derived from listening carefully is that you can weigh all sides of an issue before making decisions. Your decisions will be better as a result.

Be Aware of Body Language

You will learn more about body language later in this chapter. When you are in a meeting, remember to use body language that projects a positive attitude and an interest in what is happening. Use your knowledge of body language to detect the need for clarification or other action.

Attend Regularly

If you keep up-to-date by attending all meetings faithfully, you will not have to ask for explanations and clarifications. In addition, you will establish your reputation as a conscientious professional.

Understanding Body Language

Consultants keep telling us that more time is lost through miscommunication than anything else. "In a normal two-person conversation the verbal components carry less than 35 percent of the social meaning of the situation while more than 65 percent is carried by nonverbal messages."[1]

Body language is more limited than verbal language and mainly consists of posture, clothing, facial expressions, eye contact, tone of voice, and movement. An understanding of nonverbal communication, or body language, can save time because it keeps you from misunderstanding what another person is trying to communicate. For example, when an angry person says, "I'm not angry," but is so tense that he breaks his pencil, his movement should signal you to find out how he really feels. It's important to recognize inconsistency between what a person says and how he or she looks or behaves. Likewise, to maintain credibility, you need to be consistent in what you say and how you say it. Nowhere is this more important than in a meeting.

The sections that follow will discuss body language cues to look for in yourself and others while at a meeting (or anywhere).

Posture

The way you sit or stand at a meeting says a great deal. Leaning toward the speaker and looking relaxed shows that you are interested in the topic. The opposite type of posture says you don't like or agree with what is being said or the way in which it is being communicated.

---

1. McCroskey, J. C.; C. E. Larson; and M. L. Knapp. *Introduction to Interpersonal Communication*. Englewood Cliffs, NJ: Prentice-Hall, 1971.

Clothing

Clean, neat, and color-coordinated clothes say you are professional and you take yourself seriously. Unpressed, sloppy, and stained clothes tell the other person you don't care.

Facial Expression

Smiling shows interest and respect. A frowning or poker face usually means you're uninterested in what the other person is saying.

Eye Contact

Of all the aspects of nonverbal communication, I see this one as the most important. Eye contact says you're interested and you're listening. Looking away or avoiding someone's eyes says you don't like him or her or what is being said; a lack of eye contact shows disinterest. I was once told that some world leaders wear dark glasses during negotiations so that their counterparts cannot see their pupils. Large pupils would tell the other side that they approved or liked an idea; small pupils would say the reverse. It would save a lot of time if no one could wear dark glasses at the world's negotiating tables.

Tone of Voice

A calm, soft tone of voice shows that your feelings on a topic will remain neutral, even though you may agree or disagree. The opposite is a sarcastic tone. Sarcasm is anger turned inward. Rather than letting someone know you're angry, for example, you poke at them with belittling remarks. Since women have learned not to show anger, women often use sarcasm.

Gestures

Using your hands in describing an event or sharing ideas not only makes the information more interesting, but also helps bring in others' opinions. Crossed arms say you're keeping something away from the other person.

Clarify Inconsistency

If the body language of someone at a meeting is inconsistent with what he or she is saying or acting, ask for clarification. You can do this during or after the meeting. A technique to use in follow-up calls is to ask the person to comment on the way he or she thought the meeting went or about the ideas presented. The other person will usually take it from there, and real feelings will become clear.

It takes far less time to clarify a discrepancy than it takes to undo the damage that miscommunication causes.

Identifying the Types of Meetings

I have identified three basic types of meetings: planning meetings, action meetings, and social meetings. Each type has its place. You need to know why you're at a meeting and behave accordingly to maximize the benefits.

Planning Meetings

This is where you brainstorm and share examples of other businesses that have used the ideas being considered. To maximize the benefits and save time at a planning meeting, do your homework. Prepare by asking for an agenda, and thinking about what you can contribute. Do any research that's called for.

Action Meetings

This is the meeting where things get done. Research is completed and action tasks are determined. This is the time to say if something is going to work and the time to drop ideas that won't. Making realistic decisions now saves hours of thrashing through the same information later. A sublevel of the action meeting is the task force meeting. Be prepared to take action. The sole purpose of the task force is to save the group's time.

Social Meetings

This is a great place to network with old and new friends. Being able to see several people in one place saves time. Make the most of the opportunity by keeping in touch with as many attendees as you can. Use your name tag to your advantage: Rather than write your first and last name, write "Speedy Sam" if you've picked up the nickname because you work quickly. Or write "Nurturing Nancy," if you're a nurse, or "Slim Sandy" after losing twenty pounds. This is an excellent way to start conversation with new people. Tell yourself that you are going to meet three new people at the meeting and seat yourself next to someone you do not know. This is a great way to meet many new people in an hour. Stay positive and network!

Important Points to Remember

Meetings can be a problem, especially when you are not in charge, but they are essential and need to be controlled if you want to maximize efficiency and decrease the frustration caused by poor time management. If meeting participants do not arrive within ten minutes after the scheduled start time, leave.

Most meetings do not have to go over fifty-five minutes. Save time by keeping a few guidelines in mind:
- Prepare or ask for an agenda.
- Arrive early.
- Start on time and set time limits.
- Feel free to start on the quarter hour.
- Ask and answer questions, provide closure, volunteer, and listen.

Time Management Secrets for Working Women

- Understand body language and constantly assess posture, clothing, facial expression, eye contact, tone of voice, and gestures. Ask for clarification if you see discrepancies between words, behavior, and body language.
- Identify the type of meeting; plan and act accordingly.
- Make the most of your fifty-five minutes!

Chapter Nineteen

The End...
or the Beginning

A s you can probably see, achieving more in less time has a lot to do with deciding who you are in the first place.

If you are a Traditional Homemaker who is required to put a great deal of energy into a paying job, you will not be happy.

If you are a Transitional Woman who spends too much time at work, you are going to feel stress and guilt.

If you are an Achieving Woman who forces herself to emphasize the home, you will create frustration for yourself and feel overwhelmed.

Become aware of who you really are and how you really want to spend your time. I have found that any woman who is unhappy with what she is doing simply won't achieve what she wants.

Making the Most of Time

I hope you have learned in reading this book that using your time well and being time-efficient depends on six major concepts:

1. Making a commitment to be happy
2. Discovering your own uniqueness
3. Keeping the process in perspective

4. Understanding that time is relative
5. Staying focused but flexible
6. Honoring your feelings

Commit to Happiness

By making a commitment to be happy, you say that you have the right to be happy.

I believe true happiness is an inner feeling of calm and peace. It is the commitment to these feelings that will provide you with happiness.

Commitment is the reflection of your desires. If you desire to spend more time at home, then it is your commitment to this that will make it happen. If you desire to spend more time with special friends and family, then it is your commitment to this attitude that will bring it about.

Every twenty-four hours you spend brings you closer to who you are and what you want to accomplish in your life at work, at home, and personally. If you haven't begun to shift your time emphasis in proportion to your true character (Traditional Homemaker, Transitional Woman, Achieving Woman), I suggest you start doing it right now.

One word of warning: do not try to do everything at once. If you are a Traditional Homemaker and are spending 60 percent of your time working, 30 percent of your time on your home, and 10 percent on personal time, you can't make the changes overnight. But, by making a commitment to start moving in that direction, you will get there. Cut down a little on the working time, stop taking work home, don't work overtime, or get a new job or shift to part-time work. Remember that using time correctly means first making a commitment to be happy by living your values.

Discover Your Uniqueness

Time Management Secrets for Working Women is about becoming aware of your own uniqueness. There is no limit to who you are and your special talents and interests. However, you cannot be everything to everyone at the same time. What I suggest is that you get in touch with your own uniqueness, priorities, and motivational attitudes.

By organizing your thoughts and attitudes into one of three motivational lifestyles (Traditional, Transitional, or Achieving), you can make time work *for* you. You are unique. There are no two women alike. It is your own uniqueness that I want you to discover.

I want you to notice your uniqueness by thinking about goals and by *writing them down.* I want you to find what motivates you and why. Are you motivated to work part-time, or are you pressured into part-time work by cultural expectations and others' demands on you? Would you like to spend more time at work? Or would you like to spend more time on personal activities, such as reading, sports, gardening, or sewing? What are you doing now, and how do you *want* to spend your time *now?*

Keep the Process in Perspective

Enjoy the process. Rather than looking at waiting time in the grocery store or on a child's playing field as annoying, think of it as time to read a magazine or a reason to slow down and take a few deep breaths. Or take the time to put your arm around your child and give him or her a hug and a loving smile.

The decisions you make, the way you spend your time, the motivations behind what you do are all part of the process. Yes, you have demands placed on you; yes, your life requires change at times; yes, your motivations and attitudes bring out your true feelings about time and self; and yes, some days you get more curve balls thrown to you than average. But all of this helps you put your time emphasis and daily twenty-four hours into perspective.

I would like to share an excerpt from Leo Buscaglia's book *Living, Loving & Learning:*

Yesterday is gone, and there's nothing you can do about it. It's good, because it brought you to where you are right now. And in spite of what people have told you, this is a good place to be! But there's nothing you can do about yesterday, it isn't *real* anymore. And tomorrow? Tomorrow is a wonderful thing to dream about. It's marvelous to dream about tomorrow, but it isn't *real*. And if you spend your time dreaming about yesterday and tomorrow, you're going to miss what's happening to you and me *right now*. And that's the *real* reality, to be in touch.[1]

I wish a very dear friend of mine, an Achieving Woman, would take Buscaglia's words to heart. She spends her time in the future, always working for the next challenge. She works on borrowed energy and seems to put in more and more time at work. She is looking for the challenge rather than enjoying the process. She is always pushing herself, without learning from each step. She slows down when her body forces her to take sick days. Her latest bout of antibiotics cost her $120 for approximately ten pills.

Understand that Time Is Relative

I know how busy you are and the demands and pressures you feel. But it is time to stop feeling guilty and start taking control. The only thing you really have is time and you. Everything else is relative. Time is relative. How you view time as well as spend it makes the concept of time positive or negative. Your attitude about time can help you save or waste this precious personal asset.

1. Buscaglia, Leo. *Living, Loving & Learning.* New York: Fawcett Book Group, 1985.

This is one reason why my priorities may be very different than yours right now. It also explains why our priorities change over time, through life experiences and age passages. You can decide what your most important priorities are *right now* and develop an action plan.

The only person you can control is yourself. Therapists tell us that we allow others to upset us, control us, or waste our time. When we place the responsibility for our actions directly on our shoulders, it becomes more difficult to say, "I have to do this because so-and-so says I have to." Rather, it is more accurate to say, "I have to do this because I need or want to."

It is, indeed, a great personal victory to know that what you do, in the twenty-four hours allotted to you each of your living days, will bring you closer to your goals and in line with your values.

Stay Focused but Flexible

Staying focused on goals and values means being willing to expend energy to achieve them and being able to accept trade-offs.

I believe that if you stay focused on something you want, chances are good that your subconscious will work toward making your goal happen. The other half of staying focused is staying flexible. Focus without flexibility is similar to a rubber band stretched to its limit. Focus, by itself, restricts your choices and may tax you beyond the human capacity to respond.

As you work to stay focused but flexible, consider these ideas:

To choose your own Personal Motivational Lifestyle is to reflect on your inner feelings—your happiness, fear, guilt, loss, and so on.

To identify your primary time emphasis is to commit to a happy life.

To avoid guilt is to balance, not juggle, your time and your life.

To develop alternate plans is to gain self-esteem.

To find the time for love is to feel and nurture the real you and accept your vulnerabilities.

To negotiate flextime is to appreciate yourself as a worthwhile human being.

To take control of your schedule is to take responsibility for your life.

To spend time to save time is to recognize your own value.

To develop a home office or start your own business is to accept your strengths and weaknesses.

To organize your desk is to organize your thoughts.

To make decisions, right or wrong, is to exercise your freedom.

To clarify issues is to honor and trust your feelings and decisions.

To control the telephone is to accept it as your business associate.

To delegate is to trust in your ability to let go of control.

To use waiting time is to enjoy the process on the way to your goals.

To make a commitment is to focus your sights and expend your energy on personal priorities.

To communicate clearly with others is to be accepting of others' differences.

Honor Your Feelings

Trust your intuition and decisions. Only you can truly come up with the "right" decisions and plans for you. By trusting your feelings and decisions, you have choices. I want you to choose how you want to spend your time…your life. You have the choice to view time as your ally or as your enemy. Only through choices do you really have freedom; the freedom to be who you want to be and the freedom to live the type of life you want. Fight for your freedom. Only if you are free can you truly make life happier for yourself and those around you.

It is time to get all your senses involved in your life: sight, sound, smell, taste, touch, as well as feelings. *Now* is the time to develop high-quality relationships.

The greatest gift you can give yourself is to honor your feelings and decisions. The greatest gift you can give the people you love is you. You don't want to wait…you do not know when your twenty-four-hour clock will stop ticking. You must keep time as your ally, so that your hopes and dreams become reality. These hopes and dreams not only make you a happier person, but they positively touch the lives of those close to you.

I am on your side. I have seen many women literally change their lives by using this system. My professional, home, and personal priorities are always changing, but I keep my focus on the concepts I've shared throughout this book. Now it's your turn. And remember, every step of the way, though I can't be there in person, I'll be there in spirit, cheering you on. So, to all of you, I wish the very best!

Appendix

Six Weeks to a More Balanced, Abundant, and Joyful Life

"Life is not measured by the number of breaths we take, but by the moments that take our breath away." —Rabbi Abraham Twerski

Time management skills lay the groundwork for living a more balanced, calm, joyful, and productive life. Once you get your time schedule worked out, you then need to look at how you view the world. Do you see it as positive or negative? What type of emotions do you often find in yourself? With whom? When? Do you find yourself anxious much of the time? Fearful? Calm? Frustrated? Angry? Once you identify your time skills, your values, emotions, attitude, and health and fitness habits, you can effectively determine a tailor-made program that will take you to action now, no matter where you are in your motivational lifestyle.

There may be times when you feel that your goals are not being met. On some level, you need to ask yourself a few questions: Is your goal to meet your lover or might it be instead to become the woman your lover would be attracted to? You may have a goal for success when perhaps what you really want is a sense of genuine accomplishment? You may desire more money rather than making a change in your relationship to and perception of money? Or a certain outcome in a situation when perhaps it would be better to wish for peace of mind no matter what the outcome is.

Time, energy, and health are our three most valuable commodities. When any of them is not available, life seems to drain our energy, our life spark, so much more easily. But in order for us to lead rewarding lives capable of fulfillment and meaning, we need to set priorities, "find" more time, and have a potpourri of options to downshift our busy lives. Jobs, income goals, relationships, and other important aspects of life are the direct results of our energy being focused towards a baseline level of health and wellbeing.

This six-week program will help transform your life into a celebration that is balanced, healthy, and abundant. It will help you make better choices and enjoy your life more fully. I have used anecdotes and stories from my personal coaching sessions with clients to illustrate the theme of each week. This program was inspired by the work I do with my clients as well as my Integrate or Suffocate Action Retreat.

This is the same program I used for two readers for an article in *Prevention* magazine. The editor asked me to help these women find time in their busy schedules to exercise. Many of the ideas and exercises synthesize what you have read on previous pages. I will share with you the pages to review or tables to refer back to when applying the six-week program. This program also develops "systems" for each week that naturally become a habit in twenty-one days. These systems help to ensure that your new choices and lifestyle become part of your everyday activities.

The six-week program covers these areas:

Week One: Values Identification
Week Two: Emotional Patterns
Week Three: Time Skills
Week Four: Attitude Awareness
Week Five: Health and Fitness
Week Six: Financial Health
Let's look at them a little more closely.

Week One

Week one delves into your values which show up in your spirit. When you live close and consistent with your values, you tend to lead a more passionate and value-driven life.

I am convinced that when you stay on your values track, you naturally gain more momentum to get things accomplished and reach your goals. Your values are tightly attached to your spirit. Your spirit soars when you speak and act consistently with what is truly important to you. Who you are, what you say, and what you do are congruent.

You know when you're living in your "values zone" when you feel calm and at peace in your heart of hearts. When you live in sync with your values, you are living with your spirit and you shine, you radiate, you have energy.

You "check in" with your value system with most of what you do and say. When you feel guilty, it is usually because you are going against what you feel is right, ethical, or value-driven for you. Or we may temporarily have our priorities mixed up and get that "guilty" feeling. I believe that the only true motivator is our values. When things are really important to us, we do what we need to do. True motivation comes from within—that special place in our hearts that make us who we are. I also believe that living our values, not just knowing what they are, is what brings us true happiness and joy.

How close to living your values are you? When you have truly identified your values and decide to live them, you'll change your behavior. Living your values will make you the master of yourself.

Here is a beautiful poem that came my way, author unknown.

To realize the value of ONE YEAR
Ask a student who has failed his final exam.
To realize the value of ONE MONTH
Ask a mother who has given birth to a premature baby.

To realize the value of ONE DAY

Ask a daily wage laborer who has ten kids to feed.

To realize the value of ONE HOUR

Ask a couple waiting for the wedding ceremony.

To realize the value of ONE MINUTE

Ask a person who has missed the train.

To realize the value of ONE SECOND

Ask a person who has survived an accident.

To realize the value of ONE MILLISECOND

Ask the person who has won a silver medal in the Olympics.

There are several ways to "get in" or recapture the feeling and "high" of being in the zone. The following ways listed are ones in which I have used with clients that helped immensely.

- What would you most want to **Accomplish** daily, weekly, monthly, yearly, in a half-decade, a decade, two decades, three decades, and in a lifetime at work, at home, and personally?
- What would you like to **Achieve** most at work, at home, and personally?
- What would you like to give to your **Community**?
- What types of **Creativity** would you like to bring into your life?
- How much **Energy** and **Health** would you like on a daily basis?
- What brings you the most **Enjoyment** and **Peace of Mind**?
- What type of **Experiences** do you crave?
- How would you most like to spend your time and interact with your **Family**?
- How would you like to connect and develop your **Friendships**?
- How would you become **Independent** in creating your own life?
- What would it take to live a life of **Integrity**?
- Where would you love to **Live**?
- How much **Money** do you want? How much do you need?

- How much more **Personal** time do you need to live a more relaxed and balanced life?
- What would you like to have **Responsibility** over?
- What do I feel **Safe** or **Secure** with?

ACTION Sheet #1:

- List ten values that are important to you
- Choose your top five values
- Move your values to action

Here is how Shelly, a Traditional Woman, filled out this sheet:

My ten most important values

Family	Creativity
Personal Accomplishment	Personal Responsibility
Friendship	Safety
Independence	Experiences
Integrity	Peace of Mind

Top five values

Family	Personal Accomplishment
Integrity	Independence
Creativity	

Move Your Values to Action (as though you were already there)

My family comes first. I live my creativity, loyalty, and integrity every minute and hour of every day. I select projects where I can use my creativity and integrity whether it is in writing, art, management, family, or anything else I take an interest in.

ACTION Sheet #2:

- When do you most feel that your life is meaningful?
- If you could live your life over, would you change anything?
- What is the most important decision I need to make this year?
- If you could give your children, or your friend's children, only three pieces of advice, what would they be?

Shelly writes:

1.Making life meaningful

"Life is most meaningful for me when I am interacting with my children and when working on my own home business. I help over-forty women redirect their lives. I was surprised how many women were looking for this service. I see things being accomplished, and know I am meeting my goals.

2.Living life over

"I wouldn't do much differently. I certainly would have paid more attention to my children and tried to start doing my own thing earlier. I would have liked to have begun my home career in my twenties. Then, perhaps I wasn't mature enough then to see the opportunities.

3.The most important decision I need to make this year

"Do I expand or do I simply continue doing what I am doing? Right now I give all classes at home. If I expanded I would need to rent a facility. Of course, my children are in high school now so I can arrange my schedule so as to be here when they come home.

4.Giving your children three pieces of advice

1. Be true to yourself.
2. Don't be too quick to follow someone else.
3. Constantly strive to learn new things.

ACTION Sheet #3:

You have three wishes—How would you use them?

Shelly continues...

Three Wishes

- I wish to expand my business
- I wish to see my daughters graduate
- I wish to continue to work for myself

ACTION Sheet #4:

What are two of your top priorities in each area?

Personal

- To take more time for myself—thirty minutes every day
- To pamper myself with more vacations starting this summer

Family:

- Manage my business to make more time for my husband and daughters;
- Have the family home for dinner at least four nights a week

Spiritual:

- To give my daughters a sense of God and of living a good life; To give back to others by joining a local mentor program

Work

- To reach more people with my message of living a fuller life after forty
- To take more time for myself during the year—take a three-day weekend every other month

Play

- I haven't had a vacation with my husband in ten years. To take several vacations to Europe in the next few years
- To take up the game of golf this spring

Fitness

- I intend to sign up for a fitness program at the local gym next Monday morning
- Take thirty-minute walks Monday through Friday morning and night

Health

I intend to take better care of myself. I am going to take off forty pounds in the next year

I will eat healthier foods and not send out for fast foods as often

Money

I intend to save an extra $160 per month. I will put $40 a week in our investment account. I will buy two less coffees per week.

Time

I intend to balance my time better between personal and work by taking forty-five minutes each day for myself and by taking mini three-day vacations every other month

I am especially going to take more personal time in the next year by scheduling this into my calendar now

Now using these examples, make up your own value action sheets.

Week Two

"There are only two ways to live your life. One is as though nothing is a miracle, the other is as though everything is a miracle." Albert Einstein

Week two looks at our emotional patterns. Do you find that a great deal of your energy and health has been wasted because of certain emotional patterns? Do you find yourself judging what happens as good, bad, awful, or something else? Do you laugh more than you cry or vice versa? It is one thing to feel sad or hurt by someone's actions or words, but it takes it to a whole different level if you allow those words and actions to bring you down for several hours, days, or years. You end up putting yourself in bondage.

Do you find yourself filled with anxiety? Fear? I once heard that nothing in life is to be feared, only to be understood. Do you wake up every morning appreciative of the gift of life? Do you see the next day as a new beginning, where you can start again? Do you feel that you have one more day to live a purposeful life? Do you express your appreciation for waking up every morning or do you just think it's another day and you must get to work?

Do you find you're an emotional eater? Do you feed your feelings with food? We certainly know our comfort foods. If you go for ice cream, you may need something soothing and comforting...or you may be pregnant—just kidding.

A key to understanding your emotional patterns is to know what your emotional thermostat is. In other words, what does it take to get you to boiling? Once you find where your level is, it is important to learn ways to bring your anger, anxiety, and fear down to a level that still allows you to work through these emotions. Certainly, a key element in the quality of your life is the mental and emotional patterns that you experience and create!

It is important to identify your daily stress load. When you feel that stress is getting close to overload, you need to stop what you're doing, take three deep breaths, and identify the feeling—sad, angry, frustrated, irritable, and so forth. Once you know what you are dealing with then make the decision to stop the cycle of emotion and do something to lessen the feeling. If you leave these strong negative feelings unattended and continue to harbor anxiety, frustration, or depression, then your body becomes upset as well.

Neuropsychology is the study of how our emotions and our self-talk interact with our internal organs physically, as well as our brain, our subconscious self, our verbal behavior, our actions, and our attitude. This interaction is what can help us get well or help us get sick.

When you sense you are involved in a toxic situation or you're with toxic people, don't walk away—run! Avoid toxic surroundings as much as possible.

We know that our mental health profoundly impacts physical diseases ranging from heart attacks and strokes to asthma, arthritis, and diabetes. It is estimated that 90 percent of what we have learned about the brain is the product of the last ten years or so of studies. Much of this interdisciplinary approach to health is being driven, in many ways, by financial savings. It has been shown that a coordinated effort to treat mental and physical problems reduce treatment costs to individuals and employers.

ACTION Sheet #1:

1. What do you say to yourself when things go well?
2. What do you say when things don't go as planned or as you like?
3. What do you think when people thank you?
4. Keep a tape recorder going for a couple of days and let people know that it is on—you will be amazed!

Sandy, a Traditional Homemaker answers

1. **When things go well**: *"It's certainly about time."*

Reframe the sentence to a more positive and "real" statement: *"Life works beautifully and I appreciate life."*

2. **When things don't go as planned.** *"I'm fine, then my husband walks in and I blow up at him."*

Reframe the sentence to a more positive and "real" statement: *"Honey, I have had a very chaotic day today. I need some emotional support tonight."*

3. **When people thank me.** *"I'm uncomfortable. For many years I stumbled and sputtered. Now I just say, 'You're certainly welcome' and let it go at that."*

Reframe the sentence to a more positive and "real" statement: *"Just say 'thank you' and enjoy the compliment and positive energy it brings."*

ACTION Sheet #2: Energy Sheet

Make two headings at the top of the page, Positive and Negative.

List your coworkers, family, and friends you see or talk to often and calibrate how much energy they give you or take away from you. Rate them from zero to ten, ten being the highest.

 SAMPLE ENERGY SHEET

Who	Positive	Negative	Comments
Husband	4	6	It's gotten so I constantly criticize my husband. It's become a habit with me.

SAMPLE ENERGY SHEET continued

Who	Positive	Negative	Comments
Carol (friend)	8	1	Carol always compliments me, encourages me, and shares. She buoys me up when I'm feeling bad. I couldn't get along without her.
Cynthia at work	1	9	Cynthia criticizes what I do constantly and compares my personal lifestyle to hers. I don't buy my clothes at the right places. I don't go to the right hairdresser. The few times I have driven her in my car, she keeps telling me where to turn. "That's not where I would turn."

ACTION Sheet #3:

1. How often do you express your feelings to those who mean the most to you?
2. What would bring you more happiness than anything else in the world?
3. How many hours sleep do you get on a regular basis weekly? On the weekends?

1.Express my feelings.

"I guess the only feelings I express to my husband are my negative feelings. He really is a good guy. But when things aren't going right I jump on him."

Three actions I will take to change my emotional patters: 1) I will start counting to ten before I say anything to my husband when I'm about to blow up, 2) I will ask my husband for help around the house and remember to thank him for his help, and 3) I will start to be more conscious and take more responsibility for the words that come out of my mouth.

2.Bring me happiness

"I guess I just want things to go well. I don't want to face any problems, ever. And I certainly don't want anyone to criticize me. That would bring me happiness."

3. Hours of sleep?

"I probably only get about four hours of sleep a night. I stay up till one o'clock. I really have to scramble to keep the house running. And, of course, my husband keeps getting in my way. On the weekends I go to bed early and spend the next day with my daughter shopping or going somewhere. That's the only way I can make any sense out of my life."

Week Three: Time Skills

I want you to spend the third week identifying where your time is going by using the Daily Time Sheet as described on page 27. Fill this out for two weeks—every thirty minutes—and work with the results on week three. Here is a Daily Time Sheet filled out by Janey, a Forty-Something Achieving Woman with four small children:

DAILY TIME SHEET

Tuesday, June 30

6:00 a.m. wake up

6:30 a.m. take shower

7:00 a.m. get kids ready for school

7:30 a.m. kids

8:00 a.m. take kids to school

8:30 a.m. clean house

9:00 a.m. have coffee, eat breakfast

9:30 a.m. checked email

10:00 a.m. make a few calls to clients

10:30 a.m. still calling

11:00 a.m. John comes to the office

11:30 a.m. still with John

12:00 p.m. eat lunch

12:30 p.m. meet clients for big house

1:00 p.m. go home and get changed

1:30 p.m. call client for escrow

2:00 p.m. spoke to some clients on the phone

2:30 p.m. glance at the MLS book

3:00 p.m. pick up kids from school

3:30 p.m. get Shan a gift

4:00 p.m. do homework with kids

4:30 p.m. go to the store

5:00 p.m. start to make dinner

5:30 p.m. making dinner still

> 6:00 p.m. eat dinner with kids
>
> 6:30 p.m. do more homework with kids
>
> 7:00 p.m. watch some TV
>
> 7:30 p.m. TV
>
> 8:00 p.m. get kids ready for bed
>
> 8:30 p.m. get kids in bed
>
> 9:00 p.m. go to bed—I'm exhausted

I know it can be challenging, but this is vital in being able to see where your time is goes and how much time you do have if you need to use some of it a little differently. I'll provide you with several clients with whom I have done this. I then want you to answer the question: what would you do if you had an extra two hours a week? I'll share with you what some of my personal coaching clients have said and then ways in which we made that a reality without cloning them or going without sleep.

ACTION Sheet #1: My Ideal Day

I would now like for you to describe your ideal day.

I have found that a woman's ideal day is not far away from making it truly happen. Many times just focusing on creating such an ideal day is enough for the mental wheels to start running forward in thinking of different ways to accomplish this.

 ## MY IDEAL DAY

"I work but I have managed to make my work compatible with the job of getting three children off to school and my husband off to work. My ideal day would be for everything to work right. I ask my older daughter to make the sandwiches for the next day before she goes to bed and put the lunches together for the next day.

"What happens is I usually hear someone scream 'where's my lunch,' and find Jan has forgotten to do it. Then my husband is always asking me to find something. I'm usually a wreck when I go out the door an hour later. My ideal day would be for everything to go smoothly."

Say Goodbye to a Hectic Lifestyle with Integrate or Suffocate™

Integrate or Suffocate—small ways to integrate your life and lifestyle with planning, being present, and execution. In chapter 2 there is a list of different options and examples of Integrate or Suffocate. Remember, this is different than multi-tasking whereby you do several things at the same time and you're not present to any of them.

Just as a reminder, think Integrate or Suffocate when trying to combine how you can spend time in the kitchen cooking or baking and still be present with the children and not have to rush through preparations. Or, what can you create or do that which will give you more quality time with your children, spouse, friends, time to play piano, read, and the countless other things we want to do. One client, Jackie, a forty-something Traditional Woman, wanted to start playing piano again. She now practices for ten to fifteen minute intervals twice a day as a way to de-stress, get emotions out with different pieces, and refocus on something other than her sick spouse. "After about three weeks of practicing I'm almost able to play music without a lot of errors," she says proudly. As a by-product, her husband enjoys listening to the music.

Jackie was able to Integrate:

- Start playing piano again
- Time to relax
- Use her "brain muscles" in reading music
- Take her mind off her sick husband
- Didn't want to leave her husband to go out and relax

Here are a few more ideas to get you thinking "Integrate or Suffocate"™

I enjoy baking and have wanted to start baking challah (twisted bread loaves) for Friday although in my head I thought I didn't have enough time to bake bread so I didn't. I was in New York at my friend's house one Friday. She leaves for work at 8 a.m. and returns home around 7 p.m. but bakes bread every Friday. She starts the dough in the morning before work and allows it to rise all day, approximately nine hours. When she gets home from work Friday night she punches down the bread, braids it, and allows it to rise another twenty or thirty minutes and bakes it for about thirty-five minutes. Not only does it taste fantastic, but the aroma brings Friday night dinners to a whole new experience. I thought if she works all day and can do it, I can certainly bake challah on Fridays as well.

I started making the dough Friday mornings and I allow it to rise until I am finished with work and then punch it down, braid it, and bake it. I can't tell you how much I enjoy doing this. Because of my busy schedule, Friday night dinner is a time to enjoy family and friends. I prepare the meal in my mind the night before, go shopping for what I need, and look forward to preparing the dinner as well as having my family and friends to share this special evening with. So that I don't have dirty dishes to wake up to Saturday morning, I hire a college student to wash the dishes Friday night. This is an Integrate or Suffocate idea.

I am able to Integrate:

- Enjoyment of baking
- Start baking bread on Fridays for dinner
- Did not want my baking or cooking to interfere with my work day
- Enjoy family and friends for dinner
- Able to relax and enjoy dinner and not worry about cleaning up
- Help a college student with extra cash
- Keep my Sabbath as a celebration and relax

Carolyn is an Achieving Woman who is a CEO of a medical facility and practice. She often has back problems and a physician suggested she take up yoga. She now goes to her friend's house and they catch up on their lives and then they do yoga with an audio tape. Carolyn claims, "At the end of the two and a half hours of sharing with my dear friend and doing yoga, I feel emotionally recharged and physically relaxed. I hate missing these, but I do so much traveling. I try, if I can, to keep my Monday evenings clear."

Carolyn was able to Integrate:

- Takes time to relax on Monday evenings
- Enjoys the company of a good friend who she can confide in
- Enjoys the physical benefits of yoga on her back
- Tells her family this is her "girls night out"

Time Is Energy

Time management as I see it, is really about life management and your life energy. Let's look at five ways to make more time and energy in your life.

1. Telephones—"Let the answering service get it!" Today, most doctors have worked out rotating schedules so that if a patient enters the hospital and they are not on rotation for that night, the other doctor sees his/her patient. If doctors can take a break from the 24/7 cycle, why can't you? Ask yourself, "Is this really necessary?" If the answer is, "No," then turn the phone off.

2. Email—Do you check your email first thing in the mornings when you start your day? If you do, you will get off track faster than a derailed train. Do your planned work the first two hours of the day, and then check your email. Do not have the sound on identifying all new email messages—it will make you crazy. Ask yourself, "Is it really necessary to check email first thing in the morning or am I just used to doing it that way?"

3. Sleep—You may have a brand new car, but if you don't put the energy or gas in it, then it won't go anymore. The same applies to sleep and women. No fuel, no go. Figure out how many hours of sleep you need nightly and count backwards to let you know what time you need to get to bed. That's right, I'm suggesting that you don't do that last bit of laundry or clean up, but go directly to bed.

4. Eating—Just as in the gas scenario with your new car. If you don't put good gas in the engine, then you don't get good mileage. The same applies to our eating habits. What you put in your body for food will either give it lasting endurance or give you a quick spurt of energy and then will slow you down. Do you need to take the time to eat? I'll let you answer that one.

5. Attitude—The way you look at the world determines your attitude. We have a choice every morning to choose how we will respond or think of a situation or comment. A positive attitude will give us more energy and a negative attitude will rip our energy in half. It's your choice.

Now that we have more time and energy in our day, let's look at several specific time tools that will help us accomplish what we need to do within that time and energy span:

The Rule of Two

I have found that choosing only two items that if you do them, or at least start them, will lower your stress level immeasurably and get you closer to your daily goals. The Rule of Two is used in deciding which two emails to return first, calls, projects, errands, and the like. Once you have finished those two, then choose another two and complete those. The question I often get is, "Ruth, what two items should I choose?" My answer is, choose those two items that if you had no time to do anything else, you would at least feel as though you had accomplished something. How many times during a day do we find that we were busy but we don't feel any less stressed or feel we haven't really completed anything of importance? This is how the Rule of Two came about. My clients find it is an important daily time-skill tool.

Ten-Minute Planning Session

1. **Focus on the Rule of Two** What are the two things that you need to focus on today?
2. **Identify** Identify the top two items, whether they are calls to make, calls to return, or email. It could also be to start or continue projects, two ideas you want to share with your spouse on how to better communicate, or to thank your children for two things they may have said or done…you get the idea.
3. **Stop to Think and Plan** What is the best way to go about this? Ask yourself, what if anything do I still need before I can go forward at this time? Do I need to make one or two calls? Find a certain resource? Take the time to think and then do.
4. **Positive Self-Talk & Visualization** Most of our self-talk causes

us anxiety and stresses us. However, true leaders and achievers work at positive self-talk. If you need a little help in getting started with positive self-talk, here is a beginning list of what you could say to yourself several times a day:

- "I have the information or know where to find the information to start or complete this project." VISUALIZE THIS WORKING
- "I have the time that I need to work on this project, make these calls, see clients, etc." I use this one several times a day. VISUALIZE
- I know I am the best person with the best products/service for this client. VISUALIZE
- I am capable and confident in what I am doing. VISUALIZE
- I am making a positive difference in helping others with this product/service. VISUALIZE
- I am making excellent movement on this project, survey, proposal, speech, etc. VISUALIZE

ACTION Sheet #2

1. What project(s) or goal(s), if left undone, will I most regret in the coming six months? Year?
2. What are my three major goals in life? What am I doing to achieve them?

1. Projects left undone

Sharon, a Transitional Woman says, "I am a columnist for a newspaper part time. My pet project has been to start a community newspaper. This has been my project for six years now and I haven't really gotten started. If I don't move forward in the next six months or year I will be really disappointed in myself."

2. Three major goals

"My first goal actually is to have my children grow up to be responsible adults. I try to make sure that I sit down and talk to them regularly. I sometimes go to school and talk to their teachers. When they have a problem I try to give them some ways they can solve it.

"My second goal is to move to the seashore. This has always been a dream of mine. At this time I'm not doing anything to achieve this.

"My third goal is to start a small newspaper. I promise I will move this forward this year."

Action items I will do NOW to reach these goals:

Goal 1: Have my children grow up to be responsible adults

1. Spend more quality time talking and playing with them five evenings a week
2. Stay open and available to listen to the children when they speak or tell me stories
3. Set up dinnertime at 6 p.m., with everyone in the family present and helping set the table

Goal 2: Move to the seashore

1. Spend time speaking with a realtor in the area I would like to live in
2. Talk to a financial advisor as to the financial options available to us
3. Start collecting information about the area and visualize the family living there

Goal 3: Start a small weekly newspaper

1. Create a twelve-month editorial calendar
2. Start interviewing interesting people in the community
3. Call businesses for advertising revenue

ACTION Sheet #3

What would your perfect day look like?

"Actually it is a day when I would have time to do what I want to do. I don't want my editor at the newspaper throwing something at me that takes forever. I don't want my kids to make things so complicated that I have to spend hours working out the problems, like 'Where is my homework?' Just let me spend my day working on what I want to do."

Action items I will do NOW:

1. Schedule "my time" and let the family know the times in advance
2. Help the children put their homework away in one safe spot
3. Start walking in the morning to help clear my head

Week Four: Attitude Awareness

"The greatest revolution of our generation is the discovery that human beings, by changing the inner attitudes of their minds, can change the outer aspects of their lives." William James, Harvard psychologist

Are you purposeful and joyful in your present lifestyle? I have worked with several Achieving Women who have decided after many years in the workforce that they would like to change their lifestyle to a Traditional Homemaker. I have also worked with Traditional Homemakers who have decided for whatever reason to become an Achieving Woman or a Transitional Woman. Great! There is no right or wrong, good or bad—it just is. However, we need to do a little planning and take action to make the desired changes.

Earlier, you identified your ideal day. Now, I would like for you to write down the ideal you. Remember to include your values, how you would handle things emotionally, your attitude, lifestyle, fitness, time skills, spirit, appearance, and anything else you would like.

ACTION Sheet #1: The Ideal You

Tammy, an Achieving Woman, says,

"The ideal me is someone who is constantly smiling and who keeps saying, 'no problem' when obstacles come up. I always look good and can raise my children without any real hassles. I have plenty of time to do the things I want to do. Inside I love myself—outside I am always trying to make other people's day better."

Your thoughts are the number one part of your life that you can change right now, without going to school for further training, taking more classes, waiting until your children are grown, or anything else. The first step is that you simply decide to make your thoughts either positive, viewing the glass half full, or fill our thoughts with negativity, viewing the glass half empty. The responsibility lies with you—not your parents, or your spouse, or your bosses, but you! You first need to make the choice and then you need to understand that your choice has consequences and it is those consequences that help you to live a more joyful life.

Some of you may remember Norman Lear, a noted TV producer, comedy writer, and screenwriter. He created such TV icons as *The Jeffersons*, Mary Hartman, and Archie Bunker. He was recently interviewed as he entered his octogenarian decade and said he starts every day with hope. "I start every day saying, 'Here is a day, what are you going to do with it?'"

There is more and more research that shows that what you impress upon your mind will usually come about. It seems to be a psychological law that whatever you wish to accomplish or become, you must impress upon your subconscious mind through repeated self-talk.

I believe so much of your attitude is really gratitude. What are you truly thankful for? In most cases, you have more to be grateful for than not. Here is a partial poem I wrote for a parenting magazine:

I am so grateful for:
* going grocery shopping because I know I have loved ones to feed and I have the ability to feed them
* hearing my dad pick up the phone when I call because I know he's still living
* finding out about the school carnival from my children because they are in school
* helping to pay tuition for college because my children decided to go to college
* washing my hair and blowing it out because I have my hair
* washing a lot of dishes after dinner because I know I have friends and family to share meals with
* sneezing when I'm around cats because I know my immune system is doing what it needs to do
* taking my daily walks because I have the freedom and health to do it
* listening to a child laugh because I know how precious children are

The best way to be grateful is to say "thank you" and appreciate what you do have.

ACTION Sheet #2

In your "heart of hearts," what do you need to do to make your life more joyful and balanced?

"I believe I need to spend more time nurturing and taking care of my own needs. I am so busy thinking of others that I find my needs many times get left behind. Plus, I need to say 'no' more often."

ACTION Sheet #3

What is your predominant life attitude at work, at home, and personally? Do you see the glass half-full or half-empty most of the time?

"Most of the time my attitude at work, home, and personally it is half-empty. I didn't realize that I see my life this way until I did this assignment. Wow, what an eye-opener. Before this, I would have definitely said that I see life as half-full."

Week Five: Health & Fitness
Health and Fitness:

Research everyday contributes more knowledge of the strong link between your mind, your body, and your spirit. In fact, medical literature is increasingly saying that chronic stress and its consequences such as anger, depression, binge-eating, etc. are linked to high levels of upper body fat and a myriad of potentially serious illnesses. This link is related to the hormone cortisol, known as the "no-confidence" hormone, which kicks in and at high levels, tends to store fat in your "feeling" zone, deep in the abdomen. This fat causes the spare tire around your waist. Dr. Redford B. Williams, MD, professor of psychiatry at Duke University Medical Center, says, "Stress actually seems to cause our bodies to redistribute our fat, relocating it from other areas, such as the thighs, to the tummy." Other research confirms this and adds that the additional hormones of adrenaline and sex hormones contribute to this layer of fat as well.

It takes twenty-one days to establish a habit. If you want to start eating healthier or start exercising more, then look at your month-at-a-glance calendar and place an "x" on the next twenty-one days. This x symbolizes twenty-one consistent days of implementing your new habit. If you forget or stop, then be kind to yourself and start all over again. As they say, "nothing ventured, nothing gained."

Here are just a few health basics for you to remember:

1. Eat nine servings of fruits and veggies daily
2. Eat protein with each meal to give you more endurance
3. Read labels on food and stay far away from hydrogenated oils or partially hydrogenated oils (margarine is all hydrogenated), high fructose corn syrup, fast food, sugar
4. Eat organic dairy, fruits, and veggies if possible—less toxic chemicals to overload your liver

I have found that my clients who start eating healthier have a higher rate of staying involved in exercise and vice versa. Those clients that maintain a steady schedule of exercise and fitness usually start to make wiser food choices.

ACTION Sheet #1:

How can you integrate exercise and healthy food choices in your daily schedule?

1. Can you bring your lunch to work?
2. Can you park your car further away or take the stairs?
3. Can you walk for twenty minutes before work, during lunch, or after dinner?
4. Can you drink three to four cups of green or white tea daily at work?
5. Can you take vitamins before leaving for work or keep them at your desk to take during the day?
6. Can you take five minutes in the morning to get centered and breathe deeply?
7. Can you take three big breaths first thing in the morning when you get out of bed and stretch for two minutes?
8. Can you do some form of exercise twenty minutes a day?

What I can do?

Take the questions above and turn them around to say:

"I bring my lunch to work."

"I park my car further away and take the stairs."

"I walk for twenty minutes before work, during lunch, and after dinner."

"I drink three to four cups of green tea daily at work."

"I take multivitamins before leaving for work."

"I take five minutes for myself in the morning to get centered and focused."

"I take three large breaths in the morning and stretch for several minutes."

"I walk briskly twenty minutes in the evenings."

Remember, your subconscious doesn't know what is real until you tell it.

ACTION Sheet #2:

A wonderful way to get back into shape or maintain a fun attitude while you maintain a healthy lifestyle is to think of what you enjoyed doing as a child.

What things did you enjoy doing as a young child?

"I enjoyed playing basketball with my brother and my friends in the neighborhood, says Joan, a Transitional Woman.

What active things did you enjoy doing as a child? I loved to run. In high school? I played tennis with friends. College? I continued to play tennis.

ACTION Sheet #3:

What would the healthy and fit you look like? (Say it as if it were already true.)

"I weigh about 128 pounds and wear a size six dress. I run at least a mile a day without breathing hard and swim thirty minutes every day. I look good for my age."

Week Six: Financial Health

Congratulations, you've made it to week six. We are going to spend time, perhaps for the first time, to focus on your financial health. Many women spend more time watching television than watching where their money goes or how to make it grow.

It's important to realize that money has many faces. For example, money can be counted by greenbacks, coins, stocks, commodities, mutual funds, time, energy, and health. We have been talking about time, energy, and health.

A primary reason many of my clients and women, in general, do not sleep well is that they are nervous or anxious about their financial health. This may be true whether you're single or married. The sleeping zzz's don't come easily when you're thinking about how to make ends meet or how to protect the money you've made. One of the best ways to stop the cycle of anxiety is to take action, one step a time. What keeps the anxious cycle going is thinking versus acting. Some of the action items you can take for your financial health are:

1. Pay Yourself First

Develop an automatic system whereby you pay yourself first, as in a 401K plan, an IRA, or any other program that allows you to take your hard-earned money before taxes and shelter it. By paying yourself first, you lower your tax liability and the money you save or invest will make money for you.

2. Give to Charity

When I was a little girl I thought that anyone who gives to charity deserves to be wealthy. Little did I realize how true this is. When you give to charity, the law of abundance goes into play, and the more you give out the more you receive. This is true with any type of generosity, as in generosity of heart, attitude, love, money, volunteering your time, etc.

3. Make Money While You Sleep

Many women are adding to their income by starting "on the side" or "in addition to"… an eBay business, buying real estate, creating an

Internet business, working in direct sales with an international down-line, and other options. These types of businesses increase your income.

4. Invest Using Compound Interest

Set a goal to save X amount of dollars and start a CD (certificate of deposit), savings account, and any other savings arm that allows you to compound your interest every day just by saving your money.

5. Let Your Fingers Go Window Shopping

A great way to see what the new colors and looks are for a season is to check them out in a magazine. It helps to prevent "spontaneous buying," as I am fond of saying.

6. Pay Cash for "I Want" versus "I Need" Purchases

If you don't want to find yourself overloaded with debt each month, then try to use cash when buying anything other than absolute necessary purchases. If the purchase is an "I want" versus "I need," then buy it with cash. When we can see how much cash goes into an item and how quickly our hard-earned cash leaves our wallet, we may think twice before buying something.

7. Put Two Items Back

I have clients that love to shop and find that they have buyer's remorse afterwards. And if they don't, then their spouses do. So, I have suggested that when they make the purchase for clothes, shoes, etc. that they put two items back. It works!

8. Start Funds

At the beginning of my marriage, my husband and I started several "funds," even though we were not making much money at the time. It was fun to select an amount to put away from our miserly beginnings and we did this in separate envelopes with fund titles names Vacations, Taxes, For Me. We took this money right of the top of our paychecks and never really missed it. However, when we didn't have the money to go on vacations in our checking account, then we would go to our vacation envelope and decide where we could go with that amount of money. It was fun.

9. Relinquish and Replenish

When you think you need a new pair of shoes, a new blouse, or a suit, remember to give one away to someone who needs it or to a non-profit organization and replenish with a new pair of shoes, blouse, or suit. Remember, if you don't relinquish, you can't replenish. It's a fun, useful and helpful system to put into place.

10. Think small "accents" vs. big purchases

Many outfits only need an accent to update it or bring color to your face. For example, a cool pin added to a shawl or a jacket draws interest, possible discussion, and a fresh update to your "old" look. The same idea applies to jewelry in the form of necklaces, earrings, bracelets. This also applies to shawls draped around a black dress adorned with a neat updated brooch.

11. Think Healthy Food

Healthy, whole food is usually less expensive than unhealthy, prepackaged goods in most cases. A fresh apple is less expensive in money and calories than a piece of apple pie, for example.

ACTION Sheet #1: Savings Plan

Ask yourself if you can save $2 a day. If the answer is "yes," then ask yourself if you can save $4 a day, and keep going up until you reach the amount that you are willing to save daily.

Jessica, a Transitional twenty-something, worked at a credit union and wanted to buy a home with her boyfriend. She said she didn't know how it would work, but after she looked at how much she spent during the day, she was able to save $50 a week by bringing her lunch to work, drinking coffee at work instead of stopping by for an expensive cup at a local coffee house, and buying fewer clothes on the weekend. Jessica says, "I can't believe I have been able to increase my saving to $60 a week—my boyfriend is very happy."

ACTION Sheet #2: Pay cash for 25 percent of what you buy

Try to pay cash for one of every four purchases you make. At first it will seem strange if you're used to using credit cards, but after a while, it will become very clear as to how much money you're spending. Jackie, half Traditional and half Achieving Woman, said after starting this plan, "I can't believe how many items I end up putting back when it's time to pay cash—the item I'm about to purchase seems like so much more money when I pay cash versus throw out my credit card."

In summary

As with all gifts, half the fun and excitement is unwrapping the box to see what you received. I hope that you take the time to slowly unwrap all the gifts you receive daily. It will help you to identify the most important people in your life and the important goals to move you forward. The beauty of today is that every day is a new beginning. If you did not make the changes you wanted to today, that is okay, because God willing, there will be tomorrow. There are no guarantees about the number of hours, days, or years we have, but we do have a guarantee of this moment. You need to give yourself permission and love to be kind to yourself and recognize that you may still want to make changes or do some things differently.

May you find your life blessed with a calmer and less frantic pace, quality relationships where you make the time to connect and to reconnect, a healthy mind and body that is not ravaged by stress and the accompanying dangerous hormones that prolonged stress emits, and behavior that is consistent with your values that in turn energizes and motivates your spirit.

May you also continue to reach your potential in all the areas of your life with less stress and a more integrated plan and celebratory spirit consistent with your unique qualities and your authentic self. And most importantly, may you find joy and peace in the present.

I would like to share with you a poem I wrote and is close to my heart. It was inspired by the poem, *Children Learn What They Live* by Dorothy Law Nolte.

Gifts of Love

Love is the Universal Language of Inner Peace, Health and Gratitude. Our hearts are reflections to all we hold dear.

When you live with Love, you live a life full of Gifts

When you live with Passion, you live a life full with Feeling

When you live with Understanding, you live a life with Meaning

When you live with Gratitude, you live a life full of Blessings

When you live with Truth, you live a life with Inner Peace

When you live with Compassion, you live a life Without Judgment

When you live a life with Self-Esteem, you live a life that Inspires Others.

When you live with Spirit, you live a life full of Inspiration and Dreams

May your Life be full of Gifts of Love!

About the Author

R uth Klein is the president of the award-winning firm The Marketing/Time Source, an integrative and strategic marketing firm providing time management, public relations, Internet marketing, business and consumer behavior trends, generational marketing, and sales and personal coaching to businesses, professionals, moms, and college students. She lives in Santa Monica, California.

Mailing Information

If you or your business is interested in reaching the next level of performance and goals, join Ruth's de-stress community (www.destressdiva.com), receive her e-zines *Business & Consumer Trends Today!* or *The De-Stress Diva Secrets to Downshift Your Life,* or book Ruth for speeches. Please contact her at: rklein@ruthklein.com or www.ruthklein.com.

Index

Q

quarter-life crisis xi, 9

R

reality checks 159
Redbook magazine viii
returned decade 10
Robbins, Alexandra 9

S

Second Shift, The ix
Self magazine x-xi, 3
self-talk 21
Seniors xi, 6, 50
sexuality 15–16, 79, 88–91
"should-driven" behavior 155–157
starter sheets 205–206
Steinem, Gloria 2
Still Have Kids at Home 8
stress 61–66, 137–150
stress-busters 140–150
SWAT team 42, 44, 51, 70–78
synchronicity 153

T

task sheets 205
Time magazine 8–9
time-log sheets 205–209
tips for expanding home time 43–47
tips for expanding personal time 48–50
to-do list 162
Traditional Homemaker xi, 3–4, 7–9, 22–24, 29–31, 42–45, 48–49, 51, 57–58, 61, 83, 117, 130, 135, 143–144, 152, 155, 168–169, 196, 199, 208, 235, 240, 243, 277, 278–279
Transitional Woman xi, 4–5, 8–9, 22, 24–25, 29, 32–33, 42–45, 48–49, 51, 56–58, 61, 84, 101, 142–144, 152, 156, 168, 169, 177, 196–197, 199, 206, 209, 211, 215, 235, 239–240, 243, 277–279
Twentysomething Inc. 10
Twenty-Somethings 9–10

V

visualization 18, 20–21

W

weight loss 15–16, 18, 65
Wilner, Abby 9
Women in Midlife Crisis 8

Y

You Can If You Think You Can 21